I0748999

F.BELLEW

D. APPLETON & Co

NEW-YORK

Knick-Knacks

FROM AN

Editor's Table.

BY

L. GAYLORD CLARK.

'Mislike me not that I've essayed to please ye;
Some things herein may not offend.'

FLETCHER'S 'MEDLEY.

NEW-YORK:

D. APPLETON AND COMPANY, 200 BROADWAY,

AND 16 LITTLE BRITAIN, LONDON.

1852.

TO

SAMUEL D. DAKIN, Esq.,

THE FAITHFUL FRIEND OF HIS EARLIER AS OF HIS RIPER YEARS,

This Volume

IS MOST AFFECTIONATELY INSCRIBED BY

The Author.

Words Preliminary.

THE present volume is given to its readers with the old excuse of first-book adventurers—'solicitations of friends;' not however without the hope that it may be found in some degree to justify their judgment, or palliate their partiality. During some nineteen years, sitting alone or with company in the 'sanctum' of the *Knickerbocker Magazine*, or circulating in the society of a great metropolis, or sojourning at intervals in the country, the writer has seen and heard much that has awakened mirth, and felt much that has elicited tears. Looking back now upon these records, many of them almost forgotten, the old emotions with which they were originally jotted down come back again freshly upon him. It has always been his belief, as it certainly is his experience, that any one man who feels and enjoys—who can neither resist laughter nor forbid tears, that must out, and will have vent—is in some sort an epitome of the public.

So thinking and so hoping, the writer has been induced to lay this, his first humble 'venture,' before his readers; relying more upon the expressed judgment of others in the matter, than upon his own. 'I am glad to hear'—writes an American author whose favorable estimate would reflect honor upon a far worthier literary project than the present—'that you are preparing one or two volumes for publication from your 'Table.' You will perhaps remember that I once spoke to you upon the subject, and advised you to this course. I have often thought it a great pity that the sallies of humor, the entertaining incidents, and the touches of tender pathos, which are so frequently to be met with in your 'Gossip,' should be comparatively lost among the multitudinous leaves of a Magazine.'* Kindred suggestions have been received from similar flattering sources, and are at last acted upon.

Of one thing at least the reader of this volume may be assured—and that is, abundant variety. There are sad thoughts and glad thoughts recorded in these pages; influenced by all seasons, and jotted down at all seasons; scenes and incidents in town and country, and all over the country; familiar 'home-views,' anecdotes and 'stories' not a few; many and multifarious matters, in fine, original or communicated, that have made the writer laugh; and many, moreover, that have moistened his eyes, as he wrote and read and re-read them; the whole forming a dish of desultory 'GOSSIP,' in which it is hoped that every body may find something that shall please, and no one any thing to offend him.

* WASHINGTON IRVING.

CONTENTS.

Gossip about Children.

A FAMILIAR EPISTLE.

GOSSIP ABOUT CHILDREN.

A FAMILIAR EPISTLE.

LET us begin at the beginning. 'The child is father of the man;' and by permitting us to commence with the following letter to a brother-editor, written in the first person singular—a thing in itself very 'singular' in the present book—the reader will have at once before him the longest paper he will be called upon to encounter 'from title-page to colophon.'

MY DEAR FRIEND:

I LOVE children. I used to think when I was a bachelor, (it is a good many years ago now,) that there was something *rather* presuming in the manner in which doating fathers and mothers would bring their 'wee things' around them, and, for the especial edification of us single fellows, cause them to 'mis-speak half-uttered words,' and to go through with divers little lessons in manners and elocution. But both parents and children were made so apparently happy by it, that I never could think, as certain of my irreverent companions were wont to think, and to say, that it was 'a bore.' No, I never thought, or said that; but I *did* think, I remember, as I have said, that there was a little bad taste, and not a little presumption, in such a course.

I don't think so now.

When a father — and how much *more* a mother — sees for the first time the gleam of affection illumining, with what the Germans call an 'interior light,' the eyes and features of his infant child; when that innocent soul, fresh from heaven, looks for the first time into yours, and you feel that yours is an *answering* look to that new-born intelligence — then, I say, will you experience a sensation which is not 'of the earth earthy,' but belongs to the 'correspondences' of a higher and holier sphere.

I wish to gossip a little with you concerning children. You are a full-grown man now, my friend, yet you were once a boy; and I am quite certain that you will feel interested in a few incidents which I am going to relate, in illustration of my theme; incidents which I hope you will judge to be not unfruitful of monitory lessons to 'children of larger growth' than mere girls and boys.

Don't you think that we parents, sometimes, in moments of annoyance, through pressure of business or other circumstances, forbid that which was but innocent and reasonable, and perfectly natural to be asked for? And do not the best of parents frequently multiply prohibitions until obedience to them becomes impossible?

Excuse me; but all your readers have been children; many of them are happy mothers; many more that are not *will* be in GOD'S good time; and I cannot but believe that many who shall peruse these sentences will find something in them which they will remember hereafter.

'The sorrows and tears of youth,' says WASHINGTON IRVING, 'are as bitter as those of age;' and he is right. They are sooner washed away, it is true; but oh! how keen is the *present* sensibility—how acute the *passing* mental agony!

My twin-brother WILLIS — may his ashes repose in peace in his early, his untimely grave! — and myself, when we were very little boys in the country, saw, one bright June day, far up in the blue sky, a paper-kite, swaying to and fro, rising and sinking, diving and curveting, and flashing back the sunlight in a manner that was wonderful to behold. We left our little tin vessels in the meadow where we were picking strawberries, and ran into a neighboring field to get beneath it; and, keeping our eyes continually upon it, 'gazing steadfastly toward heaven,' we presently found ourselves by the side of the architect of that magnificent creation, and saw the line which held it reaching into the skies, and little white paper messengers gliding upward upon it, as if to hold communion with the graceful 'bird of the air' at the upper end.

I am describing this to you as a boy, and I wish you to think of it as a boy.

Well, many days afterward, and after various unsuccessful attempts, which not a little discomfited us — for we thought we had obtained the 'principle' of the kite — we succeeded in making one which we thought would fly. The air was too still, however, for several days; and never did a becalmed navigator wait more impatiently for a breeze to speed his vessel on her voyage than did we for a wind that should send our paper messenger, bedizened with stars of red and yellow paper, dancing up the sky.

At last it pleased the 'gentle and voluble spirit of the air' to favor us. A mild south wind sprang up, and so deftly did we manage our 'invention,' that it was presently reduced to a mere miniature-kite in the blue ether above us. *Such* a triumph! FULTON, when he essayed his first experiment, felt no more exultant than did we when that great event was achieved! We kept it up until ''twixt the gloaming and the mirk,' when we drew it down and deposited it in the barn; hesitating long where to place it, out of several localities that seemed safe and eligible, but finally deciding to stand it end-wise in a barrel, in an unfrequented corner of the barn.

I am coming now to a specimen of the 'sorrows and tears of youth,' of which Geoffrey Crayon speaks. We dreamed of that kite in the night; and, far up in the heaven of our sleeping vision, we saw it flashing in the sun and gleaming opaquely in the twilight air. In the morning, we repaired betimes to the barn; approached the barrel with eagerness, as if it were possible for the kite to have taken the wings of the evening and flown away; and, on looking down into the receptacle, saw our cherished, our beloved kite broken into twenty pieces!

It was our man Thomas who did it, climbing upon the hay-mow.

It was many years afterward before we forgot the cruel neighbor who laughed at us for our deep six months' sorrow at that great loss; a loss in comparison with which the loss of a fortune at the period of manhood sinks into insignificance. *Other* kites, indeed, we constructed; but *that* was the kite 'you *read* of' at this present.

Think, therefore, O ye parents! *always* think of the acuteness of a child's sense of childish grief.

I once saw an elder brother, the son of a metropolitan neighbor, a romping, roystering blade, in the merest 'devilment,' cut off the foot of a little doll with which his infantine sister was amusing herself. A mutilation of living flesh and blood, of bone and sinew, in a beloved playmate, could scarcely have affected the poor child more painfully. It was to her the vital current of a beautiful babe which oozed from the bran-leg of that stuffed effigy of an infant; and the mental sufferings of the child were based upon the innocent faith which it held, that all things were really what they seemed.

Grown people should have more faith in, and more appreciation of, the statements and feelings of children. When I read, some months since, in a telegraphic dispatch to one of our morning journals, from Baltimore, if I remember rightly, of a mother who, in punishing a little boy for telling a lie, (which, after all, it subsequently transpired that he did *not* tell,) hit him with a slight switch over his temple and killed him instantly — a mere accident, of course, but yet a dreadful casualty, which drove reason from the throne of the unhappy mother — when I read this, I thought of what had occurred in my own sanctum only a week or two before; and the lesson which I received was a good one, and will remain with me forever.

My little boy, a dark-eyed, ingenuous, and frank-hearted child as ever breathed — though perhaps 'I say it who ought not to say it' — still, I *do* say it — had been playing about my table, on leaving which for a moment, I found, on my return, that my long porcupine-quill-handled pen was gone. I asked the little fellow what he had done with it. He answered at once that he had not seen it. After a renewed search for it, I charged him, in the face of his declaration, with having taken and mislaid or lost it. He looked me earnestly in the face, and said:

'No, I *didn't* take it, father.'

I then took him upon my lap; enlarged upon the heinousness of telling an untruth; told him that I did not care so much about the pen; and, in short, by the manner in which I reasoned with him, almost offered him a reward for the confession — the reward, be it understood (a dear one to him,) of standing firm in his father's love and regard. The tears had welled up into his eyes, and he seemed about to 'tell me the whole truth,' when my eye caught the end of the pen protruding from a port-folio, where I myself had placed it, in returning a sheet of manuscript to one of the compartments. All this may seem a mere trifle to you — and perhaps it is: yet I shall remember it for a long time.

But I desire now to narrate to you a circumstance which happened in the family of a friend and correspondent of mine in the city of Boston, some ten years ago, the history of which will commend itself to the heart of every father and mother who has any sympathy with, or affection for, their children. That it is entirely true, you may be well assured. I was convinced of this when I opened the letter from L. H. B——, which announced it, and in the detail of the event which was subsequently furnished me.

A few weeks before he wrote, he had buried his eldest son, a fine, manly little fellow, of some eight years of age, who had never, he said, known a day's illness until that which finally removed him hence to be here no more. His death occurred under circumstances which were peculiarly painful to his parents. A younger brother, a delicate, sickly child from its birth, the next in age to him, had been down for nearly a fortnight with an epidemic fever. In consequence of the nature of the disease, every precaution had been adopted that prudence suggested to guard the other members of the family against it. But of this one, the father's eldest, he said he had little to fear, so rugged was he, and so generally healthy. Still, however, he kept a vigilant eye upon him, and especially forbade his going into the pools and docks near his school, which it was his custom sometimes to visit; for he was *but* a boy, and 'boys *will* be boys,' and we ought more frequently to think that it is their *nature* to be. Of all unnatural things, a reproach almost to childish frankness and innocence, save me from a '*boy-man!*' But to the story.

One evening, this unhappy father came home, wearied with a long day's hard labor, and vexed at some little disappointments which had soured his naturally kind disposition, and rendered him peculiarly susceptible to the smallest annoyance. While he was sitting by the fire, in this unhappy mood of mind, his wife entered the apartment, and said:

'HENRY has just come in, and he is a perfect fright! He is covered from head to foot with dock-mud, and is as wet as a drowned rat!'

'Where *is* he?' asked the father, sternly.

'He is shivering over the kitchen-fire. He was afraid to come up here, when the girl told him you had come home.'

'Tell JANE to tell him to come here this instant!' was the brief reply to this information.

Presently the poor boy entered, half perished with affright and cold. His father glanced at his sad plight, reproached him bitterly with his disobedience, spoke of the punishment which awaited him in the morning, as the penalty for his offence; and, in a harsh voice, concluded with:

'Now, Sir, go to your bed!'

'But, father,' said the little fellow, 'I want to tell you ——'

'Not a word, Sir: *go to bed!*'

'I only wanted to say, father, that ——'

With a peremptory stamp, an imperative wave of his hand toward the door, and a frown upon his brow, did that father, without other speech, again close the door of explanation or expostulation.

When his boy had gone supperless and sad to his bed, the father sat restless and uneasy while supper was being prepared; and, at tea-table, ate but little. His wife saw the real cause, or the additional cause of his emotion, and interposed the remark:

'I think, my dear, you ought at least to have heard what HENRY had to say. My heart ached for him when he turned away, with his eyes full of tears. HENRY is a good boy, after all, if he *does* sometimes do wrong. He is a tender-hearted, affectionate boy. He always was.'

And therewithal the water stood in the eyes of that forgiving mother, even as it stood in the eyes of MERCY, in 'the house of the Interpreter,' as recorded by BUNYAN.

After tea, the evening paper was taken up; but there was no news and nothing of interest for that father in the journal of that evening. He sat for some time in an evidently painful reverie, and then rose and repaired to his bed-chamber. As he passed the bed-room where his little boy slept, he thought he would look in upon him before retiring to rest. He crept to his low cot and bent over him. A big tear had stolen down the boy's cheek, and rested upon it; but he was sleeping calmly and sweetly. The father deeply regretted his harshness as he gazed upon his son; he felt also the 'sense of duty;' yet in the night, talking the matter over with the lad's mother, he resolved and promised, instead of punishing, as he had threatened, to make amends to the boy's aggrieved spirit in the morning for the manner in which he had repelled all explanation of his offence.

But that morning never came to the poor child in health. He awoke the next morning with a raging fever on his brain, and wild with delirium. In forty-eight hours he was in his shroud. He knew neither his father nor his mother, when they were first called to his bed-side, nor at any moment afterward. Waiting, watching for one token of recognition, hour after hour, in speechless agony, did that unhappy father bend over the couch of his dying son. Once, indeed, he thought he saw a smile of recognition light up his dying eye, and he leaned eagerly forward, for he would have given worlds to have whispered one kind word in his ear, and have been answered; but that gleam of apparent intelligence passed quickly away, and was succeeded by the cold, unmeaning glare, and the wild tossing of the fevered limbs, which lasted until death came to his relief.

Two days afterward, the undertaker came with the little coffin, and his son, a play-mate of the deceased boy, bringing the low stools on which it was to stand in the entry-hall.

'I was with HENRY,' said the lad, 'when he got into the water. We were playing down at the Long Wharf, HENRY, and FRANK MUMFORD, and I; and the tide was out very low; and there was a beam run out from the wharf; and Charles got out on it to get a fish-line and hook that hung over where the water was deep; and the first thing we saw, he had slipped off, and was struggling in the water! Henry threw off his cap and jumped clear from the wharf into the water, and, after a great deal of hard work, got Charles out; and they waded up through the mud to where the wharf was not so wet and slippery; and then I helped them to climb up the side. Charles told Henry not to say any thing about it, for, if he did, his father would never let him go near the water again. Henry was very sorry; and, all the way going home, he kept saying:

"'What will father say when he sees me to-night? I wish we had not gone to the wharf?''

'Dear, brave boy!' exclaimed the bereaved father; 'and *this* was the explanation which I so cruelly refused to hear!" And hot and bitter tears rolled down his cheeks.

Yes! that stern father now learned, and for the first time, that what he had treated with unwonted severity as a fault, was but the impulse of a generous nature, which, forgetful of self, had hazarded life for another. It was but the quick prompting of that manly spirit which he himself had always endeavored to graft upon his susceptible mind, and which, young as he was, had already manifested itself on more than one occasion.

Let me close this story in the very words of that father, and let the lesson sink deep into the hearts of every parent who shall peruse this sketch :

'Every thing that I now see, that ever belonged to him, reminds me of my lost boy. Yesterday, I found some rude pencil-sketches which it was his delight to make for the amusement of his younger brother. To-day, in rummaging an old closet, I came across his boots, still covered with dock-mud, as when he last wore them. (You may think it strange, but that which is usually so unsightly an object, is now 'most precious to me.') And every morning and evening, I pass the ground where my son's voice rang the merriest among his play-mates.

'All these things speak to me vividly of his active life ; but I cannot — though I have often tried — I *cannot* recall any other expression of the dear boy's face than that mute, mournful one with which he turned from me on the night I so harshly repulsed him. . . . Then my heart bleeds afresh !

'Oh, how careful should we all be, that in our daily conduct towards those little beings sent us by a kind PROVIDENCE, we are not laying up for ourselves the sources of many a future bitter tear ! How cautious that, neither by inconsiderate nor cruel word or look, we unjustly grieve their generous feeling ! And how guardedly ought we to weigh every action against its motive, lest, in a moment of excitement, we be led to mete out to the venial errors of the heart the punishment due only to wilful crime!

'Alas! perhaps few parents suspect how often the fierce rebuke, the sudden blow, is answered in their children by the tears, not of passion, not of physical or mental pain, but of a loving yet grieved or outraged nature!'

I will add no word to reflections so true — no correlative incident to an experience so touching.

Knick-Knacks

FROM AN EDITOR'S TABLE.

KNICK-KNACKS.

NUMBER ONE.

A REVERIE OF BOYHOOD AND POLITICAL ECONOMY: A NEW ERA AMONG CHRISTIANS: EXECUTION OF GROUND-MICE: AN HOUR IN SING-SING PRISON — MONROE EDWARDS: NARCOTIC INFLUENCE — A 'REGULAR BU'ST': GEOFFREY CRAYON AND 'OLD KNICK' IN SLEEPY HOLLOW — HEREDITARY LIGHTNING: A FEW THOUGHTS ON DEATH: ANECDOTE OF JARVIS THE PAINTER: A GHOST-STORY: COOL REPLY TO A DUNNING-LETTER: CHILDREN — HOME FEELING IN OLD AGE: A 'CUTE' YANKEE CLOCK-PEDLER: AUTUMN IN THE COUNTRY, AND ITS INFLUENCES: A STRANGE HORSE-ADVENTURE: AN INVOLVED 'COMMERCIAL TRANSACTION.'

WHEN there comes a warm autumnal rainy day, it gives us great enjoyment to go over (*omnes solus*) to Hoboken, and repair to a gable-angle of the Swiss châlet, built by the tasteful STEVENS, and there, under an open 'weather-board' canopy, gaze for hours upon the distant city, spreading before us like a map, and our noble harbor and bay, covered with tall ships, their tapering masts and cordage pencilled against the sky, or the lighter craft, with their white sails glinting for an instant in the fitful sunlight that steals through a broken cloud. There we watch the rain sift in long slanting lines across the bay, and over the town, and along the majestic Hudson, and think 'on diverse things foredone,' when we were as yet but a little boy; especially of early days in the country, when with departed 'OLLAPOD' we used to perch ourselves upon the top of a fresh hay-'barrack,' (soft and fragrant couch!) and from underneath its straw-thatch roof look out through the gently-falling rain upon the fading yellow woods, the meadows of dim dying green, and russet stubble-fields. That remembrance links with others of the country, until it merges in a sort of mental essay on Political Economy. One thinks of the reapers cutting the golden grain; of man and boy rolling the round fat 'murphies' out of the black loamy soil; of gathering in the yellow-green oats, so smooth, and so pleasant to 'cut, rake and bind;' of the Liliputian forests of tall silky flax-stems; of the yellow-corn, so delightful to husk at night, with a barn-floor full of girls and boys, waiting joyfully amidst the sweet 'husky' odors for the subsidence of the big 'heap,' that they may partake of the repast of pies and cakes and sweet cider that is spread 'in the house.' All these various labors 'in due season' freight the vessels which you see tending to the vast metropolis; some in the far distance, some huddled close together, some wide apart, but all making for one port; while there, in the great town before you, men and 'prentice-boys in dingy shirt-sleeves, at hours when the farmers, their 'patrons,' are in bed, 'ply their busy tools of trade;' cabinet-makers are sending off furniture; druggists are arming country practitioners with 'engines of destruction' against the 'great enemy' — or their patients; hardware dealers are sending out pots, kettles, and pans, for 'stewing, baking and boiling' in far western wilds — and so forth; which, in connection with general commerce, as dry-goods, tin-plates and spelter, groceries, hay, cutlery, 'grits' and 'shorts,' sarsaparilla, turpentine-gum, putty, 'ging-shang' root, codfish, hops, brads, bees-wax, soft-shell almonds, gun-powder, osnaburgs, fustic, corks, madder, hackled hemp, dried beef, nail-rods, staves and heading, varnish, and Brandreth's pills, constitute what is most usually supposed to compose the main elements of 'Political Economy!'

It was a pleasant thing to read, in a late number of a metroplitan religious journal, an account of four clergymen, of widely different denominations, meeting weekly at each other's houses, in a New-England village, for religious communion and prayer. The liberal Christian spirit which prompted this act did not exist formerly in that section, nor indeed any section, of the Union; and we hail its appearance with sincere pleasure. '*Other* sheep I have,' said our SAVIOUR, 'which are not of *this* fold; them also I must bring, and they shall hear my voice; and there shall be one fold and one shepherd.' Why should they, who profess to lead and point the way to heaven, dwell upon mere differences of doctrine, which touch neither the heart nor the life? Let them rather say, looking up to a common REDEEMER:

'O CRUCIFIED! we share thy cross,
Thy passion too sustain;
We die THY death to live THY life,
And rise with THEE again.'

L——'s '*Reminiscence of Boyhood*' was a positive treat. Well do we remember the '*Execution of the Ground-Mice*,' as performed by 'OLLAPOD' and the writer hereof, when we were 'wee things.' The prisoners were caught in the act of theft, under a 'shock' of cut-corn, after an ineffectual attempt at escape, and were confined in a square stone prison, 'digged i' the earth' of the meadow. We slept but little the first night of their confinement; we thought of them during the night-watches, and talked of them, as Giant DESPAIR talked with his wife of CHRISTIAN and HOPEFUL, shut up in Doubting-Castle. In the morning we visited the prison betimes, and fed the 'plaintiffs' and 'examinationed' them as well as DOGBERRY himself could have done. We continued to visit them for several days afterward; and their bearing evincing no penitence, they were condemned to be hung, and a day was appointed for their execution. We had seen a model of a gallows on the cover of the 'Story of Ambrose Gwinett,' and 'Ollapod' constructed a very secure 'institution' of that kind; and when the fatal morning arrived, with all due privacy the culprits were brought forth, the thread of death which was to clip the thread of their lives being round their necks. They were addressed in moving terms by Ollapod, and assured that all hope of reprieve was ridiculous; it could not be thought of by the 'authorities' for a moment. 'They must prepare to mount the scaffold!' They walked, 'supported' partly by the 'rope' around their necks, with firm hind-legs, up the ladder, and the 'fatal cord' was adjusted to the transverse beam. It was a moment to be remembered. At a signal given by the jotter-down hereof, the trap-door fell, and they were launched into — liberty! For the thread broke, and the 'wretched culprits' were soon safe in the long grass of the meadow. It was a narrow escape for 'em!

We passed an hour in the Sing-Sing State-Prison the other day; and while regarding with irresistible sympathy the wretched inmates, we could not help thinking how little, after all, of the actual suffering of imprisonment is apparent to the visitor. The ceaseless toil, the coarse fare, the solemn silence, the averted look, the yellow-white palor, of the convict; his narrow cell, with its scanty furniture, his hard couch; these indeed are 'visible to the naked eye.' Yet do but think of the demon Thought that must 'eat up his heart' during the long and inconceivably dismal hours which he passes there in darkness, in silence, and alone! Think of the tortures he must endure from the ravages of that pleasantest friend but most terrible enemy, Imagination! Oh, the height, the depth, the length and breadth, of a sensitive captive's sorrow! As we came away from the gloomy scene, we passed on a hill, within the domain of the guard, the Prison Potter's-Field, where lie, undistinguished by head-stone or any other mark, the bones of those who had little else to lay there, when their life of suffering was ended. There sleeps Monroe Edwards, whose downward fate we had marked in successive years.

We first saw him when on his trial; a handsome, well-dressed, black-whiskered, *seeming* self-possessed person, with the thin varnish of a gentleman, and an effrontery that nothing could daunt. Again we saw him, while holding court with courtezans at the door of his cell, at 'The Tombs,' the day before he left for Sing-Sing; clad in his morning-gown, with luxurious whiskers, and the manners of a pseudo-prince receiving the honors of sham-subjects. The next time we saw him he was clad in coarsest 'felon-stripe;' his head was sheared to the skull; his whiskers were no more; a dark frown was on his brow; his cheeks were pale, and his lips were compressed with an expression of remorse, rage and despair. Never shall we forget that look! He had a little while before been endeavoring to escape, and had been punished by fifty lashes with a cat-o'-nine-tails; four hundred and fifty stripes on the naked back!

Once again we saw him, after the lapse of many months. Time and suffering had done their work upon him. His once-erect frame was bowed; his head was quite bald at the top, and its scanty bordering-hair had become gray. And thus he gradually declined to his melancholy 'west of life,' until he reached his last hour; dying in an agony of terror; gnawing his emaciated fingers, to convince himself that he was still living; that the appalling change from life to death had not yet actually taken place! And now he sleeps in a felon's grave, with no record of his name or fate. Is not the way of the transgressor 'hard?'

'THIS pipe 's my pillar of clouds,
Such meteors I love to utter:
More than Welsh-men do cheese,
Or an English-man ease,
Or a Dutchman loves salt butter.

'If riches be but a smoak,
And fame be but a vapor,
Here's a rich mine indeed
In this fumy weed,
And honor enough in a taper!'

WE are reminded by these quaint stanzas, from 'The Christmas Ordinary,' of a circumstance mentioned to us by an old bank-notary of this town. He says that he has seldom presented a notice of protest, to a large amount, wherein he did not find the delinquent smoking a cigar. The bankrupt had made up his mind to the dread alternative of failing, and his chief solace was the fumes of the narcotic weed. Such a philosopher it was, who, when our notary presented him with the protest of a note for twenty thousand dollars, with the salvo, that 'he presumed it was a mistake, or an oversight,' replied, 'Oh, no; no mistake; it's a reg'lar bu'st!

'YON murky cloud is foul with rain' that here at Piermont we see rolling slowly over the hills that environ Sleepy-Hollow, on the other side of the river. Even while we watch it, it begins to shake its skirts, and to sift down upon the fading landscape its 'superflux of shower.' Looking at this, we cannot choose but think of a memorable excursion which the writer hereof once made with GEOFFREY CRAYON through the wizzard region of Sleepy-

Hollow, a neighborhood which his own pen had made world-wide famous. The morning had been thunderous and showery; nor did it entirely brighten up until the removal of the first champagne-cork at the hospitable table of 'Sunnyside;' always a precursor, as the host remarked, of 'pleasant weather about this time.' After dinner, preceded by the ladies of the household and another guest in the family-carriage, Mr. CRAYON, in a light open wagon, 'tooled' the 'Old KNICK' over the high eastern hills that enclose the sheltered valley where in their day lived and flourished old BALTUS VAN TASSEL, and his blooming daughter KATRINE. The sun came out between the pearl-colored opaque clouds; the birds began to sing in the trees; a bobolink was 'rising and sinking on a long flaunting weed' in an adjoining field; and every thing in nature was bright and smiling. Now it came to pass, howbeit, that when, beguiling the way with much rememberable converse, we came to the brow of the last hill that overlooks the turn of the road into the valley, one of the aforesaid opaque clouds, at first no bigger than a man's hand, but which had been gradually 'gathering fatness,' suddenly darkened, and presently 'opened upon us;' also there were thunderings and lightnings; and trees, singly and in ranks, tossed their plumes of green, and battled with the storm. Moreover, the rain now descended amain; insomuch that Mr. CRAYON wheeled suddenly into an angle of a rail-fence that skirted an umbrageous grove, dismounted, clambered over, and took shelter under an adjacent tree, holding over his head meanwhile the cushioned wagon-seat, adown which, as from a spout, the rain poured from his back. 'Why don't you come under here, and be comfortably housed, as *I* am?' asked the Sleepy-Hollow historian, with amusing mock gravity: 'Whereto thus then' 'Old KNICK:' 'Dare n't do it, dear Sir; 'fraid of the lightning, now playing about us; had a near relation once struck with the 'electric fluid' (the kind always mentioned by country newspapers as the most fatal) while standing under a tree; came near dying — but didn't.' 'Oh!' answered Mr. CRAYON, 'that alters the case: '*it runs in the family, eh?*''

Well, well; the idea of lightning 'running in a family;' the odd appearance of the speaker, with his inverted leathern cushion on his head, under which he looked like a Roman beneath his tortoise-shell shield; the after excursion through the valley, with all that we saw and heard by the way; the appearance of a saturated guest about the hearth of 'Sunnyside' that night, clad in roomy habiliments of the host; all these manifold recollections have arisen in about the space of a minute.

'Cur'ous' and very pleasant are the matters lodged in the thousand cells of memory!

'*Thoughts on Death*' are well intended, but they do not contain any thing very original. This is the only subject upon which every body speaks and writes without a possibility of having experienced what they undertake to discuss. Certainly it is an awful moment when the last flutter expires on the lips; when the incomprehensible soul solves the solemn secrets of nature, and blends the past, the present and the future together. 'If death,' says an old author, 'puts an end to the enjoyment of some, it terminates the sufferings of all. I care not what becomes of this frail bark of my flesh, so I but save the passenger.' When 'gray hairs besnow the brow, and grayer thoughts the heart,' how many there are, as they lay their heads nightly upon their pillows, who could wish that the slumbers which fall around their heads were the forerunners of that sleep which shall restore their borrowed powers to their original non-existence! They have come to consider life as but a momentary convulsion between two tranquil eternities; an avenue to death, as death is the gate that opens to a new and enduring life. 'Ever close by the gate of the tomb,' says the thoughtful TEUFELSDRÖCKH, 'I look upon the hostile armaments and pains and penalties of tyrannous life, placidly enough, and listen to its loudest threatenings with a still smile.' The world is a prison, out of which many are daily selected for execution:

——— 'DEATH anon must come
To all; hot tears shall macerate

Each hardened cheek of this vain multitude.
When you are dancing, by and by, that fop,
Wilted with grief, will lean upon an urn!
All days are some one's black day; this is ours,
To-morrow theirs. The Cap-and-Bells will drive
Boys from the window where his child is dying.'

Who does not sometimes 'think on these things?' Who does not, in his thoughtful hours, at summer even-tide, when the great sun has gone down the glowing west, or in the still night-watches, or on awakening in the serene morning, call to mind the solemn truth, that 'we must *all* lie down alike in the dust, and the worms shall cover us?' But 'the shortest life is long enough if it lead to a better, and the longest life is too short if it do not.'

'*Sitting for a Portrait*' is an old subject, not very felicitously handled. 'Speaking of portraits,' there is a very good story told of JARVIS, the painter, which we think will be new to many of our readers. When his bacchanalian propensities had rendered him rather an unequal if not an unsafe artist, he was employed by a gentleman in a Southern city to paint his wife, a miracle of plainness, under the stipulation that a pint of wine, at a single sitting, must be the extent of his potations. JARVIS assented, and in due time produced a perfect fac-simile of the lady. On exhibiting it to the husband, he seemed disappointed. It was *too* literal a transcript of the original. 'Couldn't you have given it,' said he to the painter, 'a *little* less —— that is, couldn't you give it *now* a little more ——.' 'If you expect me,' interposed JARVIS, seeing the husband's drift at once, 'if you expect me to make a *handsome* portrait of your wife, I must have more than a *pint* of wine at a sitting! I couldn't get up imagination enough to make her even good-looking, under *a quart* at the very least!' The gentleman 'left the presence.'

WE are not, as a general fact, a believer in ghosts; but the following circumstances will, we think, stagger the incredulous reader, as we confess it staggered us. The relator, when a boy, lived in the country. While somewhere in his early 'teens, he was sent by his father, on a dim half-moonshiny November evening, to accompany a young girl, the daughter of a distant neighbor, to her home. The road in one place led along the side of a stone wall, which surrounded a grave-yard in a sparse grove, on a breezy eminence, about half-way to their place of destination. Having company, he thought little of the grave-yard, until he arrived opposite to it, on his return alone. He was a brave lad; but his heart beat thick and fast when his progress was suddenly arrested by a prolonged groan, proceeding from the 'place of graves.' His first thought was to run; the next, that his father's old negro-man 'JAKE,' who was up to all sorts of practical jokes, had got into the grave-yard, on purpose to frighten him, as he came along back. This idea put him upon his mettle. He picked up three or four 'rocks,' as they say at the South, and clambered up on the wall. Looking down upon the field of irregular tomb-stones, some rising high in the faint moonlight, and others shrinking away in shadow, he called out: 'You can't come it JAKE! *I* know you! And if you do that again, I'll fix your black flint for you! I've got some stones here, and I'll make you *feel* 'em, you blasted nigger!' But there was no response; only a deep groan. He forthwith dispatched a 'rock' in the direction whence the sound proceeded. Nothing moved — not a sound was heard. 'Now be done, JAKE!' exclaimed the now slightly terrified boy, 'or I'll throw again: *these* stones will kill you in a minute, if they hit you!' The answer to this threat was an agonizing sound, something between a groan and a long subdued howl; the unearthly voice ending in a trembling cadence, as though there had a

> 'A GUST of wind sterte up behind,
> And whistled through the bones'

of some poor ghost, shaking with the cold of a November night; but there was no other reply. On looking more closely, however, the trembling lad distinctly saw a body, all in white, lying between two graves, not far off, and beckoning to him with long, attenuate arms, and occasioal groaning in spirit, as a spirit would naturally do. 'Well, who's afraid?' reasoned the lad; 'if it *is* a ghost, it can't hurt *me;* if it *ain't* a ghost, blast the critter! I can hurt *him*—and I will!' He now jumped down from the wall, and advanced to the spot; and there he found, sprawling on her back, between two grave-hillocks, her head twisted round against the inner-side of one of the marble head-stones, *his father's old white mare!* She had met with a sad accident while wandering among the tombs, and cropping the fall-growth of timothy and clover 'which grew thereby.' She had fallen, rolled over upon her back between two graves, and was unable to rise. The secret was now out. He had often heard the distressing groans of a horse in pain, and saw how easily he had mistaken the slow-moving legs of 'Old White' for the beckoning of ghostly hands.

We have seen, and read of, some 'cool' things in our day, but the following, which we derive from an esteemed and always entertaining correspondent, is positively 'iced.' A young lawyer got his first note for collection. It was against a country customer; so he sat down and wrote him a letter, in due form, advising him that his note was left for collection, that it 'had run a long time,' and required immediate attention to 'save costs.' In about ten days he received this answer:

'*Valley Forks, November* 15, 1849.

'F. T. H., ESQ.: DEAR SIR: I received your polite note of the fifth instant this day. It was directed to the post-office at Freetown. The mail comes from your village to Tompkinsville every day by the stage, which runs from your place to Owego, leaving your village at six o'clock in the forenoon. From Tompkinsville there is a mail every other day to Freetown, and also to Valley Forks. From thence there is a cross-mail around the hills through the lower towns in this county to our place once a week, but the post-masters on that route can't read very well, and sometimes keep a letter over one mail to spell out the direction. By directing your letters to this office, where I get my papers, I should get them generally in about three days after you mail them, and about a week or ten days sooner than if directed to Freetown; which delay might, in some cases, be of considerable consequence. I hope, my dear Sir, you will not suffer any inconvenience from it this time; but I thought it best, as you seemed a little ignorant of the geography of this part of the country, to give you this information, that you might in future know how to direct to, dear Sir,

'Yours respectfully,

'JOHN CALKINS.

'P. S.—As to that note: you say 'it has run a long time.' I can only say, as the boy said of the molasses, '*Let her run!*'

It strikes us that it would be rather sharp practice to serve a summons and complaint on that customer!

RARE little 'plants' for the immortal gardens and groves of the 'better land' are children! How continually we 'oldsters' go back to our earliest days! Take up, over your morning meal, a daily journal, and running your eye, faint-readingly, along what may interest you pleasantly, perhaps exultantly, you casually glance (in passing most likely to some other department of the paper which has also an especial charm for you) at the deaths. *There* is recorded the demise of a metropolitan merchant. You knew him, when a boy, in the country; you knew him also, when, rising by regular steps, from a toiling clerk to an eminent master of scores of such as he himself had been, he walked a monarch in the mart of trade, and his voice was potent among 'multitudes of men commercing.' You read, that on such a day, amidst the crowded thoroughfares of the town in which he had lived so long, he died. Perhaps you had not even missed him from the crowded streets; yet he died; and you remark, in the notice of his funeral, that 'his remains are to be taken, by the evening boat, or cars, to —— for interment.' Ah! yes; —— is a small hamlet; far removed from the restless din, the ceaseless turmoil, of the great city, where your friend's gainful and active life has been passed; but there, there at the old homestead, lies in 'cold obstruction' an aged and honored father; there rests the 'mother who looked on his childhood, who smoothed his pillow, and administered to his helplessness;' a sister, tenderly beloved, sleeps there; a fair flower, nipped too early by the untimely frosts of death; there too is buried a brother, whose place was never, never supplied; and there would *he* rest; *there*, while the slow-counted hours of illness were notching the progress of his earthly decline, he turned ever his thoughts of final repose. He knew he was soon going to renew the childhood of his soul in the undiscovered country; and he would rise, at the last great day, to the consciousness of a new existence, on the very spot where GOD first breathed into his earthly body the breath of life, and he became a living soul. We *began* this, to introduce an amusing anecdote of a child; but we could n't do it.

A FRIEND tells us a good story of a Yankee clock-pedler down south, which, among other things, may perhaps account for the peculiar favor with which that class of chevaliers are regarded in that region. He took with him, in a long Connecticut covered-wagon, forty clocks, and sold and 'put 'em up' along the country, in one direction, warranting them to keep 'fust-rate time.' He exhausted his supply, with but a single exception; and then, with unparalleled assurance, he turned about and retraced his course. The last person to whom he had sold a clock hailed him as he was going by: 'Look o' here, stranger, that clock you sold me ain't worth a continental cuss. 'T wont go at all!' 'You don't say so! Then *you* must ha' got it, Square! See, the fact is, I find by my numbers that there was *one* o' my clocks — I had forty on 'em when I fust sot out — that I am a leetle afraid on: it was condemned to-hum 'fore I come away; but some how or 'nother it got put into the wagon. What's the number o' your clock, Square?' 'Fourteen thousand and one,' replied his victim. 'That's jest the blasted thing!' exclaimed the pedler. 'I'll chang' with yeöu; yeöu take my last one, and I'll take this hum. The *works* is good, I guess; on'y want fixin' a leetle.' The exchange was made: and all along the road the pedler was similarly arrested by his dupes, who were similarly duped in return. He took every successive bad clock to his next customer, and received another bad clock for the next. And this was mentioned and laughed at as 'Yankee 'cuteness.' It strikes us forcibly, however, that 'swindling,' of the meanest kind, would be a more appropriate designation for such a transaction.

WALKING over the hills to-day, at the Ferry of DOBB, that looks down upon the broad Tappaän Zee, and the distant shores of the lordly Hudson, holding 'Young KNICK.'s little brown hand in ours, as we traversed the faintly-fading fields, we began to meditate upon *why* it is, that even the precursors of Autumn are so melancholy. The wind has a different sound in the trees; it *sighs* as 'fall' approaches, and the leaves respond but slightly to its most fervent kiss: moreover, there is a hushed silence in the air which belongs not to Summer. And these outward things beget an irresistible inward sadness: and as we walked, these lines of TENNYSON came to mind:

'TEARS, idle tears, I know not what they mean,
Tears from the depth of some divine despair,
Rise in the heart and gather to the eyes,
In looking on the fading autumn fields,
And thinking of the days that are no more!'

There are no two sadder words in the English language than these: 'no more — no more!'

A LADY-FRIEND, not a thousand miles from Gotham, relates the following, which has struck us, rightly considered, as possessing an element of the pathetic in no ordinary degree. An old horse, that had served his master faithfully for some twenty-five years, was sold to a drover from one of the little Long-Island Sound villages near New-Haven, and taken to that pleasant town for shipment to the West Indies. As the old fellow went away, in new hands, he seemed to have a kind of instinctive presentiment that he was to return no more. He cast 'many a longing, lingering look behind,' and whinnied his apprehensions so

affectingly, that his old owner almost relented, and but for seeming childish, he would have followed and revoked the bargain, a course which his children, who were watching the old horse depart, strenuously urged him to adopt. He disappeared, however, with his new master, and soon after, in company with a large drove of other horses, he was placed on board a vessel, which, one afternoon in March, set sail from New-Haven for the West Indies. The vessel had hardly reached the open Sound, at night-fall, before a storm began to 'brew,' which by nine o'clock became so violent that the safety of the ship, captain and crew, was placed in imminent jeopardy. The craft labored so heavily that it was found necesary to throw over much of the live freight, which greatly encumbered the deck. The oldest and least valuable horses were selected, and among them was our four-legged 'hero.' The stormy waters of the Sound received the poor old fellow; but his 'destiny' was not yet to be fulfilled. The shore, which the vessel had 'hugged' in the tempest, was only three miles distant, and this, with more than '*superhuman* effort,' he was enabled to reach. That very night his old master was awakened by the familiar 'whinnying' of his faithful beast, over the long-accustomed door-yard gate; saying, like the old 'gaberlunzie-man' in the Scottish song,

'Get up, good man, and let me in!'

The familiar sound came like the voice of NAT. LEE'S 'spirit-horse,' as described by DANA in 'The Buccaniers,' to that remorseful master. He *did* 'get up,' and led the old steed into his wonted stall, which he thereafter occupied undisturbed until his death. With an unerring instinct, that animal had travelled twenty-two miles, after reaching the shore, before he arrived at the door of his old master. 'I shall never sell another old horse,' said the original narrator of this story to our friend, 'the longest day I live!'

IT will be some time, if not longer, before we shall awaken the echoes of our quiet sanctum with a laugh so irrepressible as a guffaw which has just escaped us, at a mercantile anecdote inimitably related by a German friend. An old fellow living at Frankfort-on-the-Main, sent to a business-correspondent at Frankfort-on-the-Oder, a large consignment of cotton stockings, and at the same time, to another correspondent in the same place, an equally large consignment of cotton night-caps, the product of his own manufactory. He wrote to each the price at which they were to sell, but the sum designated was found to be too large, of which fact they took occasion to inform him. He yielded a little in his demand, but still there were no offers for his fabrics. Again he writes, in reply to other letters of his correspondents, naming a yet smaller amount; but weeks elapse, and still no sale. At length he writes to each correspondent to make *some* disposition of his manufactures; if they can't get money for them, at least to exchange them, no matter at what reasonable sacrifice, for any other goods. Under these instructions, the stocking-factor calls upon the night-cap agent, both unknown to each other in connection with their principal, and 'names his views;' he wishes to exchange a lot of superior cotton stockings for some other goods; he is not particular what kind, as the transaction is for a friend, who is desirous of 'closing his stock.' The man at first can think of nothing which he would like to exchange for so large a supply of stockings; but at length a bright thought strikes him. 'I have,' said he, 'a consignment of cotton night-caps from an old correspondent, which I shall not object to exchange for your stockings.' The bargain was soon closed. The stocking-factor wrote back at once that he had at length been enabled to comply with the instructions of his principal. He had exchanged his stockings for 'a superior article of night-cap,' in an equal quantity, which he was assured were likely to be much in demand before a great while!

The next day came a letter from the night-cap agent, announcing his success, and appended to the letter was a big bill for commissions! As YELLOWPLUSH would say, 'Fanzy that gent's feelinks!'

WE suggested, not long since, that a simplification of the nomenclature of the law would not be amiss; and we ventured to offer a few arguments in support of that position. We are quite of the opinion that a similar simplification of *Medical Nomenclature* would prove of service to the masses. We have sometimes seen the necessity of this very ludicrously illustrated. Very much confounded was our friend Doctor DOANE, a few years since, by a remark of one of his patients. The day previous, the Doctor had prescribed that safe and palatable remedy, the 'syrup of birch-thorn,' and had left his prescription duly written in the usual cabalistic characters: '*Syr. Rham. Cath.*' On enquiring if the patient had taken the medicine, a thunder-cloud darkened her face; lightning flashed from her eyes; and she roared out: 'No! I can read your doctor-writing — and I aint a-goin to take the *Syrup of Ram-Cats* for any body under GOD's heaven!' 'Hence we view the great necessity there is' of a material change in our medical nomenclature.

NUMBER TWO.

AN INDEPENDENT STAGE-COACH DRIVER: THE RETORT CONCLUSIVE: THE SEA AND ITS INFLUENCES: THE DELUDED DOG AND REFRACTORY LOBSTER: DEATH OF THE FIRST-BORN — AN AFFECTING INCIDENT: A DRY PUMP: EXPERIMENT UPON THE MUSICAL ORGANS OF A JACK-ASS: THE 'CLOUDLESS SKIES' OF PARADISE: A RAIL-ROAD 'RECUSSANT:' A LITTLE EVENING-SCENE IN THE SANCTUM: HUMORS OF AN ELECTION — THE CHALLENGED 'FRIEND:' THE TRUE HERO — AN AUTHENTIC ANECDOTE: NATURAL HISTORY — THE FLAMINGO: PUZZLING QUESTIONS IN 'LOGIC:' REMINISCENCES IN THE LITTLE CHURCH AT LAKE-GEORGE.

MANY readers will remember Mrs. KIRKLAND's story in her '*New Home*,' of the Michigan stage-driver, who 'drew rein' in a violent autumn-storm at the gate of one of the far-scattered cabins of a western forest, into which he ran, leaving his passengers, a burly Englishman and two querulous, 'stuck-up' daughters, to follow him, as best they might. The doughty JOHN BULL came in after him, leading his daughters, with rueful faces and sadly bedraggled skirts, all three looking grouty and glum enough. 'I say,' said the Englishman to the driver, who had ensconced himself in a warm and cozy seat by the fire, 'I say, that luggage ought to be brought in, ye kno'.' 'Wal, *I* should think so, tew. If 't was mine, *I* should bring it in, any how. 'T may get sp'ilet.' 'Well, fellow, why *don't* you bring it in?' 'Why don't I *bring it in?*' said the other, slowly and with an unmistakable sneer; 'why, I aint your servant, *be* I? Guess *not:* that's a berry that don't grow on the bushes about these diggin's. I *drive* you, Square, and I don't do nothin' else!' This incident came to mind a few moments ago, on hearing a friend relate the following anecdote. He said, that soon after the revolutionary war, a brave Yankee officer, a former captain in the service, happened to be at St. Petersburg, in Russia, and while there was invited to dine at the table of a distinguished merchant. There was a large number of guests at the table, and among the rest an English lady, who was anxious to appear as one of the 'knowing ones.' On understanding that an American was sitting near her, she expressed to one of her friends a determination to quiz him. She fastened upon him like a tigress, making numerous inquiries touching our habits, customs, dress, manners, modes of life, education, amusements, etc. To all these queries the officer gave courteous answers, which seemed to satisfy all the company with the exception of the lady herself. She was determined *not* to be satisfied, and went on: 'Have the rich people in your country any carriages? — for I suppose there are *some* who call themselves rich.' 'My residence,' replied the captain, 'is in a small town upon an island, where there are but few carriages kept; but in the larger towns and cities on the main land there are quite a number maintained, suited to our republican manners.' 'Indeed?!' replied his fair questioner, in a tone that was both interrogative and exclamatory: 'I can't fancy where you find coachmen: I should n't think the Americans knew *how* to drive a coach.' 'We find no difficulty on *that* account, Madam,' calmly rejoined the captain; 'we can have plenty of drivers by sending to England for them.' 'To England!' exclaimed the lady, speaking very quickly; 'I think the Americans ought to drive the English, instead of the English driving the Americans.' 'We *did*, Madam, in the late war,' rejoined the officer; 'but since the peace, we have permitted the English to drive us!' There was no more 'quizzing' of our American during the dinner. He waited in vain, like SAM WELLER in 'BARDELL *vs.* PICKWICK,' for the next question.

'THE sea is HIS, and HE made it!' Now there is conveyed in this sentence, to our poor conception at least, a kind of mysterious sublimity; and we never stand by the solemn shore of the great ocean, without hearing in every wave that, as it rolls pouring onward and expanding side-wise, breaks at the ends of its emerald cylinder into a musical foam, without taking up the burthen of that pervading Voice, and exclaiming, '*The sea is His, and He made it!*' And it is pleasurable to think that this impression, if not general, is at least not uncommon. We have remarked, with unwonted sympathy, in Dickens's last story, how the waves, 'hoarse with the repetition of their mystery,' affect his heroine, as they roll the dank sea-weed at her feet, while she stands by the resounding shore. Even thus, too, had they awakened a vague yet sublime sense of the 'Infinite and the Eternal' in the minds of Florence and her 'little brother, gone home to God.' What thoughts of the departed, what spirits of the Past, what dim foreshadowings of the Future, are evoked by the sight of the illimitable ocean, and the 'voice of all his waves!' Tennyson, in a few brief lines, which we have repeated alone on the sea-shore, we know not how often, touches this chord, whose vibrations are so melodious to the soul:

'Break, break, break,
On thy cold gray stones, O Sea!
And I would that my tongue could utter
The thoughts that arise in me.

'O well for the fisherman's boy,
That he shouts with his sister at play!
O well for the sailor lad,
That he sings in his boat on the bay!

'And the stately ships go on
To their haven under the hill:
But O for the touch of a vanish'd hand,
And the sound of a voice that is still!

'Break, break, break,
At the foot of thy crags, O Sea!
But the tender grace of a day that is dead
Will never come back to me.'

THERE was much surrounding cachination where this circumstance was mentioned the other evening: A man who was 'somedele' fond of lobsters, was wistfully regarding a basket of them in the market, with his dog by his side, while another by-stander was sticking the end of his cane into one of the disengaged claws of a big fellow at the top. 'How he does hold on!' said the man with the cane. 'Yes,' responded the man with the dog, 'but it 's because he '*dents* the cane, and his claws won't slip on the wood. But he could n't hold on to a critter, or you or I, in that way. When he feels any thing *givin'*, a lobster always stops pinchin'.' 'Guess *not*,' said the owner of the basket: 'you put your dog's tail in that there claw, and you 'll *see* whether he 'll hold on to 't or not.' No sooner said than done: the lobster-lover lifted up his dog, dropped his tail into the open claw, which closed instanter, and the dog, 'as smit by sudden pain,' ran off howling, at the top of his speed. 'Hello!' exclaimed the owner, 'whistle back your dog: d—n him! he 's runnin' off with the lobster!'. 'Whistle back your *lobster!*' rejoined the other; '*that* dog aint coming back; that dog 's *in pain.* I can't git him to come near me when he 's in pain.' That humane citizen dined that day upon as fine a lobster as there was in *that* basket, 'any how!'

THERE is an affecting passage in one of the letters of Mrs. GRANT of Laggan, recently published, describing the death of Mrs. BRUNTON, author of 'Self-Control,' 'Discipline,' etc. Being for a long time without offspring, she signalized herself by her tender care of the forlorn and helpless children of others. At length, after being nineteen years married, her only earthly wish seemed about to be granted. 'Why,' says Mrs. GRANT, 'should I tell you of our hopes and joys on this occasion? After three days of great suffering, she gave birth to a still-born child. She insisted on seeing it, held its little hand, and said, 'The feeling this hand has caused to my heart will never leave it.' Shortly after a relative came in, and spoke tenderly of her loss. 'There was nothing so dear to me as my child,' she replied, 'and I make my SAVIOUR welcome to it.' She 'sorrowed most of all,' as she lay on her death-bed, for her bereaved husband; thinking sadly with the tender English poet:

'HALF could I bear, methinks, to leave this earth,
And thee, more loved than aught beneath the sun,
If I had lived to smile but on the life
Of one dear pledge; and shall there then be none
In future times, no gentle little one,
To clasp thy neck, and look resembling me?''

THE '*Lay of the Pump*,' in all its *thoughts* is a rank plagiarism from HAWTHORNE'S admirable 'Rill from the Town-Pump.' The author may really be, for aught we know, what he claims to be, a 'Temperance Man;' but he is a thief, notwithstanding. By the by, speaking of pumps, there is a very mysterious contrivance of this sort in the village of Cherry-Valley. When the good citizens are pumping it, it utters a sort of subdued screech, that seems to be a cross between the guttural caterwaul of an enraged grimalkin and the opening bray of a donkey. We heard it three or four times with increasing amazement; and at length ventured to ask of a by-stander, who was watching the Richfield cohorts winding their way down 'White's Hill' into the village, 'In the name of Discord, friend, is that a pump or a jack-ass?' 'It 's a pump, I guess; though it doos sound something *like* a jack, that 's sartin.' Our informant was a singular-looking genius. He had a jolly, twinkling eye, a broad-brimmed, low-crowned old hat, a nose that turned under instead of up, and a face that *laughed* in every line of its surface. He wore, moreover, what we had often heard of, but had never seen before, a pair of leather-rimmed spectacles, with round blue-green glasses, as if cut from a coarse window-pane. 'We had a curious jack,' he continued, 'down in our town. He belonged to a terrible obstinate man, who kept him in a lot back o' the meetin'-house. Every Sunday, when the hosses was druv under the shed along the back-eend o' the meetin'-house, that tarnal jack would begin to bray, and keep it up all sermon-time. In summer, when the windows was open, you could n't hear nothin' else, scasely. The man that owned him hated the minister as he did pizen, and he would n't put the blasted critter into any other lot, out o' clear spite. But the folks could n't stand it; and one day one of the deacon's sons catched the jack, and putting a knife up his nose, cut out a piece of the dividin'-*grissle*, about the size of a dollar, so 's to prevent his braying any more; and he *did 'nt* make a great deal o' noise while 't was gettin' well; but when it healed, and he tried to play a bray on it, it made the *awfullest* noise you ever heer'd! It was a different instrument altogether. At first goin'-off it was a terrible bray, but it come out at the eend with the *shrillest whistle* you ever see; sharper than a fife, and as loud as the scare-pipe of a locomotive ingine. It was tew much; folks could n't bear it; and a good many of the congregation j'ined together, and went to buy the plaguy nuisance off. The owner laäfed when they called on him and told their business; but they gi'n him his price, and put the noisy critter out o' the pale of the church!'

WE remember crossing to Hoboken one mellow autumn evening with an esteemed friend, one among the most vigorous and popular of our American poets. There was such a pomp of golden and many-colored clouds in the track of the setting-sun as we had never seen before. 'Oh!' exclaimed our companion, 'what a beautiful world this is! They tell us of the balmy airs and the 'cloudless skies' of Paradise: then,' he added, pointing to the infinitely beautiful and glowing west, 'then they have not *that* there: and what can a scene be worth that has not clouds? How can we truly appreciate the light of the blessed sun without them? And how gloriously they *illustrate* the brightness of his beams!' It has always seemed to us that heaven should seldom be compared, in its 'physical features,' if we may so speak, with the earth; but rather depicted as a place where the redeemed soul, in a new sphere of righteousness and love, shall 'look for the restoration of the old ruined earth and heaven, from which beauty and life shall have departed, and from which planets and stars have vanished away.' And this, when the fires of the resurrection morning shall redden the last day, this shall be witnessed. 'These eyes,' says a rapt master of sacred song:

'These eyes shall see them fall,
Mountains and stars and skies;
These eyes shall see them all
Out of their ashes rise:
These lips shall then His praise rehearse
Whose nod restores the universe!'

A FRIEND of ours, sojourning during the past summer in one of the far-off 'shore-towns' of Massachusett's Bay, was not a little amused one day at the querulous complainings of *one* of the 'oldest inhabitants' against rail-roads; his experience in which consisted in having seen the end of one laid out, and at length the cars running upon it. Taking out his old pipe, on a pleasant summer afternoon, and looking off upon the ocean, and the ships far off and out at sea with the sun upon their sails, he said: '*I* don't think much o' rail-roads: they aint no kind o' *justice* into 'em. Neöw what kind o' justice is it, when rail-roads takes one man's upland and carts it over in wheel-barrers onto another man's *ma'sh?* What kind o' 'commodation be they? You can't go when you *want* to go; you got to go when the bell rings, or the blasted noisy whistle blows. I tell yeöw it's payin' tew much for the whistle. Ef you live a leetle ways off the dee-pot, you got to pay to *git* to the rail-road; and ef you want to go any wheres else 'cept just to the eend on it, you got to pay to go a'ter you git *there.* What kind o' 'commodation is *that?* Goin' round the country tew, murderin' folks, runnin' over cattle, sheep, and hogs, and settin' fire to bridges, and every now and then burnin' up the woods. Mrs. ROBBINS, down to Cod-p'int, says, and she ought to know, for she's a pious woman, and belongs to the lower church, she said to me, no longer ago than day-'fore yesterday, that she'd be cuss'd if she did n't *know* that they sometimes run over critters *a-purpose* — they did a likely shoat o' her'n, and never paid for 't, 'cause they was a 'corporation' they said. What kind o' 'commodation is that? Besides: now I've lived here, clus to the dee-pot, ever sence the road started to run, and seen 'em go out and come in; but *I* never could see that they went so d — d *fast*, nuther!' Now here, it strikes us, is an individual example of the feeling which constituted the combined sentiment that has consigned the Michigan rail-road conspirators to a long and gloomy imprisonment.

A DEAR little bright-eyed girl, of some five years, who has been lying upon the fur-rug before the sanctum fire, suddenly pauses in her disjointed, innocent chat; says 'Little BLINKEY has come to town,' and that her eyes are heavy; creeps up to the paternal knee, and half asleep, repeats, very touchingly to us, we must say, and certainly in the most musical of all 'still small voices,' these lines, which a loving elder sister has taught her:

'JESUS, tender Shepherd, hear me,
Bless THY little lamb to-night;
Through the darkness be THOU near me,
Watch my sleep till morning light.

'All this day THY hand hath led me,
And I thank THEE for THY care;
THOU hast clothed me, warmed and fed me—
Listen to my evening prayer.'

The prayer itself dies upon her lips, in almost indistinct, sleepy murmurs; only, when KITTY, who has come for her, is taking her away to the nursery, she says, half awakened:

. . . 'take me, when I die, to Heaven,
Happy there with THEE to dwell!'

Since little JOSE went up stairs, we 've been thinking of this, and because it interested *us*, we thought we would iot it down.

THERE are certain '*Humors of an Election*' that are worth watching by a lover of the burlesque. 'I challenge that man's vote!' said a fellow with 'building materials in his hat,' at an up-town poll last month. The person challenged lived in a princely mansion in the middle of an entire square, which contained the original soil and the original trees of Manhattan Island. 'Look o' here' said the challenger, 'what street do you live in?—what's the number of your house?—on which side of the street is it?' 'There *is* no number on my house, and it is on neither side of the street.' 'I *thought* so! Do n't know which side o' the street you live, and hain't got no number onto your door! You can go home to your house, if you can find it; you can't vote the Tig-whicket, nor no *other* ticket at *this* poll!' The challenger was walked out by the officers in attendance, and the last we saw of him, he was looking up under the hat of a friend, his body at a reeling angle forward, and trying to persuade him to go to a drinking-shop near by, and get a 'scottle of Botch ale!' Speaking of challenging votes, a friend has just mentioned to us a clever anecdote of a trick served upon a challenger by an English Quaker, several years ago, before the city was divided into numerous election districts. 'I challenge that man's vote: he is not a naturalized citizen,' said a rough-spoken individual to the quiet Friend in question. 'Thee must *know* that I am, I think.' 'If you *are* a citizen, where 's your papers? We want your *papers*,' interposed the challenger. 'They are at my residence.' 'Well, you 'll have to *bring* 'em 'fore you can vote here.' The old gentleman went home for his papers, but when he returned, the polls were closed. The next year party spirit ran very high, and the elections were bitterly contested; and again the English Friend was challenged as before, by the same person, and for the same alleged cause. 'Now thee *does n't* want me to go back *this* year to my house for my papers, does thee? Thee knows I came only a little too late with my papers last year. Does thee require me to bring them *again?*' 'To be sure I do,' replied the challenger: 'you can 't vote till you *show* your papers.' 'Well,' said the Quaker, with a faint smile on his face, 'I *thought* that perhaps thee might insist upon seeing them, and so I brought them *with* me this time!' They were 'all correct,' his vote was deposited, and as he turned round to go out, he said to the discomfited challenger, 'Farewell, friend: thee had better luck last year!'

'THERE is an endearing tenderness,' says WASHINGTON IRVING, 'in the love of a mother for her son, that transcends all other affections of the heart.' We have just heard a touching illustration of the fact, that the love of a son for his mother may also transcend and swallow up all other affections, at a moment, too, when he might well be pardoned for remembering only his own great trials. Some two years ago, a young man, belonging to Philadelphia, was returning by rail-road to that city from the town of Reading, Pennsylvania. By an accident which happened to the train as it was approaching town, and while he was standing upon the platform, he was thrown off, and fell partly under the wheels of the succeeding car; and his right arm, 'marrow, bones, and all,' was crushed to a jelly, and dropped uselessly at his side. This, however, was fortunately his only injury. He was a young man of determined nerve, and of the noblest spirit. He uttered no complaint — not even a groan. When the train arrived at the dépôt, a carriage was immediately called, when, attended by his friend, he said to the coachman, 'Drive at once to Dr. M——'s, in Walnut-street.' 'Had n't you better go immediately home?' asked his friend. 'No,' said he, 'I don't want them to know any thing about me until it is all over.' 'Our hero,' for he *was* a hero, was deaf to all the counter-remonstrances of his friend, and they drove rapidly to the house of the eminent surgeon alluded to. They were shown into the parlor, and the doctor was summoned. After an examination, 'Well, my dear fellow,' said the surgeon, for he was well acquainted with his patient, 'you know, I suppose, what must be done?' 'I do,' he replied, 'and it is for the purpose of having it done that I am here.' 'My surgical-table,' said the doctor, 'is below.' 'Can it not be done without that?' asked the sufferer. 'I cannot be tied — I cannot be held. Amputate my arm here, doctor,' he continued, holding out his dangling limb over the back of the sofa. 'Do it *here*, Doctor, I shall not flinch; I shall not interfere with your operations.' The limb was bared; two attendants, medical students in the house, were summoned; the arm was taken off above the elbow, while the patient sat as he had requested, uttering no groan, nor speaking a single word, while the operation was being performed. The dressings were applied; and, attended by his friend, the patient had reached the door on his way to his own house, which was very near by, when he turned round to the surgeon, and said: 'Doctor, I should like to look at my arm once more: pray let me see it.' The surgeon raised the mangled limb: the patient glanced at the bloodless hand, and said, 'Doctor, there is *a ring* upon the middle finger of that hand; won't you take it off for me? My MOTHER gave me that ring when she was on her death-bed. I can part with my arm, but while I live, I can't part with that ring!' The ring was slipped from the cold, white finger: 'Put it on *that* finger,' said he, holding out the same finger of his left hand. As he was leaving the door, with his attendant, to enter the carriage, he said, '*How* shall I break this thing to my poor sister?' Is not this a *true* 'hero,' reader?

'DID you ever see a wild-goose a-sailing on the ocean?' That is 'a sight,' no doubt; but it strikes us that the amphibious stalking Flamingos around the fountain at the Bowling-Green are objects even more to be admired. Nothing can exceed their singularly grotesque appearance. A Transcendental correspondent of ours, who had just been reading a 'chorus of spirits' in a new German play, improvised the following lines the other day, while looking through the rusty iron pickets at that bit of 'chaste practice' in fountain-architecture, the pile of rocks that rises in 'ragged majesty' within the pales:

NATURAL HISTORY: THE FLAMINGO.

FIRST VOICE.

'OH! tell me have you ever seen a long leg'd Flamingo?
Oh! tell me have you ever seen in the water him go?'

SECOND VOICE.

'Oh! yes, at Bowling-Green I've seen a long-leg'd Flamingo,
Oh! yes, at Bowling-Green I've seen in the water him go.'

FIRST VOICE.

'Oh! tell me did you ever see a bird so funny stand-o,
When forth he from the water comes and gets upon the land-o?'

SECOND VOICE.

'No! in my life I ne'er did see a bird so funny stand-o,
When forth he from the water comes and gets upon the land-o.'

FIRST VOICE

'He has a leg some three feet long, or near it, so they say, Sir,
Stiff upon one alone he stands, t'other he stows away, Sir.'

SECOND VOICE.

'And what an ugly head he's got! I wonder that he'd wear it,
But rather *more* I wonder that his long slim neck can bear it.'

FIRST VOICE.

'And think, this length of neck and legs, (no doubt they have their uses,)
Are members of a little frame, much smaller than a goose's!'

BOTH.

'Oh! is n't he a curious bird, that red long-leg'd Flamingo?
A water bird, a gawky bird, a sing'lar bird, by Jingo!'

MOST likely many of our readers will remember this 'vexed question' in logic: 'It either *rains* or it does *not* rain: but it does *not* rain; therefore it rains.' This used to puzzle us hugely; as did also the mathematical problem, in simple equations, which ensues: '*A cat* has one more tail than *no* cat; no cat has two tails; ergo, *a cat has three tails!*' The conclusion is irresistible. Here is something, however, which is of deeper import: 'JOHNSON studied law with DOBSON, under the agreement that he should pay DOBSON, when he (JOHNSON) *gained his first cause.* After a time DOBSON got tired of waiting for the conditions of the contract, and sued JOHNSON for his pay. He reasoned thus: 'If I sue him I shall get paid at any rate, because if I *gain* the cause, I shall be paid by the decision of the court; if I *lose* it, I shall be paid by the conditions of the contract, for then JOHNSON will have gained his first cause; therefore I am safe.' JOHNSON, on the other hand, being prodigiously frightened, sought counsel, and was told to reason thus: 'DOBSON reasons well, but there must be a flaw in his argument; because *I* and not *he* will gain the victory. If the suit goes in my favor, I shall gain it by the decision of the court; if it goes against me, I shall gain it by the terms of the contract, not having yet won my first cause. Of course I shall not have to pay him!' *Vive la Logique!*

SITTING in the little church near the 'Lake House,' Lake George, to-day, with congenial friends, we were taken back, on the wings of memory, to the days and the scenes of our boyhood. We were once more at the old homestead, once again at the old country-church; for here were the high-back'd pews, of the native color of the wood; the pulpit without adornment; the jack-knife initials of boys, carried about by no 'wind of doctrine' heard at conventicle, but contrariwise, full of the very 'old Scratch' during sermon-time; nay, here were the very psalm-and-hymn books, in the 'identical' sheepskin-binding of yore. But no MOTHER came into that homely pew with us, unfolding from around her fan the sweet-smelling white handkerchief, redolent of the aroma of dried orange-peel, that scented the very drawer whence it was taken, and taking thence sprigs of fragrant 'caraway' and 'fennel' to give to her little twin-boys; no BROTHER sat there, with his young heart even then full of unuttered and unwritten poetry, as he looked through an open window upon the green contented fields of summer,— shimmering in the hot haze that hung over them, like the tremulous rays which overhang a furnace — or surveyed on the fan the fair pictured damsel in vermillion rrobes and blue hat, assisting a little boy, in bright yellow round-about and white sailor-trowsers, to fly a scarlet kite with a green tail. All these associations were of the Past:

> 'OH, TIME! how in thy rapid flight
> Do all Life's phantoms flit away:
> The smile of hope, and young delight,
> Fame's meteor-beam and fancy's ray!'

'Onward driveth Time, and in a little while our lips are dumb!' All things have their season, and ripen toward the grave: ripen, fall, and cease.

NUMBER THREE.

A MATTER-OF-FACT GUEST: RAIN UPON THE ROOF: A MOTHER'S GRIEF: THE MISSION OF LITTLE CHILDREN: ACEPHALOUS — A NEW DEFINITION: INFLUENCE OF THE GREAT METROPOLIS UPON THE QUIET COUNTRYMAN: A 'DREADFUL ACCIDENT' — A YANKEE'S REVENGE: SUGGESTION OF A LOCOMOTIVE ON A WINTRY NIGHT: A SCOTCH 'CONSOLATION' FOR A SLIGHT: THE YANKEE IN POWERS'S STUDIO: NEW READINGS IN HAMLET: AN 'UGLY' CUSTOMER — FEARLESSNESS OF RIVALRY: DEATH OF HONORA EDGEWORTH: EXCUSES FOR DRINKING: 'OLD MURPHY' OF THE MOHAWK: THE FEMALE SMUGGLER.

THERE is an amusing character in a sketch we have just read: one of those stupid matter-of-fact persons, who can never appreciate a figure of speech, or understand the simplest jest. A 'benign cerulean,' enthusiastic for the 'rights of the sex,' remarks that woman's rights and duties are becoming every day more widely appreciated. 'The old-fashioned scale must be re-adjusted; and woman, noble, elevating, surprising woman, ascend to the loftiest eminence, and sit superior on the topmost branch of the social tree.' The ear of the matter-of-fact man catches the last simile, and he ventures to say: 'Uncommon bad climbers, for the most part in general, is women. Their clothes is n't adapted to it. I minds once I seen a woman climb a pole after a leg of mutting!' If looks could have killed the mal-apropos speaker, he would not have survived the reception which this ridiculous remark encountered from every guest at the table. He was himself struck with the mournful silence that followed his observation, and added, by way of explanation: 'That was a thing as happing'd on a pole; in coors it would be werry different on a tree, because of the branches.' At length, however, the theme of woman is renewed by the former advocate: 'Woman has not yet received her full development. The time will come when her influence will be universal; when, softened, subdued, and elevated, the animal now called Man will be unknown. You will be all women: can the world look for a higher destiny?' 'In coors,' observed the 'actual' man, 'if we are all turned into woming, the world will come to an end. For 'spose a case; 'spose it had been my sister as married my wife, instead of me; it 's probable there would n't have been no great fambly; wich in coors, if there was no population ——'

What the result of this supposed case would have been, was not permitted to transpire. The feminine part of the company immediately rose and left the table, and the matter-of-fact man to the ridicule of the male guests.

WE sat the other evening, listening to the warmish autumn rain that was falling without; and while we listened, we thought of these lines, from the pen of A. Z. LORDNOZOO:

'WHEN the humid storm-clouds gather
Over all the starry spheres,
And the melancholy darkness
Gently weeps in rainy tears,
'Tis a joy to press the pillow
Of a cottage-chamber bed,
And to listen to the patter
Of the soft rain over-head.

'Every tinkle on the shingles
Has an echo in the heart,
And a thousand dreary fancies
Into busy being start;
And a thousand recollections
Weave their bright hues into woof,
As I listen to the patter
Of the soft rain on the roof.

'There in fancy comes my mother,
As she used to years agone,
To survey the infant sleepers
Ere she left them till the dawn.
I can see her bending o'er me,
As I listen to the strain
Which is played upon the shingles
By the patter of the rain.

'Then my little seraph sister,
With her wings and waving hair,
And her bright-eyed cherub brother,
A serene, angelic pair,
Glide around my wakeful pillow,
With their praise or mild reproof,
As I listen to the murmur
Of the soft rain on the roof.'

WE stood by a western window of the pretty Episcopal church at Binghamton, on a recent Sunday morning, and saw a funeral procession enter the gate, and defile under the spring-time trees, just putting forth their first tender verdure. The day was sunny and beautiful; a soft wind was playing amidst the leafy foliage and the grass; and as the sympathizing concourse gathered around the freshly-opened grave, we could not help thinking how darker must be the hearts of the bereaved parents, who stood in suppressed anguish at its head, from the very beauty and brightness around them. The little coffin was lowered into the grave; the hollow sound of falling sand and gravel fell faintly upon the ear; and that only child of loveliness and promise was left in its cold and narrow bed, until earth and sea shall heave at the trump of GOD. As we turned away from the window, and awaited the morning service of the sanctuary, we thought of that desolate mother and that bereaved father, and how impotent would be all attemps at consolation for the loss of an only and darling child. And therewithal came to mind the reflections upon a similar scene of sadness by the eloquent author of '*The Mission of Little Children*:' 'No one feels the death of a child as a mother feels it. The father cannot realize it thus. True, there is a vacancy in his home and a heaviness in his heart. There is a chain of association that at set times comes round with its broken link; there are memories of endearment, a keen sense of loss, a weeping over crushed hopes, and a pain of wounded affection. But the *Mother* feels that one has been taken away who was still closer to her heart. Hers has been the office of constant ministration. Every gradation of feature developed before her eyes; she detected every new gleam of infant intelligence; she heard the first utterance of every stammering word; she was the refuge of its fears, the supply of its wants; and every task of affection wove a new link, and made dear to her its object. And when her child dies, a portion of her own life as it were dies with it. How can she give her darling up, with all these loving memories, these fond associations? The timid hands that have so often taken hers in trust and love, how can she fold them on its sinless breast, and surrender them to the cold clasp of DEATH? The feet whose wanderings she has watched so narrowly, how can she see them straightened to go down into the dark valley? The head that she has pressed to her lips and bosom, that she has watched in peaceful slumber and in burning sickness, a hair of which she could not see harmed, oh, *how* can she consign it to the dark chamber of the grave? It was a gleam of sunshine and a voice of perpetual gladness in her home; she had learned from it blessed lessons of simplicity, sincerity, purity, faith; it had unsealed within her a gushing, never-ebbing tide of affection; when suddenly it was taken away, and that home is left dark and silent; and to the vain and heart-rending aspiration, 'Shall that dear child never return again?' there breaks, in response through the cold gray silence 'Nevermore—oh, *nevermore!*' The heart is like a forsaken mansion, and that word goes echoing through its desolate chambers.

THERE is in WEBSTER's old spelling-book a spelling and defining lesson of words of four syllables. A friend mentions a ludicrous mistake made by a district-school-boy in the country, in the exercises of this lesson. One of the words happened to be '*Acephalous* without a head.' It was divided as usual into its separate syllables, connected by a hyphen, (which 'joins words or syllables, as sea-water!') which probably led the boy to give a new word and a new definition: '*Ikun* spell it and d'fine it!' said a lad, after the boy above him had tried and missed; '*Ikun* do it;' and he did: '*A-c-e-p-h, cef*, ACEPH—*a lous without a head!*' ''Most all of 'em laughed,' our informant says, 'when the boy said that!'

THE following opinion of our Great Metropolis is recorded with a diamond on a pane of glass in a room of the Astor House, which commands BARNUM'S 'Curiosity-Shop' in front, and is 'right fernent' ''York Meetin'-'ouse' on the other. The writer rang for his boots one morning about day-light, paid his bill and left, vowing that he had 'made his first and last visit to New-York.' From his wild look and 'used-up' manner (nothing farther having been heard of him,) it is feared he has 'made way' with himself:

'O GOTHAM! thy eternal roar
  Keeps me in constant pain;
I never was in 'York before,
  And I'll never come again!'

'Small blame to him;' for it *is* enough to set even the sedatest countryman crazy to enter the great thoroughfares of 'a city that is full of stirs, a tumultuous city.' How sober soever his mind, the prevailing excitement will seize him, and he will mingle with the conflicting currents like a straw revolving in the hurrying eddies of a running stream. In the evening, especially, when

—— 'all the spirit reels
At the shouts, the leagues of light,
The roaring of the wheels,'

the town, to one unused to its busy scenes, is absolutely overwhelming.

'Can you show me Main-street?' said an ingenious, fresh-looking young man to us, the other morning, near Hudson-Square, as we were walking down to the publication-office. 'Main-street?' we asked; 'New-York *has* no Main-street: you are thinking of Broadway, perhaps?' 'Oh, yes; Broadway — that 's it. I did n't know; I never ben in a city afore.' We accompanied him to and down Broadway, and enjoyed *his* enjoyment at all the strange sights he saw. We almost envied him the romantic *newness* of his sensations. He was positively eloquent, in his simple way, as he depicted his emotions on nearing the metropolis in the morning steamer. As he approached this 'London of America' the cloud of coal-reek which overhung the giant city, indicating its vicinity long before he reached the northern verge; the many sails which were tending toward it, in the expanding river and opening harbor; and at last, the broad bay, with tall ships setting in from the sea; the steamers and water-craft of every description hurrying to and fro from either shore; and the Great Metropolis itself stretching into the distance, with its domes and spires, its towers, cupolas and 'steepled chimnies,' rising through a canopy of smoke, in the gray dawn of a cloudless September morning; these, bursting upon his sensitive vision at once, had filled his mind, and almost made him a painter through the medium of words. He renewed within us our love of, and pride in, this our pleasant dwelling-place, the great metropolis of our native state. What a city shall we be by and by!

A confirmed wag it was who startled every body on the deck of the 'John Mason' steamer the other day, on her way from Albany to Troy, with the inquiry, in a loud nasal tone: 'Hear of that dreadful accident to-day aboard the Greenbush hoss-boat?' 'No!' exclaimed half-a-dozen by-standers at once; 'no!'—what was it?' 'Wal, they was tellin' of it down to the dee-pot; and nigh as I can cal'late, the hoss-boat had got within abeöut two rod of the wharf, when the larboard-hoss bu'st a flue; carryin' away her stern, unshippin' her rudder, and scaldin' more 'n a dozen passengers! I do n't know as there is any truth into it; praps 't aint so; but any way, that 's the *story.*' The narrator was less successful, according to his own account, with a rather practical joke which he undertook to play upon a Yankee townsman of his, a week or two before, in New York. 'He never liked me much, 'xpect,' said he, 'nor I did n't him, nuther. And I was a-walkin' along Pearl-street in 'York, sellin' some o' these little notions 'at you see here, (a 'buck-wheat fanning-mill,' a 'rotary-sieve' to sift 'apple-saäce,' etc.,) when I see him a-buyin' some counter goods in a store. So I went in and hail'd him: 'Says I, right off, jest as if I 'd seen him a-doin' the same thing a dozen times 'afore that mornin', says I, 'Won't they trust you *here,* nuther?' Thunder! you never *see* a man so riled. He looked right straight at me, and was 'een-amost *white,* he was so mad. The clerks laäfed, they did — but *he* did n't, I guess. 'I want to *see* you a minute!' says he, pooty solemn, and comin' toward the door. I went; and just as soon as I got on to the gridiron-steps he kicked me! I did n't care — not *much* then; but if his geese do n't have the Shatick cholera when I get home, 'you can take *my* hat,' as they say in York. I was doin' the merchant he was tryin' to buy calicoes on a good turn, any how; for I 'xpect he was goin' to get 'em on trust, and I know'd he was an all-

mighty shirk. I ruther guess he did n't *get* 'em, but I do n't know — not sartain.'

WHAT supernatural shriek is that, sounding through the murky air of this stormy February night? Twelve o'clock, too, 'by 'r Lady:' but be not alarmed. It is only the steam-whistle of the iron horse on the Hudson River rail-road, rushing into the Great Metropolis, at a 'two-forty' pace, bringing with him hundreds of passengers, some of whom, having never been to town before, are bewildered with its increasing vastness; the thickening lamps; the branching, crossing, lengthening, interminable streets; the 'leagues of light, the roaring of the wheels.' That same snorting steam-horse, scarce an hour ago, as he swept with his train through the very walls of the state's-prison at Sing-Sing, rumbled in the ears of the half-wakened captives, illustrating by his own wild freedom the liberty denied to them, and spoke of pleasant villages passed, and familiar scenes toward which he was rushing; he startled the echoes of Sleepy-Hollow, and the demons fled affrighted, for a greater than the steed erewhile bestrode by the 'Headless Horseman' was now spouting the hot white breath from his iron nostrils; onward he came; past golden 'Sunnyside,' disturbing not, let us hope, the inmates of that nest of genius and refinement; on to 'DOBB, his

Ferry,' and over the very soil of the pleasant places where 'Old' and 'Young KNICK,' and his little sisters so often walked and frolicked with the 'gooëd vrouw,' along the shores of the beautiful Tappaän-Zee. 'But what is all this *about?*' asks the reader. Nothing in the world but the shrill whistle of a locomotive, hollow-sounding on the dull ear of Night, just as we are going to bed.

IT is the custom, as we learn from a friend, in all parts of Scotland to send invitations, when a death occurs in a family, to all the neighbors to attend the funeral. On one occasion, a neighbor was omitted by the bereaved family, in the usual invitations, a feud having arisen between them. On the day of the funeral, while the people were assembling, the slighted 'auld wife' stood in her door, and watched the gathering. At length, unable to bear up under her resentment any longer, she exclaimed, 'Aweel! aweel! we 'll ha'e a corpse o' our ain in our ain house some day! — see *then* who 'll be invited!' What an exhibition of human nature!

BY-the-by, it may not be amiss to remark in passing, that it was the identical 'Greek Slave' concerning which the ensuing colloquy took place between the sculptor himself and a successful Yankee speculator, who had 'come over to see Ew-rope.' Scene, POWERS's studio at Florence: Enter stranger, spitting, and wiping his lips with his hand: 'Be yeöu Mr. PEÖWERS, the Skulpture?' 'I *am* a sculptor, and my name is POWERS.' 'Y-e-ä-s; well, I s'pected so; they *tell'd* me you was — y-e-ä-s. Look here — drivin' a pretty stiff business, eh?' 'Sir!' 'I say, plenty to du, eh? What d's one o' them fetch?' 'Sir!' 'I ask't ye what 's the *price* of one o' them, sech as yeöu 're peckin' at neöw.' 'I am to have three thousand dollars for this when it is completed.' '*W-h-a-t!!* — heöw much?' 'Three thousand dollars.' '*T-h-r-e-e t-h-o-ö-u-s-a-n-d d-o-l-l-a-r-s!* Han't statewary *riz* lately! I was cal'latin' to buy some; but it 's *tew* high. How 's paintin's? 'Guess I must git some paintin's. *T-h-r-e-e t-h-e-ö-u-s-a-n-d d-o-l-l-a-r-s!* Well, it *is* a trade, skulpin is; that 's sartain. What do they make yeöu pay for your *tools* and *stuff?* S'pect my oldest boy, CEPHAS, could skulp; 'fact, I *know* he could. He is always whittlin' reöund, and cuttin' away at things. I wish you 'd 'gree to take him 'prentice, and let him go *at* it full chisel. D' you know where I 'd be liable to put him eöut? He 'd cut stun a'ter a while with the best of ye; he would — and make money, tew, at *them* prices. *T-h-r-e-e t-h-e-ö-u-s-a-n-d d-o-l-l-a-r-s!*' And the 'anxious inquirer' left the presence. He now exhibits a 'lot' of 'fust-rate paintin's' to his friends.

WE beg leave to present two new 'renderings' from 'HAMLET,' which an innovating Yankee actor at the West considers authentic readings. He defends the first, upon the ground that the same spirit which had 'abused' HAMLET had previously treated his friends discourteously, kept them up at night, and prevented their sleeping on their posts. Hence 'thus HAMLET:'

> —— 'THE spirit that I have seen
> May be a devil; and the devil hath power
> To assume a pleasing shape; yea, and perhaps,
> Out of my weakness and my melancholy,
> As he is very potent with such spirits,
> Abuses *me* too — damn-me!'

This is quite different from the usual reading, and is as much an 'improvement' upon the original as any of Mr. HUDSON'S modern versions. The rendering in the subjoined passage from the same play is defended on the ground that HAMLET looked up to HORATIO, in his 'weakness and his melancholy,' as *a father*, and therefore he addressed him by a diminutive of that endearing term:

> 'HAM. Dost thou think ALEXANDER looked o' this fashion i' the earth?
> 'HOR. E'en so.
> 'HAM. And *smelt* so, *Pa!*
> 'HOR. E'en so, my lord.'

We submit these readings to the hosts of SHAKSPERIAN commentators who infest society.

The play of 'HAMLET' was being enacted, and thereabout of it especially where GUILDENSTERN is employed by the DANE to play upon the pipe, just to oblige him. He is very importunate for the music, it will be remembered; and on this occasion he was accommodated to his heart's content. GUILDENSTERN replied to his earnest solicitations, that since he was so very pressing, he *would* give him a tune; and forthwith accomplished, to the best of his small ability, that sublime national air 'Yankee Doodle,' together with certain extempore flourishes, which he termed 'the variations.'

'THE WEST is a great country, Friend C——,' writes a clever correspondent. 'Tall things happen there now and then. Here is a specimen: Having occasion to pass through the Upper Lakes last June, I was happy enough to find myself a passenger on board that palace of a boat the 'EMPIRE,' Emperor HOWE commanding. My travelling companion for the time happened to be a thoroughbred 'Hoosier,' a prince of a fellow; one who feared GOD and loved fun and the ladies, but who was withal a most abominable stammerer. We had n't been long aboard, when the captain called our attention to a most remarkable-looking individual seated at the end of the cabin. I am not myself particularly handsome, and have seen some ill-looking men in my day; but so ugly a man as this had never crossed the scope of *my* vision. HOWE declared him emphatically 'the ugliest man that ever lived;' whereupon my friend TOM offered to wager a half dozen of champagne that he had seen a worse one in the steerage. The bet was at once accepted, and TOM started for his man, who was to be brought up for comparison. He found the fellow a bit of a wag, as an intolerably homely man is apt to be, and, after the promise of a 'nip,' nothing loth to exhibit himself. As they entered the cabin door, my friend, with an air of conscious triumph, turned to direct our attention to his champion, when he discovered the fellow trying to insure success by making up faces. '*St – st – st – stop!*' said he; '*no – no – none of that! You st – st – stay just as God Almighty made you! You ca – ca – ca – ca – can't be beat!*' And he was n't!

IS N'T this a touching picture of the death of HONORA EDGEWORTH, as described by her husband? It so strikes us: 'after having sat up all the night, I was suddenly called at six o'clock in the morning. Her sister was with her. The moment that I opened the door, her eyes, which had been fixed in death, acquired sufficient power to turn themselves toward me with an expression of the utmost tenderness. She was supported on pillows. Her left arm hung over her sister's neck, beyond the bed. She smiled, and breathed her last! At this moment I heard something fall on the floor. It was her wedding-ring, which she had held on her wasted finger to the last instant; remembering with fond superstition the vow she had made, never again to lose that ring but with life. She never moved again, nor did she seem to suffer any struggle.' 'They loved in life, and in death they were not divided!'

IN a certain town in New-Hampshire, a certain inhabitant thereof required for his comfortable enjoyment at least a pint of 'white-faced New-England,' daily. He had become reduced in his pockets, so that it became necessary for him, like the Israelites of old, to procure somehow a double portion on the day before the Sabbath, that he might quietly enjoy his church, of which he was a constant attendant. On one Saturday he had been very unfortunate; for the shades of evening began to fall, and yet he had not gathered his 'spiritual' manna for the day of rest. A neighbor at that moment requested him to throw some wood into his shed; and after the small job was completed, gave him a few cents.. He saw that the old fellow looked sad and unsatisfied, and said to him: 'Is n't that *enough* for the work? Why, you can get half-a-pint with that money; and can't you keep Sunday on *that?*' 'Why, I suppose I *could*, 'Squire, but then,' (looking up with a disconsolate visage,) but then, 'Squire, *how* would it be kept?' This anecdote by a clever correspondent reminds us of another, which we shall venture to relate in this connection, though it must needs suffer by the juxtaposition. Mr. G——, who had by degrees become so attached to his cups that he could not comfortably go by eleven o'clock without his 'nip' of brandy, and who was yet anxious to avoid the suspicion of being an habitual drinker, was in the habit daily of inventing some excuse to the bar-keeper and those within hearing. He had used up all the stereotyped reasons, such as 'a slight pain,' a 'a kind of sinking,' not 'feeling right,' etc., etc. One Saturday, at the usual hour, he called for his brandy-and-water, saying, 'I am extremely dry; *I am going to have salt fish for dinner!*' 'No excuse was better than none,' he probably thought.

ONE of the earliest settlers of old Schoharie was a man named MURPHY, more familiarly known as 'Old MURPHY.' He was a terror to the Indians and their sworn enemy, for he had suffered much from their robberies, and wanton destruction of his crops and cattle. But his most deadly hate arose from the murder of his two brothers; for which act he solemly swore to devote his life to their extermination. 'Old MURPHY' was a wily enemy, as the Indians had well ascertained; and they sought his life by all possible artifice and strategy. On one occasion their wiles came near being successful. MURPHY had a cow, which wandered from his cabin during the day to browse in the woods, with a bell suspended from her neck to indicate her whereabout; returning always at night to be milked, and with 'udders all drawn dry' to stand and 'inly ruminate' by the hut until morning called her to sally forth again. One evening she failed to return; another day passed, and with it the hour 'when the kye came hame' usually, but *she* came not. Fearing that she had met with foul play, MURPHY started, with his rifle on his shoulder, to 'look her up,' following the direction she was taking when she left the hut. After several hours of fruitless pursuit, the faint sound of her familiar bell in the distance gladdened his ear. 'It's all right!' said he, in his delight at finding her; and he rapidly neared the spot whence the sound proceeded, a thicket of close undergrowth, in the heart of the forest. All at once he stopped short. That is 'Old Spot's *bell*,' said he, 'but it's not on *her neck;* she do n't swing her bell in *that* way when she browses. There 's mischief here!' Cautiously approaching the spot whence the slow and regular 'ting-a-ling' proceeded, he saw at some sixty yards distant two Indians seated upon an old mossy log, peering intently now and then into the recesses of the wood, and at intervals of three or four minutes slowly swinging the cow-bell, which they thought would bring 'Old MURPHY' into their toils, 'as a bird hasteth to the snare.' But it was *his* hour of joy, not theirs. He watched the movements of the red rascals as a cat watches a mouse when safe in her claws. Secure from observation behind a large tree, he selected the 'bell-wether,' and with deliberate aim sent a bullet through his heart. The Indian uttered one shriek, sprang three feet or more upward, and dropped dead beside the log upon which he had been sitting. His comrade looked round in amazement to gather the direction of the shot, and then shouldered the dead body of his comrade, and was moving off, when a second shot from the musket which MURPHY had by this time loaded, laid him and his dead companion lifeless together. There were two withered scalps hanging on each smoky jamb of Old MURPHY'S fire-place for more than twenty years: and he always regarded them with a 'grim smile' when he was rehearsing the history of their acquisition.

'*Poetry Run Mad*' is inadmissible, on two accounts. In the first place, it strikes us we have met *parts* of it at least before; and in the second, the style has 'outlived our liking.' Nobody but HOOD manages well this ragged species of verse; a very clever specimen of which is contained in his '*Custom-House Breeze*,' the story of a lady-smuggler who would not go ashore at Dover, because there was 'a *searching* wind' blowing, which might expose the lace-swathings of her person:

'IN spite of rope and barrow, knot, and tuck,
  Of plank and ladder, there she stuck!
She could n't, no, she would n't go on shore.

  'But, Ma'am,' the steward interfered,
  'The wessel must be cleared.
You mus' n't stay aboard, Ma'am, no one do n't!
  It 's quite ag'in the orders so to do,
  And all the passengers has gone but you.'
Says she, 'I cannot go ashore and won't!'
          'You ought to!'
            'But I can't!'
          'You must!'
            'I sha' n't!''

NUMBER FOUR.

THE QUACK-DOCTOR: NAPOLEON AND HIS BATTLES: MAL-ADROIT COMPLIMENT: THE LIVING-DEAD: PURSUIT OF KNOWLEDGE UNDER DIFFICULTIES: A TEMPERANCE STORY: COMFORT OF COMMON THINGS: A HOG IN ARMOR: POETRY OF THE ALPHABET: AUTHENTIC ANECDOTE OF THE DUKE OF WELLINGTON: PERILS OF A JACKASS: A MAN'S OWN HOME: INSIGNIA OF 'HENPECKERY' — THE HELPLESS 'HELP-MATE': SONNETEERING, WITH A SPECIMEN: REMINISCENCES: DEATH OF A GOOD MAN.

'I STUMBLED on a character the other evening,' writes a friend, 'on board a steam-boat, which presented some traits that I thought rather original and unique. I daguerreotyped him on the spot. I had just finished supper, and was quietly enjoying my cigar on the deck, when I heard an individual declaiming in a loud tone of voice to some two or three attentive listeners, (but evidently intended for the benefit of whomsoever it might concern,) on pathology. Being as it were thus invited, I also became a listener to something like the following: '*There it is now!* Well, some people talk about *seated* fevers. I do n't know any thing about *seated* fevers; there aint no such thing as seated fever. A musquitoe-bite is a fever; cure the bite, and the fever leaves you. So with a *bile*—just the same thing; their aint no *such thing*, I tell you, as seated fever.

The fact is, your regular doctor practizes according to books. I practize according to common sense. Now there was Dr. RUGG, of our village, the Sampson of the Materier-Medicker. Well, *he* treats fevers according to the books; consequence is I get all the patients: and he says to me one day, says he, 'why,' said he, 'how *is* it, you get all the fever cases?' And I told him exactly how it was; and it *is* so. 'Well, Doctor, interrupted one of the listeners, 'How *do* you treat fevers?' 'Well, *there it is*, you see; you ask me how I treat fevers! If you had asked me when I first commenced practizing I could ha' told you; cant tell you now. I treat cases just as I find 'em, according to common sense. And *there it is:* now there was Mrs. SCUTTLE; she was taken sick; all the folks said she had the consumption; had two doctors to her; did n't do her a single mossel o' good. They sent for *me*. Well, as I went into the house, I see a lot o' tanzy and a flock of chickens by the door: felt her pulse: says I, 'Mrs. SCUTTLE, you aint no more got the consumption than I've got it. Two weeks, an' I cured her!' 'Well, doctor, how did you cure her?' '*How* did I cure her? *There it is* ag'in! I told you I see a lot of tanzy and a flock of chickens growing at the door. I gi'n her some of the tanzy and a fresh-laid egg — brought her right up. It's *kill* or *cure* with me! In fact, I call myself an officer. My saddle-bags is my soldiers, and my disease my inimy.

I rush at him; and 'ither he or me has got to conquer. I never give in!'

My cigar was out; and while lighting another, the doctor vanished: possibly hastened by the influence of one of his own prescriptions.'

WE always associate, and at once, with NAPOLEON'S name, the dreadful scenes presented by his deserted battle-fields; such for an example as marked the sanguinary contests of his Russian campaign. Here is a sketch of one, from the pen of an eye witness: 'The battle-field presented a terrible picture of ruin and carnage, especially on the left and centre, where the greatest efforts had been made to take, maintain, and retake the redoubts. Corpses of the slain, broken arms, dead and dying horses, covered every elevation and filled every hollow, and plainly indicated the progress of the action. In the front of the redoubts lay the bodies of the French; behind the works, showing that they had been carried, lay the Russians. On many points the heaps of corpses told where squares of infantry had stood, and plainly pointed out the size of the closely formed masses. From the relative number of the slain, it was easy to perceive that the Russians had suffered more than the French!' And this is but one of hundreds of similar scenes! Yet, 'had these poor fellows any quarrel? Busy as the Devil is, not the smallest! Their *Governors* had fallen out!' If one could indulge a 'grim smile' at any thing in relation to BONAPARTE, it would be at the potential *military* standard to which he reduced every thing. Do you remember his order on the appearance of the Mamelukes in Egypt? 'Form square; artillery to the angles; asses and savants to the centre!' Characteristic; but complimentary that, to the 'learned savants!' 'Asses and savants to *the centre!*'

'READER, did you never encounter a person who was always striving, in the presence of ladies, to lug in 'a compliment' (as that is called which compliment is none) to the 'fair sex?' Is there a greater bore in the infinite region of Boredom? Somebody has lately 'illuminated' a specimen of this class, in a pleasant anecdote. A lady, whose attention he had been trying to force all the evening, observed, in the words of an old saying, and with a slight shudder as from cold, 'I feel as if a goose were walking over my grave;' the origin, we may suppose, of the term 'cold-goose-pimple.' Sir Compliment Hunter thought of ROMEO's aspiration, 'Oh! that I were a glove upon that hand!' and replied: 'Oh! would *I* were that goose!' Goose truly he was; but the bright, clear idea of hoping he might be the interesting bird which should walk over the *grave* of one whom he professed so ardently to admire, was a notion which could only have entered a brain like his own.

IT was a sad thing just now, in the gay and busy Broadway, under a sunny, cloudless sky, with the healthful current of life coursing joyously in our own veins, to relinquish the feverish and wasted hand of a friend at whose door DEATH will call ere long, and walk with him through thc Dark Valley. 'I am going,' said he, in a voice scarcely above a whisper; 'I am fast going; I shall leave all this!' and he turned his glassy eyes upward to the calm clear heavens, and waved his hand toward the busy crowds that rolled through the street or pattered with hasty steps upon the pave; 'I shall *soon* leave all this!' 'It is but too true!' thought we, as we turned to watch his slowly-receding footsteps:

> —— 'YET a few days, and thee
> The all-beholding sun shall see no more
> In all his course; nor yet in the cold ground,
> Where thy pale form was laid, with many tears,
> Nor in the embrace of ocean, shall exist
> Thy image.'

May he be able to say with joy, when the Last Messenger shall await his departure, 'Come DEATH to this frail, failing, dying body! come the immortal life!'

STANDING with a friend the other day by the river-side, to take in the noble *coup d'œil* of the new steamer KNICKERBOCKER, we overheard a little anecdote connected with water-craft, which made our companion merry all the way home; which we shall here transcribe; '*and* which it is hoped may please.' 'It seems there was' (nay, we know not *seems*, there *was*) a verdant youth from the interior of Connecticut, for the first time on board a steamboat. His curiosity was unbounded. He examined here, and he scrutinized there; he wormed from the engineer a compulsory lecture on the steam engine and mechanics in general, and from the fireman an essay on the power of white heat, and the 'average consumption of pine cord-'ood.' At length his inquiring mind was checked in its investigations, and 'the pursuit of knowledge under difficulties' made at once apparent. He had mounted to the wheel-house, and was asking the pilot: 'What you doin' *that* for, Mister?—what *good* does 't do?' when he was observed by the captain, who said, in a gruff voice: 'Go away from there! Don't you see the sign, 'No talkin' to the man at the hellum?' Go 'way!' 'Oh! certing—yäes; I only wanted to know ——' 'Well, you *do* know now that you can't talk to him; so go 'way!' With unwilling willingness, the verdant youth came down; and, as it was soon dark, he presently went below; but four or five times before he 'turned in,' he was on deck, and near the wheel-house, eyeing it with a thoughtful curiosity; but with the captain's public rebuff still in his ears, venturing to ask no questions. In the first gray of the dawn, he was up, and on deck; and after some hesitation, perceiving nobody near but the pilot, who was turning the wheel, as when he had last seen him, he preferred his 'suppressed question' in the oblique style peculiar to his region: 'Wal, goin' it *yit* ha?—been at it all night?—*a-screëwin on her up?* eh?' What vague conjectures must have bothered the poor querist's brain, during the night, may be partly inferred from the absurd but 'settled conviction' to which he had at length arrived!

'*A Temperance Story*' relies mainly for its 'fun, which the Editor seems to enjoy,' upon an ancient JOSEPHUS MILLERIUS. The collateral anecdote, however, toward its close, is not so much amiss. Two young men, 'with a humming in their heads,' retire late at night to their room in a crowded inn; in which, as they enter, are revealed two beds; but the wind extinguishing the light, they both, instead of taking, as they supposed, a bed apiece, get back-to-back into *one* bed, which begins to sink under them, and come around at intervals, in a manner very circumambient, but quite impossible of explication. Presently one observes to the other: 'I say, TOM, somebody's in my bed.' 'Is there?' says the other; 'so there is in mine, d — n him!' Let's kick 'em out! The *next* remark was: 'TOM, I've kicked *my* man overboard.' 'Good!' says his fellow-toper; 'better luck than I; my man has kicked *me* out — d—d if he has n't — right on the floor!' Their 'relative positions' were not apparent until the next morning.

THERE is a good deal of comfort in *Common Things.* Is n't there, though? Just rung the sanctum-bell for KITTY to come up and bring us a slice of bread-and-butter. It is after twelve o'clock of a rainy October night; for we are closing the November number, and our self-imposed 'stent' is to get all through before we go to bed. When we take a 'stent,' we *do* it. We used to, when hoeing potatoes, 'cutting stalks,' pulling flax, and husking corn in 'the ked'ntry,' and we can do it yet. Well, KITTY did n't come; she had retired to 'the arms of MURPHY.' So we took the candle and went down to the kitchen to help ourselves. It was *very* clean and neat. A solitary cricket retreated under the range as we entered with our bright Carcel lamp. The white floor was 'swept and garnished;' and the week's 'washing and ironing' hung on the white-pine clothes-horse. How sweet those linen garments smelled! And 'young KNICK'S' 'sack,' and little JOSE's pink frock, and the ' wee ' one's small stockings, although the wearers themselves were rapt in rosy slumbers up stairs, were not uninhabited, to our eyes, at that moment, though they *were* hanging in the kitchen. We *enjoyed* those twin-slices of bread-and-butter, with two tender, cross-cut, crumbling pieces of corned-beef sandwiched between, and a pickled walnut. After all, many of our passing enjoyments are made up of trifles like this. Is n't it so?

We do n't know when we have laughed more heartily than at a sight which we encountered the other day in Broadway. A portly female of the *Porcine* genus, in a high state of ' maternal solicitude,' was perambulating slowly along the street, with three hoops around her expanded person. Indeed, she seemed thoroughly secured against any accident in the way of explosion. She was indebted doubtless to the hoops by escaping clandestinely from some 'tight fit' of a barrel into which she had forced herself in search of provant, and which had collapsed upon her person in the larcenous act. By-the-by, ' speaking of pigs,' we perceive that an enterprising Yankee is about revising some of the musty apothegms of the day, and verifying their absurdity. He has already made ' a whistle out of a pig's tail,' and has a very handsome silk purse nearly completed for a new-year's present, which is fabricated mainly from ' a sow's ear ! '

HE was a 'man of letters' who wrote the following. It is a new style of poetry altogether. It will be seen that every letter of the final word must be pronounced as though DILWORTH himself presided at the perusal. The letter or letters in Italics will be found to constitute the rhyme. There is a good deal more of it, but this is sufficient to serve as a specimen:

'ON going forth last night a friend to see,
I met a man, by trade s-n-o-*b*;
Reeling along the path he held his way:
'Ho! ho!' quoth I, 'he's d-r-u-n-*k*!'
Then thus to him: 'Were it not better far,
You were a little s-o-b-e-*r*?
'Twere happier for your family, I guess,
Than playing off such wild r-i-g-*s*;
Beside, all drunkards, when policemen see 'em,
Are taken up at once by t-h-*e*-m!'

THE following anecdote of the DUKE OF WELLINGTON, which we derive from an original source of the highest respectability, may be relied upon as entirely authentic: Lord WELLINGTON was dining at a public dinner at Bordeaux, given to him by the authorities, when he received a despatch from Paris, informing him of the abdication of NAPOLEON. He turned to his aid-de-camp, FREEMANTLE: 'Well,' said he, in his knowing sportsman tone, 'we've run the fox to his hole at last.' 'What do you mean?' said FREEMANTLE. 'NAPOLEON has abdicated.' FREEMANTLE uttered an exclamation of surprise and delight. 'Hush! not a word!' said WELLINGTON; 'let 's have our dinner comfortably.' He laid the letter beside him, and went on calmly eating his dinner. When the dinner was over, 'There!' said he to Monsieur LYNCH, the Mayor of Bordeaux, 'there 's something will please you.' The mayor cast his eye over the letter, and in an instant was on the table announcing the news. The saloon rang with acclamations for several minutes. The mayor then begged leave to give a toast: 'WELLINGTON, the Liberator of France!' It was received with thundering applause. The Spanish consul rose, and begged leave to give a toast. It was the same: 'WELLINGTON, the Liberator of France!' There was another thunder of applause. The Portuguese consul did the same, with like effect. The mayor rose again, and gave 'WELLINGTON, the Liberator of EUROPE!' Here the applause was astounding. WELLINGTON, who sat all the while picking his teeth, now rose, made one of his knowing civil bows to the company round: 'JACK,' said he, turning to FREEMANTLE, 'let 's have coffee.'

THE 'Pioneer Watch' will find none but admirers. We hope to hear often from the writer. He will always be cordially welcomed. His sketch of the old mule is like a pictured animal by PAUL POTTER; and if his description of the bray of a jackass is not *perfection*, we cannot conceive of such a thing: '*an asthma, carried on by powerful machinery!*' DICKENS never hit off any thing more felicitously. 'Speaking of jack-asses,' what a melancholy fact that is, which is recorded by a Louisiana journal: 'While the 'mentangentrie' was being exhibited here, an old negro man drove his cart, which was drawn by a mule, near the pavilion, with a view of taking a peep at the monkeys. The mule and cart were left alone while CATO amused himself at the 'show.' When the performance was over, the company commenced packing up for the next village, and when the canvass was withdrawn, the elephant stood naked just before the mule, which gave one single bray, and fell dead in the harness.' Who can depict the horror, the intense, the 'excreüciating' horror, which must have pervaded that poor donkey's bosom!' None but a jackass can appreciate the depth of the emotion conveyed by that sonorous bray, with its 'dying fall!'

THE following thoughts, by the author of 'Friends in Council,' are replete with the true feeling of which they are the offspring: 'A man's own home is a serious place to him. There it is he has known the sweetness and the bitterness of early loves and early friendships. There, mayhap, he has suffered one of those vast bereavements which was like a tearing away of a part of his own soul: when he thought each noise in the house, hearing noises that he never heard before, must be something they were doing in the room — the room — where lay all that was mortal of some one inexpressibly dear to him; when he awoke morning after morning to struggle with a grief which seemed as new, as appalling, and as large as on the first day; which indeed, being part of himself, and thus partaking of his renovated powers, rose equipped with what rest or alacrity sleep had given him; and sank, unconquered, only when he was too wearied in body and mind to attend to it, or to any thing.'

'I'VE always remarked,' says that profound observer, Mr. 'CHAWLS YELLOWPLUSH,' that when you see a wife a-takin' on airs onto herself, a-scoldink, and internally a-talkin' about '*her* dignity' and '*her* branch,' that the husband is inwariably a spoon.' A friend of ours says that he was reminded of this sage remark the other night, in coming down the Hudson. A large, fat, pompous woman, who was ever and anon overlooking her husband, (a thin, lank personage, with a baby in his arms, who exhibited every mark of prolonged annoyance,) in reply to a meek

5*

complaint on his part of fatigue, and the expression of a wish that the nurse might very soon get over her sea-sickness, said:

'I never saw a man conduct so before—never, on the face o' the globèd airth! If I'd ha' known that you was goin', to act in *this* way, *I certainly would n't ha' fetched you!*'

The gentleman straitway sang the 'Lay of the Henpecked' to the crying baby, and from that time forth, was as mum as an oyster.

'BYRON says, in a letter to Moore, 'I never wrote but one sonnet before, and that was not in earnest, and many years ago, as an *exercise;* and I will never write another. They are the most puling, petrifying, stupidly platonic compositions.' To which I subscribe. I do not mean to say that good sonnets have not been written. I have seen such; it is the *school* that is bad. They are like Flemish pictures, or as the painter said of the sardines, '*Little fishes done in oil.*' But as I have been requested to write a sonnet, I will not refuse you, yet I am sure I would not do so again even for a friend; that is, a friend for whom I had an especial regard: sonneteering is too nice a matter; the better done, the worse; and I think, with DISRAELI, 'Extreme exactness is the sublime of fools.' Nevertheless here is the *thing.* If you wish to put it among your

'KNICK'-Knacks, you may have consent thereto, thinking that it may do some good:'

'A SONNET?' well, if it 's within my ken,
I'll write one with a moral. When a boy,
One Christmas morn I went to buy a toy,
Or rather we; I and my brother BEN;
But so it chanced that day I had but ten
Cents in my fist, but as we walked, 'Be goy-
Blamed' if we did n't meet one PAT McCOY,
An Irishman, one of my father's men,
Who four more gave, which made fourteen together.
Just then I spied, in a most unlucky minute,
A pretty pocket-wallet; like a feather.
My money buys it. BEN began to grin it:
'You 're smart,' says he; 'you 've got a heap of leather,
But where's them cents you wanted to put in it?'

JUST been reading, and with no small interest, '*An Historical Discourse*,' giving the history of the little town of our nativity, the place where 'Aunt LUCY's twins' were baptized. The names and histories of all the pastors, from the earliest settlement of the place to the present period, are given; and as we read them, how many pictures from the 'dark backward and abysm of time' arose to view! Parson W——, for example, how well we remember him! 'A man severe he was, and stern to view,' but a good man at heart, no doubt. We recollect him so far back as the time when our childish fancy was, that when he got up to speak, he 'took his text' out of a small box under the pulpit-cushion; we forget now what we then thought the '*Text*' was; but we once saw something like what we remembered for a dim moment to have *thought* it, in a toy-store on Christmas-eve, some years ago! We were always afraid of Parson W——, 'we boys;' and many and many a time have we gone and hid when he approached the house. Religion was a 'dreadful thing' in those days. Cheerfulness was tabooed; and a solemn visage and a cold demeanor were the outward and visible signs of having 'obtained a *hope*.' A common 'professor' was not to be encountered without emotion, but 'the minister,' all in black, was a terrible bug-bear! We used to regard him, as 'an officer of the divine law,' in much the same light in which police-officers are viewed by the suspicious delinquent. But Parson W—— is gone; and we cannot but felicitate ourself, for one, that we 'did what was right' in our attendance upon his ministrations. How many hundreds of times, wrapped up in sweet-scented hay, in the bottom of a sleigh, did we ride through the howling winter storm, to sit in that old church, with nothing but the maternal foot-stove and the prevalent 'fire of devotion' to keep us from perishing; yea, even to the division 'sixteenthly,' and the 'improving' 'Hence we learn, in view of our subject, in the next and *last* place,' etc. In summer there was a pail of water with a tin-porringer by the door; so that we could quench any thirst that might arise 'from the heat of the weather or the drought of the discourse;' but winter-service, and rehearsals in that comprehensive body of divinity, the 'Westminister Shorter Catechism, ('*Shorter* catechism,' and 'nothin' shorter!') these were *too* much! There was relief only in eating our Sunday 'turn-overs' and nut-cakes-and-cheese at the neighbors' at noon-times, with faces glowing before the high-piled wood fires. Also it was extremely pleasant to go home with the prettiest girls from the evening conference-meetings held at the school-house. Ah, well-a-day! we see in the notes to this discoure the names given, and the triumphant deaths recorded, of those who were once near and dear to us; and chief among them, that near relative, whose silver hair and mild benevolent blue eyes are before us of yore. He it was who was wont to go around his pleasant orchards, full of all manner of fruits, and select the choicest varieties for the little boys, never so happy himself as when engaged in making others so. His last end was peace. A little while before his death, he called his son to his bedside, to write down his last request. 'Bring your table close to the bed,' said he; 'I want to see you write.' This was done: 'Now father,' said his son, 'what shall I write?' 'Write,' said he, 'this my last will and testament: I will myself and my dear children, and my grandchildren and their posterity, to GOD the FA-

THER, SON and HOLY SPIRIT, through time, praying that the blessing of GOD may rest upon them. Now lift me up, and let me sign that.' He was raised, and his hand trembling with age was guided as he wrote for the last time his own name. As he lay down, he said, 'My work is now done, and I am ready to go home. My way is clear. I *know* where I am going.' A little while after this, as the sun was going down, at his request he was raised up in bed: 'All seems natural out there,' said he, looking out upon his beautiful acres; 'just as it used to look. It is very pleasant; but I care nothing for it now; I am going,' said he, pointing toward heaven, 'I am going up there — I am going home!' And a little while after, the good man fell asleep in JESUS.

NUMBER FIVE.

A FRENCHMAN DISCOMFITED: AN AGREEABLE DISAPPOINTMENT: WEATHER 'COMPLAINANTS': GEOGRAPHICAL DISORDERS: 'PURSUIT OF KNOWLEDGE UNDER DIFFICULTIES': SPORTING A NEW LANGUAGE: DEATH IN THE SCHOOL-ROOM: CONUNDRUM — 'FORCED CONSTRUCTION': A CENTURY — THE PAST AND PRESENT: A DUBIOUS DINNER: TRANSPOSED 'CAUSE AND EFFECT': A BOOK-SELLER AT CAMP-MEETING: TRUE VALUE OF MONEY — 'NOTE-LIFTING': THE CATCHER CAUGHT — AN AUTHENTIC RECORD: SEEING OURSELVES AS OTHERS SEE US: JARVIS AND THE FRENCHMAN: AUTUMNAL FAREWELL TO DOBB'S FERRY.

OUR present theme is certainly a not very savory subject; but the untimely misfortune described in such unmincing Anglo-Saxon by a correspondent, tempts us to record a similar accident which we recently heard depicted by a friend, a French gentleman, whose unostentatious but princely hospitality adds (what one could hardly deem possible) even a new charm and grace to the lovely banks of the St. Lawrence, along the most delightful reach of that resplendent stream. 'It ees twànty year,' said he, 'since zat I was in New-Yo'k; and I go up one night in z' upper part de cité, ('t was 'most in de contree,) to see a fraànde. Ah! oui! W'en I com' by de door-yard, I see som'sing — I not know what he ees, but I s'ought he was leetil ràbeet;

but he was ver' *tame.* I go up sof'ly to heem : 'Ah, ha!' I say to myself, 'I 'av' gots you!' So I strike him big stroke vis my ombrel on his necks. Ah, ha! sup'pose w'at he do? *B-a-a-h!!!* He strike me back in my face wis his—— *Damn! I cannot tell:* it was *awfuls!* DREADFULS! He s-m-e-l-l so you cannot *touch* him—and I de saàme! I s'row myself in de pond, up to my necks; but it make no use. I s-m-e-l-l *seex wee-eek!* I not like go in ze room wis my fraànde. I dig big hole to put my clo'es in de grounde: it not cure zem! I dig zem up: bah!—it is de saàme! I put zem back—and dey smell one year; till zey rot in de ground. *It ees faàct!'* And so it *was* a fact; for no man born of woman could ever counterfeit the fervor of disgust which distinguished the graphic delineation of that sad mishap.

WE heard a pleasant illustration, an evening or two ago, of a peculiarity of western life. A man in one of the hotels of a south-western city was observed by a northerner to be very moody, and to regard the stranger with looks particularly sad, and as our informant thought, somewhat savage. By-and-by he approached him, and said: 'Can I see you outside the door for a few minutes?' 'Certainly, Sir,' said the northerner, but not without some misgivings. The moment the door had closed behind them, the moody man reached over his hand between his shoulders and drew from a pocket a tremendous bowie-knife, bigger than a French carver, and as its broad blade flashed in the moon-light, the stranger thought his time had come. 'Put up your scythe,' said he, 'and tell me what I 've done to provoke your hostility?' 'Done, stranger?—you have n't done any thing. Nor I ha n't any hostility to you; but I want to pawn this knife with you. It cost me twenty dollars in New-Orleans. I lost my whole 'pile' at 'old sledge' coming down the river, and I ha n't got a red cent. Lend me ten dollars on it, stranger. I'll win it back for you in less than an hour.' The money was loaned; and sure enough, in less than the time mentioned the knife was redeemed, and the incorrigible 'sporting-man' had a surplus of some thirty dollars, which he probably lost the very *next* hour.

'WHAT a perfectly *horrible* day this is!' says your complaining, querulous citizen, as he wipes the perspiration from his glowing face; 'I *detest* such weather!' Dear Sir, you should n't say so; the rivers of water which run down your body are in obedience to a law of nature that preserves your health. Moreover, the heat of which you complain is ripening the 'kindly fruits of the earth, so that in due time we may enjoy them.' Nature is getting ready to publish her 'cereals,' and her timely heat is swelling into pulpy lusciousness the great clusters of Isabella-grapes, which shut in the parlor-piazza, darken the windows of our sleeping-room in the second story, screen those of the nursery in the third from the sun, and actually hang, in all forms of grace, from the very eaves! Also the vari-colored pinks, verbenas, heliotropes, dahlias, and a large family of nameless flowers, are shedding their beautiful hues and perfume between the 'house-vine' and the 'back-vine,' which creeps over its broad trellice, and suspends there, in long pendulous 'bunches,' its rich abundance of fruit. Yes; and every day as we look out at these things, we see the green ivy visibly growing over the pinnacles of the towers of our 'Church of St. PETER' in the rear — a beautiful and graceful sight.

P. S. It *is* a pretty hot day, though, 'that's a fact.' Must go and take a 'shower' in the adjoining bath-room. Pheugh! *This* kind of heat can't ripen any thing, unless a 'blast-furnace' will do the same thing. It *is* 'horrible' hot weather!

WE remarked a very laughable typographical error in a newspaper a day or two since. It was in a paragraph which announced that a formerly distinguished southern politician had been struck with apoplexy, and had 'lost the use of *one side of his speech!*' It reminded us of the man who, having stood in the same place in a cotton factory for many years, was one day detained by illness, and wrote to his employer that he should be unable to resume his labor, as he had a painful swelling on the *east side* of his face!

NOTHING is more characteristic of your true Frenchman than his irrepressible curiosity, which he will often gratify at the expense of danger, and sometimes at the risk of his life. In matters of science, by the way, this peculiarity of the 'grand nation' has been of great service to mankind. A friend relates a story pleasantly illustrative of this insatiable national impulse. A young Parisian lawyer, accustomed only to French breakfasts, arrived in the morning at Dover on his way to London, was surprised to find a robust JOHN BULL seated at a small side-table, loaded with meats and their accompaniments. He surveyed him attentively for a moment or two, and then began to soliloquize in an 'undress rehearsal' of the sparse English at his command: 'Mon DIEU!' said he, 'can it be posseeble zat cet gentil-homme is ete hees *brekfaste!* Nevare minds: I shall, I sink I shall *ask* heem. 'Monsieur! I am stranger. Vill you av ze politesse to tell me wezzer zat is your brekfaste or your dinnà wat you eat?'' JOHN rises with indignation, his cheeks distended with a large portion of his substantial meal, and is about to resent what he deems an affront; but discretion gets the better of valor, and he sits down again to resume his meal. The Frenchman paces the floor dubiously for some minutes, until his enhanced curiosity overcomes his temporary timidity, when he again accosts the sharp-set son of 'perfidious Albion:' 'Sare, if you knew de reezon wherefor' I rek-quire for know wezzer zat is your brekfaste or your dinnà wat you ete, you would 'av ze politesse to tell me immediate, and sans offence.' JOHN was silent, as before, but his face actually glowed with excitement and suppressed passion. All these evidences of displeasure however were lost upon the curious traveller, who once more addressed his 'unwilling witness,' and this time fairly brought him to the use of his speech; for he rose in great anger, accused the Frenchman of having insulted him; a blow followed, and a duel was the 'net purport and upshot' of the affair. Had the Frenchman's curiosity been satisfied, he would doubtless have been more steady-handed: 'but Destiny had willed it otherwise.' BULL's bullet pierced him, and the wound was decided to be mortal. Englishmen are seldom ill-tempered upon a full stomach: our hero relented; he was filled with remorse at having shot the poor fellow on so slight a provocation, and was most anxious to make amends for his fault. 'My friend,' said he to the dying man, 'it grieves me much that I should have been so rash as to lose my temper in so trifling a matter; and if there is any way in which I can serve you, rest assured you have only to name it, and I will faithfully perform your last request.' '*Vill* you, my fren'? Zen,' said his victim, writhing in the agonies of death, 'if you will *be so kind as tell me wezzer zat was your brekfaste or your dinnà wat you ete, I shall die ver' mosh content!*'

SPEAKING of Frenchmen: A friend of ours records one out of a thousand instances, of daily occurrence: 'Come here, *Gas-son*,' said a young fopling, at one of our metropolitan eating-houses. A waiter presented himself. 'Your name is n't *Gas-son*, is it, Stupid? I called '*Gas-son*,' yonder'—and he beckoned to a lad, whom he had heard called garcon, the day before, to do his bidding! We have often laughed at the story of a person of pleasing address and appearance, who was encountered on board a steam-packet from Dover to Calais. It was observed, that whenever he obtained an auditor, he would address him courteously, and commence a discussion of the qualities of two carriages which were on the forward deck. 'That 'ere big coach,' said he, '*is* a nice 'un; but them 'ere scratahes on the cab, them's the vorst on't, though!' A gentleman who heard these coarse remarks thrice repeated to different individuals by a person of pleasing and gentlemanlike exterior, had the curiosity to inquire of one who seemed to be a companion voyager, why it should happen that his language was so strangely out of keeping with his general bearing; when lo! it transpired that he was a Parisian, sporting the little English he had learned of a cockney valet, in a brief stay in London, before his countrymen. Many an 'ignorant ramus' on this side the water makes himself equally ridiculous, in misapplying and mispronoùncing the language of this ambitious Gaul; speaking it like the man whom MATTHEWS describes, who boasted of his perfection in French, but gave the credit to its felicitous acquisition; he 'l'arnt it of a Garman, that l'arnt it of a Scotchman at Dunkirk!'

OH Heavens! how many bereaved hearts are bleeding at this very hour in this city: hearts made desolate in a single moment! Fifty children, studying at one instant in the hushed school-room, and the next in eternity! Sitting here to-night, with our dear ones about us, we shudder with horror while we glow with gratitude to the benevolent BEING who has 'preserved *them* hitherto.' What a sad scene will be the school-room where these departed sufferers were wont daily to meet! Their fellow-pupils and play-mates will sing, in words that 'Young KNICK.' has just been repeating to his little sister:

'OH where, tell me where have the little children gone?
Oh where, tell me where have the little children gone?

They once were sitting here with us,
  They sang and spoke and smiled,
And they loved to meet us thus,
  But they 've left us now, my child.

'Oh where, tell me where have the little children gone?
Oh where, tell me where have the little children gone?
  I seem to see their sparkling eyes,
    I seem to hear their song;
  But we'll never see them more
    In the school where we belong!'

Beard, the distinguished western artist, mentions the delivery of a conundrum which he once heard in this state. A tall, red-haired, 'serio-dubious' sort of over-grown boy, who was 'designed for the ministry,' and had just obtained his 'parchment' from an eastern college, was called upon, at a parting supper, to 'make a speech.' He excused himself by saying, 'I dont know any speech that I can say neöw.' He was asked for a song. 'No, he never *could* sing; feöund *that* out when he first went to singin'-school.' However, being hard pressed for 'something,' he said, looking at and twisting bashfully his long freckled fingers, 'I can tell a conundrum that I made myself last week. It come to me first one night when I was abed, and I made it out next day, and wrote it down on a piece of paper. I got it here neöw.' So saying, he took from his waistcoat-pocket a slip of paper, and read: 'What village in 'York State is the same name as the Promised Land?' There was some 'guessing,' but at last it was 'given up,' and a 'solution requested:' '*Canandaigua!*' at length expounded the proposer. But the company were still as much in the dark as ever: 'Canandaigua!' exclaimed a dozen in a breath; 'why — how — *where* is there any resemblance to the 'Promised Land?' 'Can't see the slightest.' 'Why, you see,' said the conundrum-maker, '*this* is the way on 't: yeŏu must divide the word, and instead of *Can*-an you must say '*Ca*-nan,' and throw the '*daigua*' away! Canaan was the 'Promised Land,' see!' A resistless and united guffaw followed this 'forced construction,' which the expounder mistook for admiration. 'Aint it a fu'st-rate conundrum?' said he, with a visible chuckle, that only increased the obstreperous cachinnation. We should n't like to look at so bright an intellectual luminary as this, except through a piece of smoked glass.

IT may be, nay doubtless it is, a morbid feeling which prompts the meditative man to pause and look up at the successive stones slowly sinking into their resting-places in some public edifice in process of erection: thinking the while how long those inanimate blocks will remain there, and how many will gaze up at them when the present beholder is mouldering into dust. Such have often been our own thoughts in looking at the public temples which have been builded in this city within the last fourteen years.

But we have been thinking to-day how (could we but know it) the fronts of our earlier edifices would be found written all over with kindred thoughts, if they who gazed at them could have left the impress of their reflections upon the stones which arrested their attention. *They* are gone: yet nature is as gay, the sun shines as bright, men are as busy in getting gain, as in the centuries that are past. Ah! well may the thoughtful man exclaim:

'WHERE, where are all the birds that sang
A hundred years ago?
The flowers that all in beauty sprang
A hundred years ago?
The lips that smiled,
The eyes that wild
In flashes shone
Soft eyes upon;
Where, O where are lips and eyes,
The maiden's smiles, the lover's sighs,
That lived so long ago?

'Who peopled all the city streets
A hundred years ago?
Who filled the church with faces meek,
A hundred years ago?
The sneering tale
Of sister frail,
The plot that work'd
A brother's hurt;
Where, O where are plots and sneers,
The poor man's hopes, the rich man's fears,
That lived so long ago?

6

'WHAT meat *is* this?' said a country farmer the other day, to a legal friend who had invited him into a French restaurant in the lower part of the city, to take a hasty dinner with him; 'what meat *is* it?' 'It 's beef, I think,' said the lawyer. The countryman replied, 'I guess not; do n't *taste* like beef to me;' and he regarded the amphibious-looking dish before him with thoughtful solicitude. At the next mouthful, he laid his knife and fork down, and asked with eager curiosity, 'An't this a *French* eatin'-house?' 'It is,' answered the lawyer. 'Then it *is* dog!' he exclaimed, removing the last morsel from his mouth, as a sailor relieves his jaws of a tobacco-quid; 'it *is* dog, and I *thought* it was! I *et* dog once at 'Swago, (Oswego) in the last war, and I know what it is.' And although it was an excellent restaurant at which they were dining, so great was his prejudice against the French cuisine, that he could not be persuaded to taste another morsel. When they were walking home he said to his friend: 'My neighbor JONES was down to 'York once, and being very fond o' sassengers, he went into an eatin'-shop to get some. While he was a-hearin' of 'em fry, hissin' and sputterin' away, a man was buyin' some of 'em raw at the counter, and while he was a-tyin' of 'em up, a chap come in with a fuz-cap and a dirty drab 'sustoot,' and laid down a little bundle at the fur-eend o' the counter, He looked at the keeper, and see he was a little busy; so he said, lookin' shy at him as he went out, says he, ''Ta'nt no matter about the money *now*, but that makes *eleven*,' p'intin' toward the bundle. JONES looked at the bundle, and he says he see the *head of a cat* stickin' out at the eend, with long smellers onto it as long as his finger! He left *that* shop 'mazin quick, and han't never eat a sassenger sence!'

MOST persons have heard, perhaps, of the direction given by a gawk to a traveller: 'You go down this road, till you come to Squire JONES' house, which always stands by a little yaller dog.' An amusing continental traveller, (who was so 'indifferent' to natural scenery that he rode around the lake of Geneva in a *char-à-banc*, with his back to the lake,) adopts a similar transposition. He tells us that the German universities are 'always placed at the *seats of celebrated beer!*' The French traveller in Scotland, who reported that at every village they kept relays of dogs to bark the feeble coach-horses on toward the next one, did not awaken more ludicrous associations.

OUR friend BURGESS, of the well-known house of BURGESS STRINGER AND COMPANY, tells a capital anecdote of himself, which should not be altogether privately 'hushed up.' He is a member of the Methodist Church ; and being at a camp-meeting near Sing-Sing, last summer, he had the misfortune, after two or three days' and nights' attendance, to fall asleep in the midst of a powerful sermon. It was just after the New-York Trade-Sale of books, and Mr. Burgess was dreaming thereof: and to the searching questionings of the speaker, 'Will you any longer delay ?—will you not choose to-day whom you are to serve ?—what course you are to take ?' '*Take the lot!—the balance to Burgess, Stringer and Company!*' exclaimed Burgess eagerly, as he awoke, and stared wildly around him, when he saw every body staring still more wildly at him, and the minister himself petrified with amazement!

The 'competence' of the tiller of the soil, the 'abundance' of the successful mechanic, and the 'sufficiency' of the tradesman, we conceive to be better calculated to promote happiness than 'great wealth,' even when unencumbered. We are not insensible to the value of money. Our remark was pointed as to the *wants* that wealth brings; but the *cares* of it are not less exacting. 'Do n't you *know* me?' said a western millionaire, soon after 'the crisis,' to a friend of ours, with whom he had formerly been intimately acquainted; 'do n't you *remember* me? My name is ——.' 'Good heavens! it can't be possible!' exclaimed our friend; 'why, what has wrought such a change in your appearance? Where's your flourishing head of hair? where's your flesh gone? what's put that bend in your back?' 'The times! the times!' replied the 'poor rich man;' 'as for my back, I broke that last year, *lifting notes;* some of them were very heavy.' A grievous and unnecessary burden no doubt they were; and how much better was the rich man's 'wealth,' with its carking cares, than the 'abundance' of the contented mechanic?

THE following amusing adventure, given by a correspondent writing from Buffalo, actually took place in the town of M——, in Ohio, two years ago. 'Farmer —— had two daughters, very interesting young ladies, yet in their teens, who were quite romantic in their notions. The father was an aristocratic member of the Baptist church, and of course was very particular as to the 'company' his girls should 'keep.' Now it happened that these two pretty girls became acquainted with a couple of young bucks, clerks in an adjoining village, and, to use a common phrase, 'took quite a shyin' to 'em.' To this the old gentleman was very much opposed, as he intended to match his daughters himself. But ''t was no use' talking to them; while week after week wore away, and found the young men constant visitors. At length, in order to enforce obedience, the old man found himself driven to the necessity of locking up the foolish children who had presumed without his consent to fall in love with a couple ot poor tradesmen. The sweet girls were accordingly confined on Sunday afternoons in the back bed-room in the second story, which fronted the barn-yard; a very romantic 'look-out.' Under the window was a pile of stones, which had been left after repairing the cellar-wall in that corner. For two or three succcssive Sabbath evenings, the usual period of visiting their inamoratas, the lovers had climbed, by means of the sheets of the bed, which were let down from the window by the heroic girls, up to the apartment of their imprisoned lovers, and from nightfall until rosy morning did revel in the 'ambrosial delight of love's young dreams.' But this clandestine courtship could not be continued without being at last discovered. One lovely Sabbath, just at twilight, the father, coming in from the barn, thought he saw something rather ominous hanging out of the back-window; so he walked noiselessly around to ascertain the 'nature' of it. There hung the fatal 'flag of surrender;' and the old man, giving it a slight jerk, commenced the ascent. He was lifted gently from off his feet, and felt himself gradually 'rising in the world.' 'T was a very heavy weight, the daughters thought; and to tell the truth, it *was* a corpulent 'body-corporate' at which they were hopefully tugging away.

But lo! his head had reached the window-sill; and now, just as his old white hat appeared above the window, his affectionate daughters 'dropped him like a hot potato;' and, with something like the 'emphasis of a squashed apple-dumpling,' the old man came in instant contact with mother Earth; while the two knights of tape-and-scissors, who were not far off, enjoying the scene, 'made hasty tracks from the settlement,' leaving nothing behind them but bodily misery, horror-stricken damsels, and their own coat-tails streaming on the cool night-air!'

A FOG lay over the broad expanse of the Tappaän-Zee, at DOBB his Ferry, the other morning. There is a small but *very* long-eared donkey at that place, the Bucephalus of a juvenile play-mate of 'Young KNICK.,' whom also *our* scion backs whenever so minded. The little animal is very strong, and 'carries weight for age;' so *we* mounted him, on the foggy morning aforesaid, and rode to the water's edge, looking into the mist, which hid the farther shore from sight. Sir JOSHUA REYNOLDS, in one of his lectures, says that the horizon-line of the 'great and wide sea,' in mid-deep, is one of the most striking emblems of the infinite and the eternal to be found in all the works of the ALMIGHTY. We thought of this while looking off upon the dim (and at the time boundless) waste of waters before us; and then came the thought of NAPOLEON at Saint Helena, musing by the solemn shore of the vast ocean which formed the watery walls of his island-prison: and so strong was the last impression, that, mounted as we were, we began to feel, in that moment of deep reverie, that we *were* NAPOLEON, taking our equestrian exercise of a morning, and looking off upon the sea; when all at once, an unmistakable juvenile voice, that is usually 'music to our ears,' 'let down the peg' that held up our musings, with the untimely, and we may add uncalled-for remark, accompanied by a loud laugh, that was surely unnecessary if not unbecoming: 'If there is n't FATHER on DUNKEY!—*how he looks!*' Our imaginary NAPOLEON vanished as quickly at this interruption as did HAMLET's father's ghost when he 'smelt the morning air;' and we 'saw ourselves as others saw us;' a biped, clad in a thin linen coat, broad-brimmed Rocky-mountain fur hat, (a present from 'BELLACOSCA,' now of that ilk,) seated on an ass, and a little one at that! As we turned him to go back, having 'satisfied the sentiment,' his saddle turned too, and we fell to the ground, a distance, perhaps, from the top of his back, of some three feet. No bones were broken; but we did n't like the report of the unimportant circumstance which 'Young KNICK.' bore to his mother: 'FATHER got threw from DUNKEY!' '*Threw!*'— that's a good style of grammar to be used by the son of an EDITOR!

Whitney & Annin fc.

All this may seem ridiculous: but why might we *not* have fancied ourself NAPOLEON, amidst the kindred outward accessories of his last position? Supposing our dress and steed were *not* warlike? Is it the *uniform* that makes the captain? If it *is*, we should like to know it!

WE heard the other afternoon, from a proved *raconteur*, who has no rival, either orally or with pen in hand, a story of JARVIS's, the distinguished painter, which made us quite 'elastic' for half a day. A mercurial yet misanthropic Frenchman, who, to 'save himself *from* himself, used often to call upon JARVIS, had an 'Old Master,' a wretched daub, whose greatest merit was its obscurity. Being ignorant of the hoax which had been played upon him in its purchase, he set a great value upon it, and invited JARVIS to come to his room and examine it. JARVIS did so; and to prevent giving its possessor pain, he avoided the expression of an opinion 'upon the merits,' but advised the owner to have it cleaned; it being 'so dirty that one might easily mistake it for a very ordinary painting.' Some four or five days afterward the Frenchman called upon the painter; and the moment he entered his apartment, he exclaimed: 'Ah! Monsieur JARVEES, I 'ave some'sing to tell you! My graänd picture is des-troy'!—no wors' a d——n any more! I get ze man to clean him : ver' good ; he wash him all out wis de turpentime ! Ah ! if I could only catch him !—I would kick him *p-l-e-n-t-y !'* 'Heavens !' exclaimed JARVIS ; 'can it be possible that that great picture is *spoiled ?* You must have been in a towering passion when it came home in that condition.' 'No, no, Monsieur,' replied the Frenchman, in a lachrymose, pitful tone ; 'I am not strong man to be angry —I was *s-i-c-k !'*

IT is one of those warm, low-cloudy, fine-rainy days of late October. Young KNICK, an hour ago, in a grassy ravine of a hill-side grove, now almost bereft of its summer honors, helped us to brush together a thick bed of faded leaves ; and, on that fragrant couch we have been lying, looking off through the thin blue drizzle upon the dying woods over the Tappaän Zee, and the patches of fall-wheat, of matchless green, that edge them, toward the river. Returning, after much pleasant chit-chat with the little Junior, we find a pacquet of letters and communications from town (to which we did not repair to-day) upon our table ; and lo ! the first one we open is what HALLECK terms

> 'A HYMN o'er happy days departed
> A hope that such again may be.'

Our esteemed correspondent has certainly touched us at

this moment in a tender point. He expresses our sentiments exactly:

'"Tis well at times to mope and sigh,
If one can give good reason why;
E'en change of scene may cause (who knows?)
A tear to trickle down one's nose:
I grant ye it is weak to sob —
O, very!
Yet must I weep to leave dear DOBB,
His Ferry!'

'October's wailing winds are here,
Its foliage pied, and meadows sere;
Gorgeous, with all its bravery on,
Crisping with frosty breath the lawn,
It endeth my gay summer job,
So merry;
And now 'Good-bye to 'Mr. DOBB,
His Ferry!''

'I shall remember well its shades,
Its CONSTANT-dells and green arcades,
Where murmuring winds on summer eves
Made music in the trembling leaves;
Those leaves, beneath whose shade the cob-
Bler-sherry
Cemented friendship's chain at 'DOBB,
His Ferry.'

'And now I stand upon the wharf,
While shoots our favorite 'ARROW' off;
And still in thought behold afar
The spot where my fond wishes are;

But steamer, stage, nor prancing cob,
Nor wherry,
May bear my yearning heart to 'DOBB.
His Ferry!'

'Tied to the roaring city's wheel,
Where omnibii their thunders peal;
Pent up mid bounds where vice is nursed,
Where man with many a care is cursed,
One lives amid a seething mob,
Half terri-
Fied with scenes unknown at 'DOBB,
His Ferry.

'Shake, shake your lazy sands, O Time!
And swiftly bring round Summer's prime;
Bring its glad gales to waft me back,
Up the broad Hudson's sparkling track!
The vision makes my pulses throb;
I bury
All work-day thoughts, and muse on 'DOBB,
His Ferry!''

Whoever shall visit 'DOBB'S' the ensuing winter, and the pleasant domicil which we inhabited there, will on examination find pieces of 'Old KNICK.' sticking to the door-posts; retained there in the disparting struggle of the final adieu.

NUMBER SIX.

THE GENTLEMAN IN BLACK: THE STABAT MATER. CONUNDRUMS — A PRACTICAL ONE: A TRIBUTE TO ART — ELLIOTT AND INMAN: AN 'ORIGINAL': A REVEREND JEREMY DIDDLER: A MORNING LOCOMOTIVE IN THE METROPOLIS: AN 'UNFORTUNATE MEMORY': INFLUENZAL POETRY: A PROFANE SWEARER NONPLUSSED: A TWO-EDGED COMPLIMENT: A MAN OF THE WORLD'S ADVICE: SENATORIAL BON-MOT: A MUSICAL ENTHUSIAST: GOD IN NATURE — A COMET: 'WHAT'S THE LAW?' — AN ANECDOTE.

WE derive the following capital anecdote from an esteemed friend who 'was there,' and who never yet permitted a good thing to escape his observant eye. A stage-coach well freighted with passengers, was once travelling from London to York. Among those on the outside was a dry-looking gentleman in rusty black, and very taciturn. According to custom, he soon got a travelling-name from his dress; and from some accidental whim, the passengers seemed to take a pleasure in playing upon it. Whenever they stopped, there would casual questions be asked: 'Where's the Gentleman in Black?' 'Won't the Gentleman in Black come by the fire?' 'Perhaps the Gentleman in Black would like a bit of the mutton?' In short, the Gentleman in Black became a personage of consequence, in spite of his taciturnity. At length, in the middle of the night, crash! went the coach, and the unlucky 'outsides' were sent headlong into the ditch. There was a world of work in repairing damages, and gathering together the limping passengers. Just as they were about setting off, the coachman was attracted by a voice from a ditch, where he found some one, white as a miller from rolling down a chalky bank. The Unknown prayed in piteous voice for assistance. 'Why who the deuce are you?' cried coachee. 'Alas!' replied the other, in a tone half-whimsical, half-plaintive, 'I'm the *Gentleman in Black!*'

ARE not these lines from the '*Stabat Mater*' felicitously translated? We have the poem entire, but segregate only the two stanzas which ensue:

STABAT mater dolorosa,
Juxta crucem lacrymosa,
Dum pendebat filius:
Cujus animam gementem,
Contristantem et dolentem
Pertransivit gladius.

O quam tristis et afflicta
Fuit illa benedicta,
Mater unigeniti:
Quæ mœrebat, et dolebat,
Et tremebat; cum videbat
Nati pœnas inclyti.

Although nothing could exceed the simple beauty of

the original, yet the reader will be struck with the true spirit of the rendering:

NEAR the cross the MOTHER weeping
Stood, her watch in sorrow keeping
While was hanging there her SON:
Through her soul in anguish groaning,
O most sad, HIS fate bemoaning,
Through and through that sword was run.

Oh how sad with woe oppressed,
Was she then, the MOTHER blessed,
Who the sole-begotten bore;
As she saw HIS pain and anguish,
She did tremble, she did languish,
Weep, her holy SON before.

ADVICE, we are well aware, is one of those things which 'it is more blessed to give than to receive;' yet we cannot help saying to our Philadelphia correspondent, that the labor he has bestowed upon his punning epistle would, otherwise directed, have sufficed for the production of an article that could scarcely have failed to reflect credit upon his evident talents. Labored puns and conundrums are very hard reading. It is not less a labor to laugh at them than it is to write them. Look at this wretched thing: 'Why is a man looking for the philosopher's stone like NEPTUNE?' 'Give it up' at once, and 'let us pass on, and not offend you' farther. ''Cause he 's a sea-king what do n't exist!' It is of kindred stuff that modern puns are made.

There is such a thing as a practical conundrum, which is not amiss. 'Look a-hea', SAM,' said a western negro one day to a field-hand over the fence in an adjoining lot; 'look a-hea', d' you see dat tall tree down dar?' 'Yaäs, JIM, I does.' 'Wal, I go up dat tree day 'fore yes'dy to de bery top.' 'W'at was you a'ter, SAM?' 'I was a'ter a 'coon; an' w'en I'd chased 'im cl'ar out to t' odder eend o' dat longes' limb, I hearn sumfin drop. W'at you guess 't was, SAM? D' you give 'm up? *'Twas dis d——d foolish nigga!* E-yah! e-yah! Like to broked he neck: been limpin' 'bout ever since!'

WE do not know when we have encountered a more forcible tribute to an American portrait-painter than is contained in the following extract from a letter which a distinguished foreigner, at present sojourning in this country, recently received from his wife, now resident in London. The passage refers to the portrait of the gentleman in question, a most speaking likeness of the original: 'At last I can announce to you the safe arrival of the long-expected treasure, your dear portrait. With what delight I greeted it, is beyond my power to express. My impatience to behold your pictured countenance induced me to attempt to open the huge packing-case unaided, and I soon succeeded in releasing it from its bondage; and to my heart's delight I once more surveyed your perfect image! To my idea, it is in all respects a complete resemblance of yourself; and every day I am more and more impressed with this opinion. I send you a thousand thanks for this to me invaluable present. It is a treasure I would not part with for any earthly consideration. Still I *must* tell you that it makes me feel more unhappy and more disconsolate at our temporary separation; and so restless am I to survey your likeness, so truly depicted, that scarce a night passes without my procuring a light and dwelling upon it, while all is stillness around me. Present my compliments to the artist, and say that I am more grateful to him than I can find words to express, and that he has conferred the greatest happiness on me that this world can afford, next to that of sending me the original.' The artist here alluded to is Mr. C. L. ELLIOTT, whose studio is in an upper room of the Art Union Buildings, Broadway. Truth to say, the encomium passed upon Mr. ELLIOTT in the foregoing fervent sentences is well deserved. We know of no American portrait-painter who has advanced with more rapid strides toward perfection; a fact sufficiently evinced by the patronage which he has secured from the best sources in the metropolis. A few weeks before the death of the lamented HENRY INMAN, that fine artist was in the studio of Mr. ELLIOTT. After surveying the portraits of his latest sitters with a painter's eye and a painter's scrutiny, he said, 'I must have you paint *my* portrait, and I will paint your's in return.' 'I shall only be too glad to do so,' replied Mr. ELLIOTT: 'I cannot help thinking that I should be able to obtain a characteristic likeness of you.' 'Yes,' answered INMAN, (in a manner which we could *see*,) passing his hand over his face, with a significant gesticulation; 'yes, I think you could; features plain and blocky — *blocky!*' Would that any New-Yorker possessed at this moment a portrait of our departed friend, such as he knew ELLIOTT could have painted!

'WHILE I am on the subject of 'originals,'' writes an esteemed Southern friend, now a Senator of the United States, 'allow me to bring to your notice a specimen: I was in the office of a legal friend some time since, when a dilapidated specimen of humanity, bearing full traces of the wear and tear of life, came in. He addressed himself at once to the proprietor of the office: 'Your servant, Sir. I see before me, I presume, that distinguished lawyer, —— ——,' naming my friend. 'I myself, Sir, am in affinity to the legal profession. I am the son, Sir, of a distinguished advocate in the Old Dominion: my name, LANCELOT LANGLEY LING — the Reverend LANCELOT LANGLEY LING. I live in the State of ——. I teach a little, I preach a little, and I plough a great deal. These combined operations have told upon me: they tell upon me now,

Sir. As the poet says, 'These tatter'd robes my poverty bespeak.' The people of my region, Sir, are poor, and can afford me but little help. I said, 'I will seek the wealthy of another State: they shall minister to my wants.' I came hither to find them: but do you know, Sir, that external appearance has its effect upon men? Yes, Sir, it *has*; and therefore, before I sought the wealthy I came to the wise, who regard not exteriors, but look to the mind. 'Worth makes the man, and want of it the fellow; the rest is all but leather;' and indeed, Sir, there is very little 'leather' about me, as you may easily perceive by looking at the tattered condition of my boots. Now, Sir, I will be grateful for *your* contribution. My wants are simple — my desires few. I have a small plantation, on the top of a high hill; the plantation very small, but the hill very high. A log-house graces its brow; a beautiful well of splendid water is there, Sir; an orchard of benevolent fruit-trees is there also, (I call them benevolent, Sir, because they give both sustenance and shade to me, and

> ''TIS sweet to sit beneath the shade
> That your own industry hath made:

Something of the poet, too, Sir, as you see:) and I am there also when I *am* there; but at present the schoolmaster (myself, Sir) is abroad, and my mission is threefold: FIRST: I want clothes: my journeyings and my labors have brought bad habits upon me. (Excuse the pun, Sir: it is a college failing. 'You may break, you may ruin the vase if you will, but the scent of the rose will linger there still.') SECOND: I want money to buy a small negro boy; one that I can call, on my return from my various travels, and say to him: BOB, SAM, TOM, or whatever his name might be, 'Take my horse and carry him to the stable:'

'THEN might I rest beneath my leafy bower,
And hug the spirit of the passing hour.

Last and not least, Sir, I want window-sashes for our church, which we call 'Mount Zion.' I want putty and glass, or money to buy them:

'THESE are my wants; all simple, and but few:
My tale is told — I leave the rest to you.'

"'And *my tale* is easily told, Mr. LING,' said my friend, 'and my duty will be quickly performed. Here are five dollars: if that sum is of any use to you, you are welcome to it.'

"'Will five dollars be of any service to me? Will a smart shower be of any service to a droughty land? Will a large slice of the staff of life be of any service to a hungry traveller? Yes, Sir, five dollars *will* be of use to me! Do you know what I will do with this sum, which I am now proud to call my own? Nay, Sir, you must know — you *ought* to know — so list to me. I will purchase a pair of boots for myself, with part: the balance shall be invested in putty and glass for the aforesaid church. And now farewell!

'A THOUSAND blessings, saith thy bard,
A thousand joys to thee;
A life-time by no sorrow marr'd,
A death from anguish free.'

If ever you come to ———, Sir, come to me. You will be welcome to the home, to the heart, to the hospitality, of LANCELOT LANGLEY LING. Once more, *Vale!*'

'And away he went. I saw him the next day in the streets. He had on a fine pair of boots, and I trembled for the putty investment. Once more we met, and he no longer looked like 'the man all tattered and torn, that kissed the maiden all forlorn,' for he was dressed in a full suit of broad-cloth; 'superfine,' and as FAGIN said, with the 'heavy-swell cut.' Whether he ever succeeded in realizing funds for all the simple and few wants and desires of his heart, I know not.'

THERE goes again that steam-shriek of the locomotive, on the Hudson River rail-road! But it is morning now; and instead of conveying wondering new-comers to the metropolis, it is carrying country-born metropolitans into the very midst of their old associations. They are passing, by the 'going-forth of the ways,' *from* the great city:

they leave the 'roaring of the wheels,' and the thousand sights and sounds which have long been familiar to them; they pass the 'out-squirts,' as Mrs. PARTINGTON terms the suburbs, and anon the horizon begins to widen; the river broadens to the Tappaän-Zee; the surburban villas, gleaming upon the shores, are left behind; the hills, the ancient hills, arise, 'whose summits freeze in the fierce light and cold;' and beyond all, 'lies the vast inland, stretched beyond the sight;' an inland, at this spring-season, where the country-bred traveller sees in his mind's eye the blue smoke curling up from the maple-sugar 'sap-works;' smells the bass-wood 'spouts,' ('gouge'-split and thin-'whittled' before the pensive evening fire of spring,) and inhales the odor of the red-cedar buckets: he recalls the deep, 'sploshy' snow, through which he tramped, 'neck-yoke' on shoulder, to bring the luscious juice to the 'store-trough,' previous to being poured into the dark-boiling, low-murmuring 'pot-ash-kettles;' and he remembers well the looks of the vari-colored *fungi*, with an under-surface whiter than the finest zinc-tints of our friend FOSDICK, which grew upon the prostrate and decaying monarchs of the forest, over which he strode, on his 'sweet' mission. Perhaps he may remember a snow-storm too, like this in which we write, when his humble cot was shut up by the elements; when the turkeys and geese, the cocks and hens, came up the high snow-banks and pecked at the windows;

when the long icicles, button-ribbed, like the end of a rattle-snake's tail, hung scarcely-dripping from the eaves; and the little folk would open the outer door, move a step or two from it, the whiff of a snow-shower-bath taking away their breath in the mean time, and, half shrinking, half in sport, pierce two or three deep yellow holes in the bank, and then rush shivering into the house again. But there's the last, the dying sound of the steam-whistle, away in the stormy distance!

HEARD a little incident to-day, which struck us as a very graphic illustration of the hurry with which surgical operations are sometimes resorted to. A brave officer, who had been wounded with a musket-ball in or near his knee, was stretched upon the dissecting-table of a surgeon, who, with an assistant, began to cut and probe in that region of his anatomy. After a while the 'subject' said: '*Don't* cut me up in that style, doctor! What are you torturing me in that cruel way for!'

'We are looking after the ball,' replied the senior operator.

'Why didn't you *say* so, then, before?' asked the indignant patient. 'I 've got the ball in my pocket!' said he, putting his hand in his waistcoat, and taking it out. 'I took it out myself,' he added; 'did n't I *mention* it to you? I *meant* to!'

'AT-CHEE! — at-chu!' We have caught the 'Idflu-edza!' That last was the sixteedth tibe we 've sdeezed id five bidutes. We 've been tryidg to si'g the followig so'g, but bade bad work edough of it:

'By BARY-ADDE is like the sud
  Whed at the dawd it flidgs
Its golded sbiles of light upod
  Earth's greed a'd lovely thi'gs.
Id vaid I sue: I o'dly wid
  From her a scordful frowd;
But sood as I by prayers begid,
  She cries, 'Oh do! — bego'de!'

'By BARY-ADDE is like the bood,
  Whed first her silver sheed
Awakes the dightidgale's soft tude,
  That else had siled't beed:
But BARY-ADDE, like darkest dight,
  Od be, alas! looks dowd;
Her sbiles od others beab their light,
  Her frowds are all by owd:
I 've but o' de burthed to by so'dg,
  Her frowds are all by owd!'

'IN Schoharie county,' writes an obliging friend, 'there lives a man whose addiction to profanity is such that his name has become a by-word and a reproach; but by some internal thermometer he so graduates his oaths as to make them apply to the peculiar case in hand; the greater the mishap or cause for anger, the stronger and more frequent his adjurations. His business is that of a gatherer of ashes, which he collects in small quantities and transports in an ox-cart. Upon a recent occasion, having by dint of great labor succeeded in filling his vehicle, he started for the ashery, which stands upon the brow of a steep hill; and it was not until he reached the door that he noticed, winding its tortuous course down the long declivity, a line of white ashes, while something short of a peck remained in the cart. 'The dwellers by the way-side and they that tarried there' had assembled in great force, expecting an unusual anathemal display. Turning however to the crowd, the unfortunate man heaved a sigh, and simply remarked: 'Neighbors, it 's no use; *I can't do justice to the subject!*'

VERY sly and 'smart' is the following anecdote, which we find unattributed to any particular source, in a religious journal of this city: 'JOSIAS WINSLOW was one of the early governors of the Massachusetts colony. It is said that at his funeral the Rev. Mr. WITHERELL, of Scituate, prayed that 'the governor's son might be half equal to his father.' The Rev. Dr. GAD HITCHCOCK observed afterward, that the 'prayer was so very reasonable, it might have been hoped that GOD would grant it; but he did n't!'

WONDER if there are not some people in the world that do actually reason after the cool manner of the philosopher who gives this sage advice to his friend? Just as likely as not. We know some citizens who *act* according to such advice, 'any way': 'The duties of life are two-fold: our duty to others and our duty to ourselves. Our duty to ourselves is to make ourselves as comfortable as possible: our duty to others is to make them assist us, to the best of their ability, in so doing. This is the plan on which all respectable persons act. Adhere strictly to truth — whenever there is no occasion for lying. Be particularly careful to conceal no one circumstance likely to redound to your credit. If it be for your interest to lie, do so, and do it boldly. No one would wear false hair who had hair of his own, but he who has none, must of course wear a wig. A wig, you see, my young friend, is simply a lie with hair on it. I do n't see any difference between false hair and a false assertion. In fact, I think a lie a very useful invention. It is like a coat or a pair of breeches: it serves to clothe the naked. But do n't throw your falsifications away. I like a proper economy. Some silly persons would have you invariably speak the truth. Now if you were to act in this way, in what department of commerce could you succeed? How would you get on in the law, for instance? What vagabond would ever employ you to defend his cause? What practice do you think you 'd be likely to procure as a physician, if you were to tell every old woman who fancied herself ill that there was nothing the matter with her? Never break a promise unless bound to do so by a previous one: and promise yourself, from this time forth, never to do any thing that will put you to inconvenience. Be firm, but not obstinate. Never change your mind when the result of the alteration would be detrimental to your comfort and interests; but do not maintain an inconvenient inflexibility of purpose. Do not, for example, in affairs of the heart, simply because you have declared, perhaps with an oath or two, that you will be constant till death, think it necessary to make any effort to remain so. The case stands thus: You enter into an engagement with a being whose aggregate of perfections is expressible, we will say, by 20. Now if they would always keep at that point, there might be some reason for your remaining unaltered, namely, your not being able to help it. But suppose that they dwindle down to 19 1-2: the person, that is, the whole sum of the qualities admired no longer exists, and you, of course, are absolved from your engagement. But mind, I do not say that you are justified in changing *only* in case of a change on the opposite side: you may very possibly become simply tired. In this case, a prior promise to yourself will absolve you from the performance of the one in question.'

WE heard a clever thing at the table of a friend at 'Shnang P'int' the other day, which is too good to be lost. It appears that one morning at the capitol, just after the Senate had organized, Senator BADGER was seized with so violent a fit of sneezing, that it caused much merriment in the galleries. Senator DICKINSON, a man of genuine humor, thereupon immediately sent him the following:

'A NOISE in the Senate is quite out of place,
If 't is one which spectators are like to be pleased at;
And a member should know, if 'out-siders' do not,
That the Senate in session is 'not to be sneezed at!'

OUR right-hand 'MAIN' mentions an amusing instance of professional enthusiasm. He was coming down from Albany the other evening, in one of our noble Hudson River steamers, and was about going to take his place near the entrance to the supper-table, when his arm was seized, almost convulsively, by a man who was watching the movements of the engine, and apparently listening intently to some unusual noise. 'Do you hear *that?*' said he; 'do you hear THAT, Sir?' 'No,' said 'MAIN,' a little scared, thinking that there might be a sound indicative of 'a b'iler a-bu'sting;' 'no, I d-do n't notice any thing unusual.' 'Wait a bit; hear *that?* 'Ko-chung! ko-chung!'—that 's a *minor-third*, Sir! — a *perfect* minor-third!' Such a musical critic as that would assign the 'yowl' of a tom-cat, the 'ye-ö-a-w!' of a pussy, or the bray of a jackass, borne on the night-wind, its specific position on the musical scale. What a beautiful thing it is to have 'an ear' for music — especially *such* music!

We were standing one evening, some years ago, in the door of the house of a friend, residing in one of the upper streets of the city, being about to take our leave of him for the night. The atmosphere was beautifully clear and the air delightfully cool. The far-off stars shone in their serene and silent spaces, with a back-ground of such deep blue as one sees when looking into the sky at midnight from the top of Kaätskill-mountain. While we were 'gazing steadfastly into heaven,' the friend by our side remarked: 'By-the-by, there is a comet predicted to appear, somewhere about this time, in the heavens. I was reading an article about it this very afternoon: it will make its first appearance, I believe, in *that* quarter of the heavens,' pointing high up, and in a south-westerly direction. We stood regarding wistfully that particular part of the evening sky, when our friend exclaimed, 'As I live, there is the comet *now!* Yes — yes: there it *is*, to a certainty!' And following his directing finger we saw, far up, and away in the south-west, a semi-luminous body, something not unlike an enlarged star, with a dim 'continuation,' like the fainter light of the 'Milky Way,' of a clear, bright night. 'Look at it! — *think* of it!' exclaimed our friend. 'There in yonder sky, is an erratic, wandering body, with no fixed orbit, uncontrollable, so far as known, by any specific law, or regular celestial mechanism, which, after sweeping its awful cycle amidst the revolving worlds above us, suddenly 'streams its horrid hair' on the midnight sky! How wide, how sublime, has been its celestial journey! And is it not a heavenly, an almost overpowering thought, that hereafter, in a world of unclouded light and knowledge, it may be vouchsafed to us to see with our natural eyes, and without the mistakes to which calculation is subject, the course of comets, the order of the solar and planetary systems, and fathom the depths of that dread arch of mystery that now hangs suspended above us!' This incident, which occurred many years ago, was forcibly called to mind a few days since, as we were steaming down from DOBB'S, on the morning of the recent partial eclipse of the sun. Here was demonstrated not only the grandeur of the divinely-ordered movements of the heavenly bodies, but the sublimity of the intellect of the creatures of the ALMIGHTY. At the very moment predicted, we saw, through a bit of smoked glass, a faint rim of shadow clip the edge of the great orb of day, and continue its encroachment upon its diminishing light, until the exact extent that had been foretold was attained. And *then* it was that we thought of those who, at that precise moment, high upon the Alps, were looking from those towering forms of Nature that 'pinnacle in clouds their snowy scalps,' to see the mighty shadow of the eclipse roll along the vast region below, blotting out whole provinces of lovely Italy in its giant-march! It were worth the toil of a twelve-month to witness that sublime spectacle.

SOMEBODY, 'we name no parties,' illustrated in our hearing the other evening the vague idea which some people, who enter into litigation, have of the powers of LAW over any and all cases, under all sorts of circumstances. A man in a state of great excitement entered a metropolitan lawyer's office, and taking off his hat, and a chair by the table at the same time, and wiping the perspiration from his forehead with a damp red-and-yellow pocket-handkerchief, asked the counsellor 'in chambers' for his 'views' as to '*the law*.' 'Well,' said the counsellor, 'as to *what* law?—under what *circumstances?* State your *case*. I 'll tell you what the *law* is, when you state your case. You want to know what the law is as to *what?*' 'Wal,' responded the client, scratching his head, and seeming to be greatly taken aback by this unexpected obstacle, 'wal, 'sposin' a man leaves the state, and do n't come back ag'in?

THEN what's the law!' 'I never shall forget,' said our informant, 'the blank disappointment exhibited in that client's face, when I told him that *that* was a case past any legal surgery of mine. 'Can't *fetch* him, eh?—and he owes me more 'n fifty dollars!' Seeing that his 'case' was 'gone,' the client left also.

NUMBER SEVEN.

CHRISTMAS GREENS — THE CROSS: A 'PICTURE IN LITTLE' OF WAR: RAFT-INCIDENT ON THE OHIO: THOUGHTS OF THE DEAD — WESLEY: 'SEARCHING THE SCRIPTURES' — A NEW READING: A PHILOSOPHER OUTWITTED: 'GREAT SHAKES' OF A DUTCHMAN'S DOG: THE MYSTERIOUS PRINCE — 'POISSON D'AVRIL': AN INDIAN ON THE GALLOWS: DEATH OF A MOTHER: THE 'YANKEE-PASS': A FEBRUARY NIGHT: A TESTACEOUS PHENOMENA: THE 'UP-SHOT' OF MARRIAGE: 'DUBIOUS' SCULPTURE: DEATH OF AN INNOCENT: 'MRS. RAMSBOTTOM' ABROAD: A CHURCH DEDICATION: 'UNDER-DONE' APOSTLES: PLEASURES OF MEMORY: RUM *versus* WATER: TRICKS UPON TRAVELLERS: NIGHT-CONFLAGRATION — THE SILENT CITY

LOOKING around, as we came in to-night, upon the annual Christmas-greens, in all tasteful forms, with which the hand of Affection annually decorates the sanctum, we met 'THE CROSS,' graceful in shape, and entwined with rosaries of red berries. Far back in memory we went instantaneously, and heard, for the first time as it were, in the little church of our 'boyhood's home,' this first verse of a hymn fall from the eloquent lips of the Rev. DERRICK C. LANSING:

> 'WHEN I survey the wondrous cross
> On which the PRINCE OF GLORY died,
> All earthly gain I count but dross,
> And pour contempt on all my pride!'

How many are the cells of memory! — how countless the things that are treasured there! — and how strangely they rise to the mind, amid one's daily cares and avocations! We shall know more of this mystery hereafter.

'THERE is tew sides to the matter of war,' says HOSEA BIGELOW, writing from Mexico; and he proceeds to illustrate the fact:

'THIS kind o' sogerin' ain't a mite like our October trainin',
Where a chap could clear right out, ef it only looked like rainin';
Where the Cunnles used to kiver up their shappoes with bandanners,
And send the Insines skootin' off to the bar-room with their banners,
(Fear o' gittin' on 'em spotted,) and a feller could cry quarter
Ef he fired away his ram-rod, arter too much rum-and-water.
Recollect what fun we had — I and you and EZRY HOLLIS —
Up there to Waltham Plain last fall, a havin' the CORNWALLIS?
This sort o' thing ain't jest like that: I wish that I was furder!
Ninepence a day for killin' folks comes kind o' low for murder.
(Why, I 've worked out to slaughterin' some, for Deacon CEPHAS BILLINS,
And in the hardest times there was I always fetched ten shillin's:)
This 'goin' where glory waits ye' hain't one agreeable featur',
An' ef it warn't for wakin' snakes, I'd be home ag'in, short metre!
O, *would n't* I be off, quick time, ef 't warn't that I was sart'in
They 'd let the day-light into me, to pay me for desartin'?'

HOSEA is not the only one, probably, who has lately ascertained that militia trainings and 'CORNWALLS' sham-fights are quite unlike the actual 'pomp and circumstance of glorious war.'

A FRIEND once informed us that one of the most ridiculous sights he ever saw was on the Ohio river. He was going up that beautiful stream in a large steamer, when the boat encountered a vast raft, something more than a mile long, and quite half a mile wide, with a small house in the very centre of it. It was coming down rapidly with the current, when the steam-boat, notwithstanding her efforts to avoid the collision, found herself in the 'toils' of the raft, having caught in such a way between its unevenly-projecting timbers as to be quite incapable of extrication. And now it was that the doughty captain, standing upon the extremest point of the bow of his boat, with doubled fist, and 'indignation in 's aspect,' apostrophized the navigator of the raft, and poured out upon his head the fiercest vials of his anger; while the proprietor of the 'well-wooded' floating acres, whose downward course it was impossible to stem, was seen slowly approaching in the distance, holding his hand back of his ear, as if anxious to hear what 'the captain said.' As soon as he came within hail, and was made fully sensible of the anathemas that were being hurled against him, he took a short black pipe out of his mouth, spat twice, and replied: 'You go to the devil with your little steam-boat! I do n't want any o' your saäce! Get eöut o' the way!' And resuming his pipe, he slowly wended his way back to his cabin. After having been borne down some eight or ten miles, the steamer was at length extricated, and the captain went on his way rejoicing.

READER, when in the providence of GOD, it shall be your fate to stand by the cold form of one whom you have loved; to gaze upon lips, oh! how pale and motionless; upon hands thin and wasted, crossed upon the silent breast; upon eye-lids dropped upon cheeks of clay, never to be lifted again; then haply you may think of these beautiful lines of the good WESLEY. Amidst remembered hopes that vanished and fears that distracted, weeping in unknown tumults, 'like soft streamings of celestial music' will come to your aching heart this serene Evangel!

How blest is our brother, bereft
 Of all that could burthen his mind!
How easy the soul that has left
 This wearisome body behind!
Of evil incapable thou,
 Whose relics with envy I see;
No longer in misery now,
 No longer a sinner, like me.

This dust is affected no more
 With sickness, or shaken with pain;
The war in the members is o'er,
 And never shall vex him again:
No anger henceforward, nor shame,
 Shall redden his innocent clay;
Extinct is the animal flame,
 And passion is vanished away.

The languishing head is at rest,
 Its thinking and aching are o'er;

The quiet, immovable breast
  Is heaved by affliction no more.
The heart is no longer the seat
  Of trouble or torturing pain;
It ceases to flutter and beat,
  It never will flutter again!

The lids he so seldom could close,
  By sorrow forbidden to sleep,
Sealed up in eternal repose,
  Have strangely forgotten to weep,
The fountains can yield no supplies,
  The hollows from water are free,
The tears are all wiped from these eyes,
  And evil they never shall see.

THE late lamented HENRY INMAN, used to relate, with inimitable effect, a story of an illiterate English Methodist minister at the West, who one night, at a class-meeting, mentioned the following affecting circumstance: 'It is but a little while-ah, since I was a-travelink along one of your great rivers-ah, surrounded by the deep forest; I stopped at a rude shanty by the low river side-ah, and there I found a poor family in grea-a-t affliction-ah. They were all sick; their children were shiverink and starving; their heads frowzy and dirty; and I was informed by the mother that they had *lost their fine-tooth comb-ah!* They was ignorant of the go-öspel, and did n't seem to care about it, 'ither; for when I reasoned with 'em-ah, the woman was all the time lamenting the loss of her fine-tooth comb-ah! 'Have you the Bible in your cabin?' said I to her, says I-ah; says she, 'Yes, theer it is, up theer on the catch-all-ah,' p'inting to a narrow shelf over the smoky fire-place, 'but we do n't often read into it-ah; ha'nt read any on't but once't, when our little BILL died with the ager, for as much as tew months-ah!' I got onto a die-tub, my friends, that stood in the corner, and reached up and took down the blessed Book, all covered with dust-ah; and what do you think it was that I opened to-ah? What do you think it *was* that I found there-ah, to satisfy the longings of that poor woman-ah? It was the long lost, the long-wanted, fine-tooth c-oo-m-b-ah! Oh, my hearers, *s'a-a-rch the skripters-ah!* If she had only s'aärched the skripters, how her mind would 'a been eased-ah!'

GREAT men, great philosophers, are sometimes beaten on their own ground, by the simplest minds and the least-instructed intellects. We 've laughed a hundred times at an illustration of this, which occurs to us at this moment. We have heard, or have read somewhere — but *where* we have not the slightest notion — that upon one occasion NEWTON, the immortal philosopher, was riding over some English plain or 'down,' when a boy who was keeping sheep called out to him: 'You'd better make haste on,

Sir, or you'll get a wet jacket.' The sky was clear; there was not a cloud, nor a speck of a cloud, to be seen: and the philosopher considering the remark a hoax, or at least an impertinence, rode quietly on; but he had not advanced six miles before a rain-storm suddenly arose, which wet him to the skin! Saturated as he was, he nevertheless rode back, to ascertain how an ignorant lad had attained a precision in, and a knowledge of, elemental calculation, of which the wisest philosopher might well be proud.

'My lad,' said NEWTON, when he arrived where 'fed his flock, the rural swain,' 'I'll give you a shilling if you 'll tell me how you foretold the weather so truly.' 'Will ye, Sir?' said the boy, scratching his head, and holding out his hand for the shilling. Having received it, he pointed to his sheep, and thus expounded his 'theory;' 'When you see that black ram turn his tail toward the wind, it 's a sure sign of rain within an hour!' Now,

> 'NEWTON'S apple, FRANKLIN'S kite
> Gave laws to lightning and to light:'

but either philosopher would as soon have consulted a hydraulic 'ram' as the best merino, for the keen *practical* knowledge got by '*Observation*,' out of '*Experience*, which was exhibited by the 'Shepherd of Salisbury Plain; for, if we remember rightly, it *was* on Salisbury Plain where the incident which we have narrated occurred.

'I SAY, Squàre, what 'll yeöu take for that 'are dog o' your'n?' said a Yankee pedler to an old Dutch farmer, in the neighborhood of Lancaster, Pennsylvania: 'what 'll yeöu take for him? He ain't a very good-lookin' dog; but what was you cal'latin', may-be, he 'd fetch?' 'Ah!' tesponded the Dutchman, 'dat dog ish n't wort' not'ing, 'most; he ish n't wort' you to buy 'um.' 'Guess tew dollars abeöut would git him, would n't it? I 'll give you that for him.' 'Yaäs; he is n't *wort'* dat.' 'Wal, I 'll take him,' said the pedler. 'Sh'stop!' said the Dutchman; 'dere 's one t'ing about dat dog I gan 't sell.' 'O, take off his collar; I do n't want that,' suggested the pedler. ''T ain't dat,' replied Mynheer; he 's a boor dog, but I gan 't *sell de wag of his dail when I comes home!'* There is some good honest Dutch poetry of feeling in that reply, reader, if you will but think of it a moment.

A GOOD story was told us the other day by Mr. WASHINGTON IRVING, of the late Mr. Fox, British minister at Washington, when at Paris, about sixteen years since. He must have been somewhat of a wag in his younger days. There was at the time an Irish lady, Mrs. G——, of some fashion, residing in Paris, who had a great passion for foreigners of rank. She had invited a large party to dinner, on the first of April, when Mr. Fox wrote her a note, in the character of a Count of her acquaintance, informing her that he had just arrived, and requesting to have the pleasure of introducing to her his Hungarian friend, the Prince of Seidlitz-Powderz, who intended to stay but two or three days in Paris. With this note was sent a card, engraved:

> The Prince of Seidlitz-Powderz.
>
> AT MEURICE'S HOTEL.

Mrs. C—— immediately replied to his note, by inviting him and his friend to dinner. In the course of the morning, she called on two or three of her fashionable friends, who were to have soirées, requesting permission to introduce the Prince to them. The hour of dinner arrived, but the Prince did not make his appearance. The viands were kept back until they were nearly spoiled; still no Prince was forthcoming. The dinner was at last served. Various speculations were indulged, in the course of the repast, about the Prince; what kind of a man he might be; whether young or old, tall or short, dark or fair, etc. A Hungarian present, did not know of such a title among their nobility, and hinted, cautiously, that it was possible he might be an impostor. Mrs. C—— would not listen for a moment to such a suggestion. At length, about nine o'clock, a letter, with a black margin, was received from the Prince, regretting that he could not avail himself of Mrs. C——'s kind invitation, as he had just heard of the death of his cousin, the BISHOP OF EPSOM-SALTZ, who had died at Cheltenham! In a corner of the note was written '*Poisson d'Avril!*'

AN Indian was executed, not very many years since, at Batavia, in this state. He was a singular genius, with all the indomitable indifference peculiar to his race. While under sentence of death, he amused himself with drawing rude sketches on the walls of his cell, with a piece of charcoal, representing himself undergoing execution. 'Here,' said he to the sheriff, one day, 'look here;' pointing to a sketch with three figures: 'See; man with sword—guess *you:* man with rope on his neck—too much choke; guess may-be *me;* see, lazy man, with book; guess, may-be minister;' and therewith he smiled grimly. He kept up this spirit to the very last. He said one day, 'No use to be feller without you *hell* of a feller;' and when standing on the gallows, he replied to the clergyman, who rebuked his indifference and stolidity with the remark, that he feared he 'would go to hell,' '*No, guess not;*' (an Indian's expression of doubt, always;) and with these words scarcely out of his mouth, he was 'launched into eternity.'

WE have always thought these lines in 'FAUST,' descriptive of the death of a mother, to be very touching.

'AH! it is the spouse, the dear one!
Ah! it is that faithful mother!
She it is that thus is borne,
Sadly borne and rudely torn
By the sable Prince of Spectres,
From her fondest of Protectors;
From the children forced to flee,
Whom she bore him lovingly,
Whom she gazed on day and night
With a mother's deep delight.'

THE '*Yankee Trick*' described by our Medford (Mass.) correspondent is on file for insertion. It is, in *one* of its features, not unlike the anecdote of an old official Dutchman in the valley of the Mohawk, who one day stopped a Yankee pedler journeying slowly through the valley on the Sabbath, and informed him that he must 'put up' for the day; or 'if it vash *neshessary* dat he should travel, he must pay de fine for de pass.' It *was* necessary, it seems; for he told the Yankee to write the pass, and he would sign it; '*that* he could do, though he did n't much write, nor read writin'.' The pass was written and signed with the Dutchman's hieroglyphics, and the pedler went forth 'into the bowels of the land, without impediment.' Some six months afterward, a brother Dutchman, who kept a 'store' farther down the Mohawk, 'in settling' with the pious official, brought in, among other accounts, an order for twenty-five dollars' worth of goods. 'How ish dat?' said the Sunday-officer; '*I* never gives no order; let me see him.' The order was produced; he put on his spectacles and examined it. 'Yaäs, dat ish my name, sartain—yaäs; but—*it ish dat d——d Yankee pass!*'

As we write (it is twelve at night,) there prevails without one of those February snow-storms that are of so marked a character as even to task the memory of the 'Oldest Inhabitant.' Truly of such it may be averred, they are not easily forgotten. Eleven years ago, we well remember, a 'like molestation of the enchaféd elements' occurred. But the present demands all our attention. Hark to the snow hissing against the window-panes; to the 'roaring wind that roars far off,' for the most part, but that now and then 'comes anear' with a '*sough*' that makes you shudder, and to the ear of the listener 'blazes' its way upon clattering window-shutters along the stormy street, as the Indian 'blazes' upon the forest trees his pathway through the wilderness! How at this moment the floods of Long-Island Sound 'clap their hands!' How the breakers roar at Sandy-Hook! How they tumble and foam and dash, at the Long-Branch of the high Jersey-coast! GOD help the brave mariners on our shores to-night!—and Heaven defend the poor and destitute, in this vast wilderness of human dwellings, over whom the Storm Spirit now sails with dusky wing! Children of Affluence! ye have 'ta'en too little care of this:'

O YE! who, sunk in beds of down,
Feel not a want but what yourselves create,
Think for a moment on his wretched fate
Whom friends and fortune quite disown!
Ill-satisfied keen Nature's clam'rous call,
Stretch'd on his straw, he lays himself to sleep,
While through the ragged roof and chinky wall,
Chill o'er his slumbers piles the drifty heap!'

To hundreds in this crowded metropolis to-night there is nothing *ideal* in this sad picture. Happy they, if, despite the wretchedness of their desolate habitations, a 'clear dewy haven of 'rest that sweetens toil' envelopes them, and fitful glimmerings of cloud-skirted dreams!'

WE do n't usually meddle with polemical matters, and have taken no part in the 'High' or 'Low Church' question; but are inclined in this connection to ask whether the 'Episcopal Floating Chapels' on the East and North rivers are not 'High' or 'Low' churches, according to the state of the tide? And speaking of tides, we have another query, of a scientific character, to propound. There is a man on the south side of Long-Island, a man the periphery of whose aldermanic 'corporation' is a marvel to strangers, who lives almost wholly upon the '*hydraulic clams*' of that region, which are so proverbially 'happy' at high water. So great is the affinity of his gastric demands with the sea, that it is a well-attested fact in the neighborhood, that his belly rises and falls with the tide. 'There is more in this than meets the eye, if Philosophy could but find it out.'

WHAT a miserable cynic of an old bachelor it must have been who wrote the ensuing description of marriage! He 'ought to be ashamed of himself:' 'Look at the great mass of marriages that take place over the whole world; what poor, contemptible affairs they are! A few soft looks, a walk, a dance, a squeeze of the hand, a popping of the question, a purchasing of a certain number of yards of white satin, a ring, a minister, a stage or two in a hired carriage, a night in a country inn, and the whole matter is over. For five or six weeks two sheepish-looking persons are seen dangling on each other's arms, looking at water-falls, or making morning calls, and guzzling wine and cakes; then every thing falls into the most monotonous routine; the wife sits on one side of the hearth, the husband on the other, and little quarrels, little pleasures, little cares, and little children gradually gather round them. This is what ninety-nine out of one hundred find to be the delights of matrimony.' We read this a moment ago in the sanctum to a young lady of eighteen with large, bright eyes, red and dewy lips, a matchless figure—as GEOFFREY CRAYON writes, 'just bursting from her boddice'—and she says she thinks it 'atrocious,' and the man who wrote it a 'very great fool!' If the writer could have seen our fair friend when she said this, we believe that that would have been *his* opinion also.

'WE were lately amused,' says a waggish contemporary, 'at an 'art criticism' delivered by a raw and unsuspecting JONATHAN, who had been quietly gazing at a garden in one of our suburban villages, which among other ornaments, boasted several handsome marble statues. 'Jest see what a waste!' observed our rural friend; 'there's no less than six scare-crows in that little ten-foot garden patch, and ary one of 'em alone would keep off all the crows from a five acre lot!' That would have been a pleasant criticism for the sculptor himself, to hear, would n't it? He would n't have sculp'd again, 'we do n't think!'

We have done evil this day at the Ferry of Dobb, and remorse sits at our heart and 'gnaws at its cruel leisure.' *Why* should we have done the deed? It was not revenge; it was not ambition; it was not exactly wantonness; cruelty was not in all our thoughts. The scene itself; the pleasant summer day; the cool woods; the murmuring brook; the happy little folk; the twittering birds in the trees, and the chirping, 'peeping' chickens, running in and out of the grass in the green glade by the brook, following their anxious 'mother,' who seemed to know at once when they were 'out;' all these things were not suggestive of cruelty. But 'Young Knick.' had a cross-bow gun, one of the right kind, with trigger and all complete. The arrow was of pine; light, and bulbous at the end. What it was that tempted us, as we took the cross-bow in hand, to aim an arrow at that young mother of a hen, we cannot tell. We did n't want to see if we *could* hit her; our object, 'if we know our own heart,' was to see if we *could n't*—and we *did n't*. But the 'fatal shaft' sped from the string, and took instant effect upon the hind-legs of a downy, tender yellow chicken, just emerging from a tuft of grass. It fell, uttering a melancholy peep, for it had received serious 'internal injury.'

It was immediately taken up and conveyed to the nearest house. We 'sat on the body' and discovered the following facts: the 'os humeri' was broken in two places; there was a compound fracture of the 'pia-mater;' the 'left clavicle,' in its 'lower limb,' was completely severed from the main trunk; and the transverse-section of the smaller intestine was collapsed at its junction with the liver and lights.

The case was hopeless. Every thing that the best unprofessional medical skill could do to save the life of the little innocent was performed. But all in vain. Its throbbing, fluttering heart ceased to beat at about one o'clock of the same day. It expired in the arms, and was washed by the pitying tears, of sympathetic little JOSE. *Then* was the time for the lesson which we inculcated upon the sensitive hearts of the little by-standers. We enlarged upon the heinousness, the guilt, of such carelessness, such thoughtless cruelty, as they had that day witnessed; until at length the tide began to turn in our favor. They began to lose sight of our practice in favor of our preaching, and to look upon us, on the whole, as an 'instrument' designed to enforce a 'great moral truth!' Well, we *did* illustrate one; namely, that any wrong-doing will always carry with it its own punishment in the shape of an unevadable remorse. We felt chicken-hearted all day, after that 'dreadful casualty.'

The '*Letter from Mrs. Malaprop*' has little to recommend it, unless it be its sufficiently wretched orthography, which certainly does not constitute wit, though it has the merit of nine in ten of the *original* Jack Downing's imitators. Mrs. Lavina Ramsbottom, now, was a model in this kind! Her mistakes were natural, and her words were never forced. Her travelling 'dairy,' containing the 'cream of her information,' overflowed with burlesque and humor. Having a little time on her hands previous to 'embrocation in the packet for Callous in France,' she 'took it by the fire-lock' and went to see the 'School for the Indignant Blind' near London, and also to Canterbury, to view its celebrated cathedral. 'The old Virgin who showed us the church, said it was an archypiscopal sea; but *I* see no sea, and I do n't think he could, for it was seventeen miles off.' After partaking of a 'cold collection,' for which 'the charge' was 'absorbent' though it were for the 'Autograph of all the Russias,' she repairs to Dover, and embarks for France. While crossing the Channel she tells us that 'a fat gentleman fell into a fit of apperplexity and lay prostitute on the floor; and had n't it have been that we had a doctor in the ship, who immediately opened his temporary artery and his jocular vein with a lancelot he had in his pocket, I think we should have seen his end. All his anxiety in the midst of his distress was to be able to add a crockodile to his will!' After arriving in Paris, she visited all the curiosities; among other things, the 'statute of LEWIS QUINZEY, who died of a sore-throat, HENRY CARTER ('no relation to the CARTERS of Portsmouth, unless his posteriors have greatly degenerated in size and figure,') etc. At Rome she was much impressed with the 'Vacuum where the POPE keeps his bulls,' but very much wearied with the *Tedium* that she heard sung at St. Peter's.

HERE is a good thing, quoted by a friend in connection with a somewhat kindred anecdote which has appeared in the KNICKERBOCKER: 'The members of a society in Maine, by dint of long exertion, had erected a small church. One of the number was dispatched to a large town to request a noted divine to take part in its dedication. Not getting his errand exactly, he simply applied to the minister to come and dedicate our new church.' 'What part do you wish me to take?' said the clergyman. 'Why, we want you to dedicate *the church*,' was the reply. 'But do you wish me to deliver the sermon, or to make the opening prayer, or only to make some remarks?' 'Why,' exclaimed the brother, piqued at the obtuseness of the parson, 'we simply want you to dedicate tbe church, the *whole* on't; it 's only seventy-five feet by fifty: want you to *dedicate* it!'

MUCH amused to-night with an anecdote told in the sanctum of an artist in ornamental glass, who was preparing pictures of three or four of the APOSTLES, for an oriel window of a church in a flourishing western city. He had just taken them from his furnace, and was showing them to some of the vestry. 'Don't say any thing about it,' said he, 'for it would n't be noticed by one person out of a hundred, but I do n't mind telling you in confidence: Saint PETER is a little cracked in the head; he was too soft in the upper end; but I 'av got a first-rate bake on PAUL. Saint JOHN, though, is n't more than half-baked; I 'll have to bake another JOHN. But d' ever you *see* a better-baked PAUL?' His remarks were entirely professional; nor had he the most remote idea of there being a double-meaning in any thing he was saying.

HE was an accurate observer and a sound reasoner, who said: 'Mankind are always happier *for having been happy;* so that, if you make them happy now, you make them happy twenty years hence, by the memory of it. A childhood passed with a mixture of rational indulgence, under fond and wise parents, diffuses over the whole of life a feeling of calm pleasure; and, in extreme old age, is the very last remembrance which time can erase from the mind of man. No enjoyment, however inconsiderable, is confined to the present moment. A man is the happier for life for having made once an agreeable tour, or lived for any length of time with pleasant people, or enjoyed any considerable interval of innocent pleasure, which contributes to render old men so inattentive to the scenes before them, and carries them back to a world that is past, and to scenes never to be renewed again.'

WE are obliged for the kind words of our '*Newburgh Friend*,' and for this anecdote of an odd character in that meridian: 'Riding in a stage-coach a short time since, we happened to have among others for a fellow-passenger an ardent teetotaller, who was descanting eloquently upon the great value and many excellent qualities of water, and especially of its prime necessity as a beverage; declaring that nothing could be substituted in its place, etc.; when an old gentleman, who had been listening with evident impatience, remarked, with rather a contemptuous look: 'I hain't nothing to say ag'in water; I think it 's very good in its place; but for a *steady drink*, give me *rum!*' I should just like you to have seen Teetotal's face when he heard this reply. All the passengers looked grave for a second or so, (for the assumption was altogether astounding,) and then burst into a roar that made the stage-coach ring again.'

SOME one mentioned to us the other day the circumstances of a fat querulous old fellow who was driven from a stage-coach by passengers whom he had annoyed with his growlings and complainings. A cigar was lighted, when at a preconcerted moment one of the passengers exclaimed, 'For GOD's sake, Sir, put out that fire! I have four pounds of powder in my overcoat pocket!' 'Driver! driver! stop! — *stop!* — STOP!' exclaimed the victim of this 'gunpowder plot:' 'Let me get out! — let me get out! There 's a man here with powder in his pockets, and he 'll blow us all to the devil!' The complainant '*got* out' accordingly, in no small hurry, and the passengers thenceforward pursued the even tenor of their way, undisturbed by his farther annoyance. This anecdote reminds us of an occurrence which once took place at the long and picturesque bridge over the Cayuga lake, that middle-western *barrière*, of which success or defeat, in times of political excitement, are now predicated. A wag from Syracuse, who with some half-dozen friends had been disporting at the pleasant and flourishing village of Seneca Falls, determined, on approaching the toll-gate in a sleigh, one stormy winter night, to 'run the bridge.' 'Lie down, boys,' said he, 'in the sleigh, and when we get under the gate, groan a little, and tremble, but do n't over-do it.' Here, get under these horse blankets.' They did so; and when the sleigh came under the picket-draw of the bridge, they began to moan and shake, so that 'it was piteous to see and eke to hear.' 'I have nothing less than this ten-dollar bill,' said our wag, handing the gate-keeper a bank-note; 'but for heaven's sake change it just as quick as ever you can! I have three friends in the sleigh who are almost dead with the small-pox, and I 'm in such an awful ——'

'Drive on! drive on!' said the terrified gate-keeper, handing back the bill; 'drive on — pay next time!' Above the whistling of the snow-laden wind which swept over that frozen lake, and the trampling of the horses' feet on the bridge that night, the gate-keeper heard the loud laugh of those wags, proclaiming that he had been 'taken in and done for!'

LOOKING down from the roof of a high dwelling at night upon a great city, partly revealed by a conflagration, is to us a sublime spectacle. In the semi-gloom, uprise the towers, steeples, domes and cupolas into the heavens, now brightening now fading in the rising and sinking flame. The far-off clanking of the engines; the subdued roar of human voices; the faint crackling of the flames, and that monotone of raging fire which rises solemnly into the empyrean, and the restless patter of a thousand feet; all these possess, to our conception, the element of sublimity. Looking up to the dark blue star-begemmed dome above, one cannot help saying with BRYANT:

'THY spirit is around,
Quickening the reckless mass that sweeps along;
And this eternal sound,
Voices and footfalls of the unnumbered throng,
Like the resounding sea,
Or like the rainy tempests, speaks of THEE!

'And when the hours of rest
Come like a calm upon the mid sea brine,
Hushing its billowy breast,
The quiet of the moment too is THINE;
It breathes of HIM who keeps
The vast and helpless city while it sleeps.'

NUMBER EIGHT.

OUR FIRST PLAY — COUNTRY THEATRICALS: 'SHORT OF BIBLE': MAYOR HARPER CAUGHT — A TEMPERENCE 'PLEDGE': WONDERFUL CURES — OILY 'GAMMON': DR. COX 'IN A BOX': 'WORD PICTURES' — LONGFELLOW: THE MACKINAW SEA-SERPENT: 'DESTINY' DOUBTED: FIRST IMPRESSIONS OF THE KAATSKILLS: 'ACCIDENT'-AL ACQUAINTANCE: AN 'AMERICAN CITIZEN': AN IRREGULAR 'REVIVALIST': SCENES IN A CITY HOSPITAL: DUBIOUS DEFERENCE: A DUTCHMAN 'DONE': A 'BAD BARGAIN': 'VISIBLE PRESENCE' OF DEATH.

WE perceive by late English journals, that DICKENS at the London Theatrical Fund dinner, among other things remarked: 'If any man were to tell me that he denied his acknowledgments to the stage, I would simply put to him one question — whether he remembered his first play. I would ask him to carry back his recollection to that great night, and call to mind the bright and harmless world which then opened to his view.' We thought of *our* first play, the other night at Binghamton. A company of perambulating actors, and some of them very good actors too, including the manager, a talented and gentleman-like person, were to perform at the court-house. So in the evening we went up with a few esteemed friends.

The stage was erected at one end, and the audience occupied the jury-box, witnesses' stand, and the side-seats for spectators. The orchestra was a single fiddle, played at intervals with great energy. Little boys were walking continually about in the open space before the stage, peddling candy and pea-nuts. The drop-curtain was a 'feature.' It had the picture of a bird that might have been intended for the Bird of JOVE, but 'by JOVE!' it was such an eagle as we never saw before — nor since! The whole scene; the actors and the acting; the fresh-hearted little boys looking on in wonderment; the tinselled dresses and decorations; all brought vividly back to us the memory of our first play. It was at the long-room of the village inn, and 'Messrs. ARCHBOLD, TROWBRIDGE and GILBERT,' among other histrions, were the performers. How wistfully did we regard, that night, for the first time, the patched and faded mottled green curtain; the flashing of shoe-buckles, the gleaming of flesh-colored 'tights,' and the sparkling of spangled garments, caught in glimpses beneath it. And the play — oh, 'it was grand!' It was 'ZANGA, or the Revenge,' and Mr. ARCHBOLD, a mouthing old Stentor, 'did' the hero. We expected much of him, for we had heard him say in the morning: 'The pawt of ZEG-GAW, Saw, is me favorite pawt. I played ZEG-GAW at Kenendegwaw; and Mr. FRENCES GREG-GHAW, one of the most intelligent of its citizens, pronounced it supawb acting.' How the old mountebank did roar and rave! Then came 'The Village-Lawyer,' another favorite 'pawt' of his; and at this moment we can hear him say, in his affected, piping voice, '*That's* my signatur'—Timo'sy Sn-a-a-rl!' There, too, we heard our first public singing, except at church. The curtain had descended upon the personages whose sorrows were our own, and 'musing in melancholy mood,' we were gazing vacantly at the long row of tallow-candles placed in auger-holes in the boards of the stage, and at the fiddler who composed the orchestra, and who was reconnoitring the house. Presently a small bell was rung with a jerk. There was a flourish or two from the 'orchestra.' Another tinkle of the bell, and up rose the faded drapery. An interval of a moment succeeded, during which half of a large mountain was removed from the scenery, and a piece of forest shoved up to the ambitious wood which had been aspiring to overtop the Alps. At length a young lady, whom we had just seen butchered in the most horrid manner by a black visaged villain, came from the side of the stage with a smile which, while it displayed her white teeth, wrought the rouge upon her face into very perceptible corrugations, and made a lowly obeisance to the audience. She walked with measured step three or four times across the stage, before the flaring candles, smiling again, and 'hemming,' to clear her voice. A perfect stillness at length prevailed: 'awed

Consumption checked his chided cough;' every urchin suspended his cat-call, and 'the boldest held his breath for a time.' The fair vocalist looked at the 'leader,' (who had nobody to follow him,) and commenced in harmony with his instrument. How touching to us was that song! We shall never have our soul so enrapt again; for that *freshness* of young admiration possessed our spirit which can come but once. The song was '*The Braes of Balquither*,' a Scottish melody as old and as lasting as the hills. We thought the audience would be precipitated into the bar-room below, by the uproarious applause of voice, feet and hands, which followed this verse:

'When the rude wintry wind
  Wildly raves round our dwelling,
And the roar of the linn
  On the night-breeze is swelling,
Then so merrily we 'll sing,
  While the storm rattles o'er us,
Till the dear shealing ring
  With the blithe lilting chorus!'

Ah, well-a-day! — that was a 'good while ago, now;' but the interval has passed away like a dream of the night!

Here is a laughable instance of '*A Man short of Bible:*' 'A reverend gentleman, while visiting a parishioner, had occasion in the course of conversation to refer to the BIBLE, and on asking for the 'article,' the master of the house ran to bring it, and came back with two leaves of the book in his hand. 'I declare,' says he, 'this is all we 've got in the house: I'd no idee we were so near out!'

THAT was n't exactly the 'right thing' that GEORGE WILKINS KENDALL, senior editor of the New-Orleans '*Picayune*' daily journal, did down at the Brothers HARPERS' private office, one pleasant morning in May, when 'JAMES' was 'His Honor the Mayor.' You see, the way of it was this: When GEORGE went into the counting-room, he asked for 'The Mayor.' 'The Colonel' pointed to the adjoining private office, or raised 'sitting-room,' and said, 'He 's in there: there 's a delegation there from the female officers of 'The MARTHA WASHINGTON Temperance Society, of which 'the MAYOR' is the honorary President.' 'I 'll go in and see him,' said KENDELL. 'Do,' said 'the Colonel:' 'I guess they 're about through; they 've kept him talking there for some time now.' GEORGE entered, his face a little flushed, from a rapid walk down to Cliff-street; and as he did so, he was made aware of the presence of some two dozen members of the 'MARTHA WASHINGTON Teetotal Association,' in solemn conclave, their President, 'the MAYOR,' in their midst, with a face, partly from the warmth of the morning, and partly from excitement, even more flushed, if anything, than KENDALL'S. GEORGE was received, beyond a slight greeting from 'the MAYOR,' with ominous silence; but he 'knew his course.' 'Come, HARPER,' said he, 'let 's go and get *another* drink: it 's 'leven o'clock,' he added, taking out his watch; 'aint *you* dry ag'in? *I* am!' 'The MAYOR' says he had been 'taken aback' before; but the coolness and outrageous impudence of that 'tack' could n't be beat! 'The women looked daggers while KENDALL was pretending to be hurrying me to go with him and take a drink called 'Moral Suasion?'

A MOST 'extr'od'nary' production is '*Betton's British Oil.*' It *must* be, judging from the very remarkable cures which it has effected, as set forth in the proprietor's circular. Do us the favor to remark the following:

'JONAS ROBERTS, Tiler, in BLINKER'S Court, St. JAMES, Bristol, was cured of a violent swelling in his right thigh; insomuch that he was obliged to cut open his breeches with a knife, in three times dressing with the 'British Oil.' Witness my hand,' etc.

'JOHN MITCHELL, of Salisbury: 'Had a violent pain in my hip, so that I went double in both of my legs with two bottles. Witness my hand,' etc.

'AN apprentice to Mr. STONE, a Tinker in Taunton: was so deaf that he could n't hear the noise of a drum with three bottles: cured. Witness,' etc.

'MR. JARVIS, belonging to the 'Tall Woman,' at Norwich, had his hand bit by a mad dog with two bottles. Witness,' etc.

'Mr. HUMPHREY COTTERILL, of the 'Royal Tun,' Coventry, by a fall from his horse, which strained his ankle; and likewise his daughter cut desperately in the forehead with two bottles: cured with 'BETTON'S British Oil.''

'ELIZABETH SLOUGH, of Wellington, in the county of Salop, entirely lost the use of her hand in three times' bathing with this Oil. Witness her *hand*,' etc.

We have no hesitation in pronouncing these 'very remarkable cures:' and to those who believe them to be veritable, we have no hesitation in commending the 'Oil' in question.

THE venerable Doctor Cox, of Brooklyn, was driving out in thoughtful mood the other day in a one-horse wagon, in a narrow street in the suburbs of the town, when two wagons, one on each side, attempted to pass him. All three got stuck fast together, 'so that they could not be movéd.' After trying for some time, a crowd began to collect around, and Doctor Cox began to grow red in the face, and to remonstrate in strong terms, and with much repetition, against the carelessness of one of the green delinquents. At last the other replied, (and we suspect the wag must have known the Doctor,) I—I—I could n't help it: you *know* I could n't; and what the d—l is the use of an old white-headed man like you standing there, *swearin'* at me in that way?—*swearin'* at me for what I could n't help? What 's the use of *swearin'*, any how? *I* could n't help it, I tell you; I did n't *go* to do it, o' course; *swearin'* away at a fellow for what he did n't *go* to do!' The Doctor blushed, and looked a little guilty:

the charge was so *outrageous*, he could n't help it; and it was made before a good many by-standers, who had often seen him in the pulpit. 'I *swear* at you!' exclaimed the Doctor, in utter amazement. 'Ye-ă-ă-ă-s!' said the other, with prolonged and potent emphasis; '*swearin'* at a fellow like a trooper, when he did n't go to get you stuck!' The Doctor shrunk away abashed, being fairly driven from the ground.

BRYANT is remarkable for the 'word-pictures,' as the Germans term it, which he strews so profusely through his poetical writings: often, by the use of a single vernacular expression, bringing before the reader the most distinct and delightful images. LONGFELLOW possesses a kindred power. One hardly knows, sometimes, how his 'effects,' in artist-phrase, are produced; but a nice study of his language will generally reveal their source. Observe the picturesqueness, the variety, the *reality* of scene, condensed in these few stanzas:

'WHEN descends on the Atlantic
The gigantic
Storm-wind of the Equinox,
Landward in his wrath he scourges
The toiling surges,
Laden with sea-weed from the rocks.

'From Bermuda's Reefs, from edges
Of sunken ledges,

In some far-off, bright Azore,
From Bahama, and the dashing,
Silver-flashing
Surges of San Salvador.

'From the tumbling surf, that buries
The Orkneyan Skerries,
Answering the hoarse Hebrides:
And from wrecks of ships, and drifting
Spars, uplifting
On the desolate, rainy seas.

'Ever drifting, drifting, drifting
On the shifting
Currents of the restless main;
Till in sheltered caves, and reaches
Of sandy beaches,
All have found repose again.'

Do you remark, reader, the wide grasp, the life, action, visible motion, that pervade these lines? They compose a succession of 'marine views' as palpable to sight as the colorings of the pencil.

THE sea-serpent has been discovered again by an English captain, officers and crew; and the illustrated London journals contain portraits, 'half-size' and 'full-length,' of his snakeship, accompanied by minute and authenticated descriptions of his 'person' and movements. We have been led to believe, from our own experience, that one may be very easily deceived in these water-reptiles. Toward the twilight of a still day, near the end of July, 1847, HORACE GREELEY and 'Old KNICK.' hereof, were seated on the broad piazza of the dark-yellow 'Mission-House' at Michilimackinac, looking out upon the deep, *deep* blue waters of the Huron, when an object, apparently near the shore, suddenly attracted our attention. We both examined it through a good glass, and came to the mutual conclusion that it was an enormous sea-serpent, elevating its head, undulating its humps, and 'floating many a rood' upon the translucent Strait. Such also was the opinion of the proprietor of the 'Mission House,' who in a ten years' residence at Mackinaw had never seen the like before. 'Away went HORACE, and away' went 'Old KNICK.' after him, down to the shore: and but for most tremendous kangaroo bounds 'on behalf of the party of the first part,' and a slight sticking in the mud of an intervening marsh, 'on the part of the party of the second part,' 'this deponent affirms and verily believes' that this deponent would have reached the beach aforesaid as soon as he, the said HORACE did. When we had arrived, lo! the object which had so excited our curiosity was nothing more than the dark side of a long undulating, unbroken wave, brought into clear relief by the level western light which the sun had left in his track as he dropped away over Lake Michigan. We felt rather 'cheap' as we came along back together; and 'allowed' that if they 'd seen at Nahant what we had at Mackinac, they 'd have *sworn* that it was the sea-serpent. 'Catch *us* doing any thing o' *that* kind!' etc.

I KNEW an old man,' writes a correspondent, 'who believed that 'what *was* to be *would* be.' He lived in Missouri, and was one day going out several miles through a region infested, in the early times, by very savage Indians. He always took his gun with him, but this time he found that some of the family had it out. As he would not go without it, some of his friends tantalized him by saying that there was 'no danger of the Indians;' that he 'would not die until his time had come,' etc. 'Yes,' says the old fellow, 'but suppose I was to meet an Indian, and *his* time had come, it would n't do not to have *my gun!*'

READER, by your leave, we will give you some 'leaves,' as we sit in the light of a transcendent morning, not yet fully dawned in its glory, surveying — whenever, for a moment, the music of the pen ceases — from an upper window of the 'Pine Orchard House,' the magnificent scene spread out below. A white fog-serpent, a hundred miles in length, is undulating his humps along the Hudson, and with head erect, is moving gradually on toward Albany. The clouds, born of yesterday's shower down the mountain, arose bright beneath us this morning, having washed their faces clean in their own rain during the night; and now they hang far below, saturate with sunlight, like illuminated billows of floating cotton. Toward noon, perchance, they will gather together again, and flecking with shadows the wide expanse beneath them, as they sail along, suddenly pause and 'discharge their cargo,' the husbandman rejoicing the while, that at last,

> 'THE gathered storm is ripe, the big drops fall,
> And sun-burnt meadows smoke, and drink the rain.'

We have just been fancying the prospects of grandeur and beauty which may be commanded from the dawn-tipped mountains that bound the view on the north and east — the Green Mountains of Vermont, old Monadnock and the mighty hills of the 'steady land,' which rise between us and the distant river, that, calmly gliding, parts the abrupt peaks of Holyoke and Tom — the wide-spread fields, the peopled villages, humming with busy industry, the shining streams, and the white churches, upon which they look down. Come hither, ye cockneys, and denizens in populous cities pent, and inhale this mountain air! How many a languid form, lying in sadness upon a bed of pain, awaiting his only solace, the footstep of his physician, 'with healing in the creak of his shoes,' would bless this invigorating breeze! What a contrast to the city is here! There, a red-nosed man, with a sandy peruke, walks about the few small and dusty patches of faded green, (called 'parks!') and tapping the reclining pedestrian with his baton, points to a by-law of the city's fathers, suspended from a stunted tree, where frowns denouncingly, '*Keep off the Grass!*' There, the *gutteral* airs, hot and sultry, would penetrate the obtusest olfactory, though guarded by a dense moustache, bristling 'like the horns of a centipede;' airs embracing every variety of *mauvaise odeur*, from the green mantle of the standing pool, to the most piquant cat-effluvia. Here, on the other hand, the whole city, placed on the vast plain below, would dwindle to a speck, and all the nations of the world might there stand assembled, without jostling. Here, there is no elaborate dirt. Here, the mountain wind,

'Most spiritual thing of all the wide earth knows,'

would well-nigh revive the dying. But we are forgetting that the Kaätskills need not our poor blazon.

'DID you know Doctor WEIR?' asked an inquisitive gentleman in one of the Philadelphia cars, of a Northampton country Dutchman. 'Doctor VEER?' he replied; 'well den, yaäs, I know'd him a little. I seen him once-t. We was on dat shteam-poat vat vash plow'd up mit te p'iler bu'stin' by Pittsburgh dere; and w'en I vash goin on de shore by de plank, he and de shmoke-pipe vash comin' down. I never seen him pefore nor since!'

THIS 'wooden country' of ours is really beginning to be thought something of 'on the other side!' As the English cockney said of Niagara Falls, 'it is very clever: very!' AMERICA!—let us think how many at this moment are 'on the seas' approaching our shores! Every hour on the coasts of the old world representatives from the different nations of the earth are departing for this republic; every hour some vessel crowded with exiles from tempestuous kingdoms and principalities is nearing our shores, or, while the 'shouting seaman climbs and furls the sail' in our harbor, is landing its human freight upon our piers. Come along, future 'fellow-citizens!' We have thousands of square miles where the epidermis of the earth has never been scratched. There is room enough and there is work enough for all: nor on *this* side of the 'big brook' shall any of you 'come nigh to perish with hunger.' What a proud thing it will be deemed, by-and-by, to be able to say, '*I am an American citizen!*'

SUPPOSE you just run your eye over this anecdote of '*Guzzling Pete*,' a half-witted country wight, and the standing jest of a little town in Connecticut, who came home one rainy Saturday night, so 'darkly, deeply, beautifully *blue*,' that he went to bed with his hat and boots on, and his old cotton umbrella under his arm. He got up about two o'clock the next afternoon, drunk with last night, and took his way to the meeting-house. Rev. Dr. B—— was at his '17thly,' in the second of six divisions of a very comprehensive body of Hopkinsian divinity, when 'Guzzling PETE' entered the church, with an egg in each hand. He saw, as through a glass darkly, and with evident commiseration, a man in black, very red in the face, for the day was oppressively warm, who seemed to utter something with a great deal of vehemence, while a considerable number of those underneath him were fast asleep; among them Deacon C——, with his shiny-bald head leaning against the wall. PETE, unobserved by the minister, balanced his egg, and with tolerable aim, plastered its contents directly above the Deacon's pate! Hearing the concussion, the worthy divine paused in his discourse, and looked daggers at the maudlin visiter. 'Never mind, uncle,' exclaimed the intruder: 'jest you go on a-talkin'; *I'll keep 'em awake for you!*' By this time the congregation were thoroughly aroused. 'Mr. L——,' said the reverend pastor, with a seeming charity, which in his mortification he could scarcely have felt, and, addressing a 'tiding-man,' near the door, 'Mr. L——, won't you have the kindness to remove that poor creature from the aisle? I fear that he is sick.' '*Sick?*' stammered our qualmish hero, as he began to confirm the fears of the clergyman by very active symptoms; '*s-i-c-k?*—yes, and it 's enough to make a *dog* sick, to 'sit' under such preachin' as your'n: it 's more 'n I can *stand* under! Yes, take me out: the quicker the better!'

WE often pause beneath the half-closed blinds of some public hospital, and picture to ourself the gloomy and mournful scenes that are passing within. The sudden movement of a taper, as its feeble ray shoots from the thickly-set windows, until its light gradually disappears, as if it were carried farther back into the room, to the bed-side of some suffering patient, is enough to awaken a whole crowd of reflections; the mere glimmering of the low-burning lamps, which, when all other habitations are wrapped in darkness and slumber, denote the chamber where so many forms are writhing with pain, or wasting with disease, is sufficient to check the most boisterous merriment. Who can tell the anguish of those weary hours, when the only sound the sick man hears, is the disjointed wanderings of some feverish slumberer near him, the low moan of pain, or perhaps the muttered, long-forgotten prayer of a dying man? Who but those who have felt it, can imagine the sense of loneliness and desolation which must be the portion of those who in the hour of dangerous illness are left to be tended by strangers: for what hands, be they ever so gentle, can wipe the clammy brow, or smooth the restless bed, like those of mother, wife, or child?

THERE are very few persons in the Empire State who have not heard of ELISHA WILLIAMS, the eminent advocate, of Columbia county. A friend has just mentioned to us an anecdote of him which is well worth recording. He had been listening to an antagonist who was rather a dull speaker, and who had infused into his summing-up a vast deal of fustian. Mr. WILLIAMS rose when he had finished, and said: 'Gentlemen of the jury, if I did not feel strong in the justice of my cause, I should fear the effect upon you of the eloquent harangue to which you have just listened. That, gentlemen, was a splendid, a magnificent performance. I admire that speech, gentlemen of the jury — I *always* admired it. I admired that speech when I was a boy!' It is needless perhaps to add, that this compliment was not lost upon the jury,

---

'THERE goes the old Dutchman who had the dangerous geese!' exclaimed a friend in the country the other day, calling our attention to a Dutchman of the oldest 'school,' who was walking slowly along the road. We asked an explanation: 'Why, when the Yankees first began to settle in here, he was joined one morning by a slab-sided specimen of 'em, as he was picking up the quills that his geese had dropped, in their chattering morning waddles, by the edges of an oblong pond at the road-side. Presently one of the geese stretched out his long neck at the Yankee, who started and ran as if a mad dog were at his heels. 'I dold him,' said the old Dutchman, 'not to be avraid; dat de geese would n't hurt um any; but de geese *did* run after him dough, clear over de hill a-ways; and none of 'em would n't give um no rest any more, whenever he come along the sdreet. I p'lieve dey had a shbite ag'in de Yankees. Mein GOTT! it 's curious, dough, but de geese always went away, and did n't come back any more!' The secret of that was, that the Yankee, who was so afraid of the Dutchman's geese, had thrown out kernels of corn, among which was one with a fish-hook attached. Once swallowed, the angry goose was soon in tow after the flying fugitive.

'THE subject of the following anecdote,' writes a friend, 'is an old and respectable physician, who is now a very strenuous temperance man, although in his young days he sometimes 'patronised the groceries' over much. On one occasion, having indulged very freely in a variety of spirituous decoctions with some boon-companions, he mounted his mare and started for home. He had not gone far before the inconsiderate 'commingling of spirits' in his stomach gave rise to such a furious rebellion that he was fain to dismount and come to an anchor against a large log by the road-side, where he commenced a process of upheaval that was truly alarming. While engaged in these spasmodic efforts at relief, he was accosted by a traveller, who, with true Yankee solicitude, enquired what was the matter. The inebriate, in an interval of his paroxysms, gruffly replied, that he 'had traded horses, and was *very sick of his bargain!*'

'THERE is perhaps no feeling of our nature so vague, so complicated, so mysterious, as that with which we look upon the cold remains of our fellow-mortals. The dignity with which DEATH invests the meanest of his victims inspires us with an awe that no living thing can create. The monarch on his throne sinks beneath the beggar in his shroud. The marble features, the powerless hand, the stiffened limb — oh, who can contemplate *these* with feelings that can be defined! These are the mockery of all our hopes and fears — our fondest love, our fellest hate. Can it be that we now shrink almost with horror from the touch of the hand that but yesterday was fondly clasped in our own? Is that tongue, whose accents even now dwell in our ears, for ever chained in the silence of death? Those dark and heavy eye-lids, are they for ever to seal up in darkness the eyes whose glance no earthly power could restrain? And the SPIRIT which animated that clay, where is it now? Does it witness our grief? does it share our sorrow? Or is the mysterious tie that linked it with mortality broken forever? And remembrances of earthly scenes, are *they* to the enfranchised spirit as the morning dream or the fading cloud?' Alas! 'all that we *know* is, nothing *can* be known,' until we ourselves shall have passed the dread ordeal!

NUMBER NINE.

A JOKE IN 'FULL BLOSSOM': A 'ROUGH GUESS': COMPARATIVE LONGEVITY: SCENE AT SING-SING STATE PRISON: THE ART OF MOWING — ENVY OF CITY 'ARTISTS': A 'SHORT-SIGHTED' LANDLORD: MOCK-AUCTIONS: 'ORIGINAL PICTURE'-DEALERS: AN AMATEUR-FISHERMAN: CRABS, AND THEIR WAYS: A 'CONTINGENT REMAINDER': THE 'LAST BITTER HOUR': IRISH 'COUSINS': A CAREFUL TINKER: 'EXERCISED IN PRAYER.'

HOW BLOSSOM of Canandaigua *did* love a joke for the joke's sake! We must mention one. Lobsters were formerly quite scarce at Canandaigua, on account of their not being found in the waters of Canandaigua Lake, nor in the streams circumjacent. BLOSSOM had been to the city, procured a fine one, packed it carefully, and took it home with him. The fact was duly proclaimed, the lobster boiled, his friends invited — and the supper came off. There was a quaint, dogmatical old fellow, a shoe-maker named JOHNSON, an authority in the village, who had lost all his teeth but two, and those were in opposite sections of his mouth. He had never seen a lobster, nor had the slightest idea of what kind of an animal it was. BLOSSOM, tipping the wink to his confréres, helped him to one of the claws, 'as large as a stone,' and about as hard. 'How do you eat the 'tarnal thing, any how?' said

JOHNSON. 'O go right ahead with it,' replied BLOSSOM, 'just as it is: need n't be afraid of it: do n't want any seasoning.'

After very diligent but somewhat protracted efforts, the old man succeeded in drilling a hole, and establishing a suck, got a taste of the interior. Seeing this position of affairs, BLOSSOM, with the most imperturbable gravity, inquired: 'Well, how do you get along? — how do you like it?' 'Waäl,' said the old man, 'I kind o' like the *peth* on 't!' The company only smiled; they did n't *laugh*, until the old gentleman left: and he do n't know any thing about it to this day — they were so polite and well bred!

BLOSSOM's spirit must linger about Canandaigua yet. A friend of ours stopped at his hotel a short time since, and took his seat near the blazing fire, and formed one of quite a large circle of smokers. Presently a fancifully-dressed young gentleman entered, and stepping within the circle, planted himself directly in front of one of the gentlemen enjoying his Havana, who was expectorating in sundry directions, between his legs, on either side, in curves, and, as it were, in a fit of desperation, after accumulating a full supply, in a direct straight line. The young dandy, apprehending the discharge, moved one side. 'Do n't stir, Sir; do n't disturb yourself,' said the smoker: 'I think I can spit *through* you!'

A legal friend of ours the other day was about entering a haberdasher's shop in Broadway, when a young buck, with a large moustache and small income, born like Jaffier with 'elegant desires,' drove up a pair of spanking bays, glittering with their splendid caparison. 'Ah, G——,' said he, 'how de do?—how de do? How d' you like me ho'ses? Fine animals, but very costly. What do you think I gave for the pair?' 'I guess you gave *your note!*' said G——. 'Good mawning!' responded the blood; '*good* mawning:'

Every thing is comparative. What is 'a long life,' for example? How old was Methuselah before he had 'sowed his wild oats?' What time did he leave off wearing frocks? He may have been a 'hard boy' at four hundred, and perhaps exhibited infant precocity even in his hundredth year! 'At the river Hypanis, (we quote from the 'Tusculan Questions,') which on the one side flows into the Pontus, Aristotle says there are little animals grow, which live only one day. Those then that die at the eighth hour, die at an advanced age; those that live until sunset, at a very old age. Compare our longest life with eternity, and we shall be found almost in the same brevity of life as these little animals are!'

If the unhappy young man who has recently filled the journals of the metropolis with the details of his folly and crime could, before yielding to temptation, have looked in upon the state-prisoners at Sing-Sing, as we did the other day, surely he would have shrunk back from the vortex before him. Poor wretches, in their best estate! How narrow their cells; how ceaseless their toil; what a negation of comfort their whole condition! It was a sweltering August day, breathless and oppressive; but there was no rest for the eight hundred unhappy convicts who plied their never-ending tasks within those walls. Stealthy glances from half-raised eyes; pale countenances, stamped with meek submission, or gleaming with powerless hate or impotent malignity; and 'hard labor' in the fullest sense, were the main features of the still-life scene, as we passed through the several work-shops. But what a picture was presented, as their occupants came swarming into the open court-yard at the sound of the bell, to proceed to their cells with their dinner! From the thick atmosphere of the carpet and rug shops, leaving the clack of shuttles, the dull thump of the 'weaver's beam,' and the long, confused perspective of cords, and pullies, and patterns, and multitudinous 'harness,' they poured forth; from murky smithys, streamed the imps of VULCAN, grim as the dark recesses from which they emerged; from doors which open upon interminable rows of close-set benches burst forth the knights of the awl and hammer; the rub-a-dub of the cooper's mallet, the creak of his shaving-knife, were still; the stone-hammer was silent; and the court-yard was full of that striped crew! GOD of compassion! what a sight it was, to see that motley multitude take up, in gangs, their humiliating march! Huge negroes, weltering in the heat, were interspersed among 'the lines;' hands crimson with murder rested upon the shoulders of beings young alike in years and crime; the victim of bestiality pressed agianst the heart-broken tool of the scathless villain; and *all* were blended in one revolting mass of trained soldiers of guilt; their thousand legs moving as the leg of one man: all in silence, save the peculiar sound of the sliding tread, grating not less upon the ear than the ground. One by one, they took their wooden pails of dingy and amphibious-looking food, and passed on, winding up the stairs of the different stories, and streaming along the narrow corridors to their solitary cells.

It was altogether too much for the tender heart of poor ELLA, this long procession of the gangs. As they passed on in slow succession, her lip began to quiver; and one after another drops of pity rolled down her cheeks: 'tears, silent tears;' but they will be held in remembrance.

REVIVED a good many pleasant memories to-day, in a walk along the Croton aqueduct, to the charming 'Sunny-side' of GEOFFREY CRAYON. Along where we once so often walked on the same agreeable errand, there have lately sprung up two or three small villages. We found farmers mowing the aqueduct in several places where it runs through meadows; clipping its steep slopes to the very top. 'Old KNICK.' went down the grassy declivity, and asked permission of a farmer, a 'nobleman of nature,' to mow a little. The favor was readily granted. With the memory of a recent achievement of the same kind freshly in mind, the jotter-down hereof addressed himself to his pleasurable task: first whetting off the scythe, 'from heel to p'int,' after the approved manner of that preparatory exercise, and then straddling forth to the mowing. After a few vigorous cuts with the scythe, we became aware of some doubts in the mind of the gentleman whose instrument we were, as we fancied, very dexterously wielding. His first words mortified us. We were doing our best. We looked for encouragement: we may say, indeed, that we fully expected applause. Judge, then, what must have been our surprise to hear these words, uttered in a tone which was scarcely less ungrateful than the language which conveyed the 'expression of the idea by articulate sounds:' '*You* do n't know nothin' about mowin'!' We thought we must have misconceived the observation, and said: 'Is n't that cut close?' '*You* do n't know nothin' about mowin'!' was now repeated, in language too plain to be misunderstood: 'sart'in, you cut *clust* enough; *too* clust, if any thing; in *our* style o' mowin', in these parts, we do n't generally care to slice the stones off like a cow-cumber. *You* can't mow! Fust place, you stand too fur off. You 'd break your back in an hour, *that* way o' mowin'. You do n't come up to your work: why do n't you come up to your work?' Come up to our *work!*—'marry, come up!' We went out of that meadow, after these uncalled-for remarks, with a very indifferent opinion of the style of mowing in that neighborhood. We did n't comment unkindly upon *their* style of mowing, although it was essentially different from ours; then why should they so flippantly criticise ours? We did our best, in our *manner*. We left the rows of sweet-scented hay-cocks, the loaded hay-wagons, the horses switching their tails and munching the new-cut grass, with a feeling of sincere regret, that mere envy of so simple a thing as that of a superior style of cutting grass with a scythe should be permitted to embitter the thoughts of the two husbandmen, who, for some reason or other, we fancied to be sneeringly jocose between themselves as we came away. We inferred so, 'from a remark they made.' 'Guess he *thought* he could mow—he *seemed* to!'

We had many delightful things to remember, as we came away from Sunnyside, by the dusty and noisy Hudson River Rail-road, the next morning; a pro-protracted sitting with our host, and other the like agreeable persons, with much memorable discourse; a pleasant sleep in the 'spare room' for a spare man, interrupted only by a visit, in the 'dead waste and middle of the night,' from the ghost of the lady who 'died of love and green apples' in the old VAN TASSEL mansion, etc.; but our pleasant reminiscences were interrupted, and our feelings 'hurt,' by the slighting remarks of those Tarrytown farmers. Agriculture can never reach any great perfection, we fear, along the line of the Croton aqueduct, between DOBB his Ferry and 'Sunnyside Cottage.' The farmers are too conceited — too much wedded to old observances.

THAT was a somewhat cool reply which was given by a boarder to a landlord in San Francisco, when he asked him for the 'amount of his little bill.' 'You have now, my dear Sir, been boarding with me for a month, and I have not troubled you; but I am now seriously in want of the money. Every thing I purchase for the house is at a high figure: and I really can't afford to lie out of your bill any longer.' 'Can't af-*ford* it!' exclaimed the delinquent; 'then why the d——l do n't you sell out to some body that *can* afford it? *That 's* your best way!'

HAS the city reader ever passed along Chatham Square, and through the street from which it derives its name, without hearing the eternal din of hammers closing bargains up, and the uproarious vociferations of the operators?—noises that, breaking upon the ear of a passer-by, who may be indulging the luxury of his own quiet thoughts, suddenly recall vivid ideas of Bedlam; an impression that is amply confirmed, by a glance at the shop's interior, where stands a lonely man, foaming at the mouth, sawing the air with his hand, and making the dirty counter before him to resound again with the noise of his mallet. The street 'crieur' is of another class. You shall see him, even of a cold winter morning, buttoned to the throat, with a waistcoat or a pair of unwhisperables whisking about on a long stick, which he holds in his hand, while he vociferates *at* the pedestrian auditory, who sometimes glance at him in passing, 'Twent'—'five! Thirt'—thirt'—thirt'-five, for them pants!' Much practice has made him an automaton, to all intents and purposes. But the most distinguished of auctioneers, is the vender of oil-paintings; and the class has greatly multiplied, since it has been ascertained that at least an hundred 'original pictures,' on one and the same subject, and by the same renowned master, may be sold here from one auction mart. GOLDSMITH speaks of a man who, having disposed of a petrified lobster, which he had accidently found, at a great bargain, straightway set about the manufacture of the article, and drove a wholesale trade in that unique line. The picture-vender acts upon this hint, and he succeeds equally well. He deals in *bugs*, well preserved; hum-bugs, of the first water. HOGARTH, we remember, has a picture of Time, with a pipe in his mouth, whiffing smoky antiquity upon a fresh painting. Your modern picture-venders better understand the matter. We have recently read, in some of our periodicals, a brief account of the knowledge of art and the great artists which they display, but it did not come up to the reality. The great successor of Madame MALAPROP, who flourished in England some ten or twelve years ago, could alone, were she among us, do justice to the autioneer of modern paintings by the old masters. 'Here,' he exclaims, holding up a rather confused and mottled composition, 'is a splendid pictur', by a very ancient master of arts. You see the frame is old and worm-eaten, and there is the year '1528' on the back of it. It is the interior of a cathedral in Spain, or else in Italy. They are a-worshippin' inside; the priest, up by the candles, is very much incensed with the smoke that the boys is a-whirlin' round his head; and the quire 's a-singin' a tedium: but look at your catalogues; it 's all in them.' 'This pictur' was exhibited fifty years in the Vacüum at Rome, where the pope keeps his celebrated bulls. What 's bid for 't? Is five hundred dollars named, to *start* it? Five hundred do I hear?' This is struck down to a spectator at the farther end of the room, and another rises to view, with two naked figures in the fore-ground: backed by trees that are very, very green, and skies extremely blue. 'This gem of painting, gen'lemen, is a *chef-dowver* of DE BUFF; his celebrated 'Adam and Eve expulsed from Paradise.' Is three hundred dollars bid for this? It was sold for six hundred guineas in London! Is *fifty* dollars bid? Fifty — fifty — going! *Yours*, Mr. SUCKEDIN.' This was followed by a painting which seemed to represent a street-view. 'Here, now, *is* a treasure! It is a scene in the su-burbs of the city of Venice, that a gen'leman, who was here to see it this morning, called the 'Place Louis Quinzy,' named after a French officer in NAPOLEON's army, who caught cold a-travellin' in the same stage-coach at night with a wet nurse, and died of the quinzy sore-throat. I did n't hear of this in time to put it in the catalogue; but they say the first thing a traveller does, when he gets to Venice, is to hire a horse, and ride out to look at it. How much for it?' The piece went for fifty dollars. 'You will find it,' said the auctioneer, 'a very cheap pictur'— and he did.

We remember to have seen an anecdote of an enthusiastic but ignorant lover of old paintings, of whose mania advantage was taken by every huckster of pictures for leagues around him; and his love of being deceived, may be gathered from the following colloquy with an amateur friend: 'Come up and see me to-morrow, my boy, and *I'll* show you a picture that *is* a picture — an undoubted original. I want your unbiassed judgment of it. TITIAN SMITH was over to look at it, yesterday, and had the impudence to say that it was a copy — the ignorant ramus! By JOVE! I'd like any *other* man to tell me so! Curse me, if I should n't be tempted to knock him down! But come up to-morrow, and give us your candid opinion of its merits. I'd like to know what *you* think of it.' There can be no doubt, we presume, that the painting was not considered a copy.

UP and away over the superb New-York and Erie Rail-road, if you would have a trip that is better worth making than any one of the same distance out of Gotham. The blue mountains, swelling hills, and fertile vales of Rockland and Orange; the vast embankments and rocky ravines, cut by the hands of man through the lofty Shawangunk; the terrific 'Glass House Rocks,' the rushing Delaware and the lonely Susquehanna, these of themselves would well repay the traveller. Much good sport had our pleasant party, fishing in the Calicoon and Shinglekill. One there was of us, a 'personable' youth, with silky moustache, and 'dark-locks flowing free,' who would have inveigled more trout to taste his hook, but for his habiliments. The 'fashionable plaid' 'clock'-stockings, of a pink stripe, and patent-leather shoes adorned his lower members: hence, accoutred as he was, 'Old KNICK.,' 'in rustic garb, thick-booted to the thighs,' listening to his urgent solicitations to be borne across the deep and boiling brook, did essay to do that same. 'As ÆNEAS did ANCHISES bear,' he took the youth upon his back and set forth for the other side. Now it so chanced (quite as unexpectedly as the elder WELLER's upset of the coach-load of voters) that when arrived at the deepest and most tumultuous part of the stream, an unlucky misstep, and some little fatigue, compelled the 'writer hereof,' although against vehement remonstrance, to set his burthen down! Have n't been so 'sorry' for several years as we were at that 'accident,' and so we remarked at the time, but with very little effect, we thought, to the 'complainant,' after he had scrambled up the bank, through the tangled bushes, and sat croaking on an old log, a 'dem'd moist, unpleasant body!'

BEEN 'a-crabbing' to-day, off the little narrow dock at DOBB'S. What 'game' they are, those sprawling shellfish! They 'll bite any thing, from an old rag up to a ragged piece of meat. They are not 'what you may call a han'sum critter:' they cannot be deemed an 'ornament to society.' They are better 'as a meat' than as a personal friend and companion. This 'red right hand' bears witness of *that*. You cannot touch a crab's better nature: 'leastways' *we* could n't. The one we tried we thought a model-specimen; but he pinched, scratched, 'dug in,' and 'held on:' upon *us*, too, who defended his whole race down at Fire-Island one day — one Fourth of July. There was a broad shallow tub of water that was full of them, in the shade of the house; and there they floated and sprawled, in true 'independence' fashion. When their claws were extended, wags of boys would set fire-crackers on end in their joints, which they would firmly grasp, 'right end up with care.' Into the claws of a big lobster, floating in their midst, a 'TRITON among minnows,' the boys placed an erect wooden pistol, with a slow match, made of a 'cracker,' having immediate connection with the touch-hole. This was the 'great gun' of the marine party. This masked piscatorial floating-battery was 'operated' at one and the same time, and a victim dropped (to the bottom of the tub) at every successive discharge. We thought this cruel sport at *that* time; but 'by this hand' we think now that it 'served 'em right!'

WE have n't heard in a good while of a more amusing take-in than was performed by an auctioneer in a small village of 'Down East.' A fiddle had just been bidden off at a 'high figure' by a 'cute Yankee; but the auctioneer was cuter still. 'How much,' said he, after passing the buyer his purchase, how much ''moffered for *the bow?*—how *much?*—how much 'moffered for THE BOW?' 'Hello! you!—that 's *mine!*' said the astonished purchaser. 'Wal, that *is* rich!' replied the auctioneer—'*decidedly* rich! Guess you must be from the ked'ntry. Who bids for *the bow?* How much 'moffered for *the bow?*—how *much?* how much for *the bow?* A-naf, naf, naf, naf: Pass up your change, you lazy devil: you would n't a-come in, 'xpect, except to git eöut o' the sun. Guess you must be from the ked'ntry. How much 'moffered for *the bow?*' The bow was finally bid off by a shrewd by-stander, who saw a chance for a little 'spec,' and sold to the victim who had bought the fiddle, at a large advance on the original cost.

To be on earth '*no more;*' to be buried in the cold ground and forgotten; to solve the great mystery of the grave; how we shrink from it!—how the best start appalled at the thought! The '*last time,*' too, how these two words fall upon the susceptible heart! To us this thought is so impressive, that if, on leaving an apartment in some dwelling that we may never visit again, the idea occurs to us that we are leaving it for the last time, we return at once to give the lie to our fears; and so in bidding farewell to a friend, if we are reminded by this spectre of '*the last time*,' we make it a point to see him once more, and bid him again, as if by accident, a hasty and less formal adieu. It is astonishing how this idea of death will *permeate* the brain. Looking, for example, at a clock, you wonder when that hour-hand or that minute-hand shall mark the end of your pilgrimage; when each shall stop; when with *you* 'time shall be no longer,' and 'the shadow shall go back upon the dial.' And as you think of this, you recall the thousand places, in all changes of the seasons, where thoughts of 'the last bitter hour' have come upon you: in the old wildernesses; by the solemn shore of ocean, where silent and thoughtful you have walked alone; or gazing from some lofty mountain-top at the great sun in the brightness of his rising, or cloud-curtained, sinking slowly in the evening west; or at the moon careering in the firmament of night, with all her attendant stars: all these, ever-living and moving, and full of life though they be, have reminded us a thousand times of death. Yet 'GOD tempers the wind to the shorn lamb:' and HE lessens the dread of the Destroyer as we gradually approach his dark domain. We do not drop at once into sleep, that 'calm relative of death,' but as slumber creeps gradually upon us, and one by one the senses yield to its sway, so Death, the antagonist of wakeful life, who walks his unceasing rounds, and sooner or later stops at every man's door, lulls us by slow degrees into that sleep which can know no waking, till earth and sea 'heave at the trump of GOD!'

DID you ever know an Irish servant that had n't a dozen 'cousins?' A friend of ours says that he once forbade them his kitchen: but it was of no use. They came, and when *he* came, they were concealed. His kitchen-chimney smoked one day, he knew not wherefore. He knows now. He says a kitchen-chimney *will* smoke when there is a journeyman-baker up the flue! This seems reasonable.

DURING the war of 1812 it chanced that an invasion was expected in the town of Lyme, situated at the mouth of the Connecticut river. The 'spirit of the times' had previously manifested itself in militia-gatherings and organizations; and the individual who had undertaken to discipline the rustics in the art of war was one Captain TINKER, who had advanced his company to a high state of 'theoretical practice,' through the aid of broom-sticks and corn-stalks, interspersed here and there with a rusty old 'Queen's-arm.' Well, several ferocious and determined 'parades' were executed, in anticipation of the enemy's advent. Balls were cast, guns scoured, flints picked, and the 'troops' were set to work in digging a trench which should command the entrance of the river, under the supervision of Colonel S——, who was a veteran of the revolution. It was not long before some gun-boats were seen approaching, closely followed by two English frigates: and as they came within range, a shot or two was fired. The 'troops' were all duly entrenched; and thrust through their embankment, the muzzles of two culverins, fully charged with death-dealing matériel, stood 'grinning grim defiance' to foreign invasion, and awaiting the charge. But at this juncture our doughty captain was not to be found. The valiant colonel had ridden up and down the lines in vain in search of him: but at length he espied in the distance a dirt-covered head bobbing up and down occasionally from the ground, whose 'continuations' were evidently busily engaged in finding the bottom of a deep hole. In the summer-tide of passion, the colonel rode up to the spot and exclaimed: 'What the devil are you doing in that hole, Captain TINKER? Why are you not at the head of your troops?' 'Troops be d—d!' replied the captain; 'it 's their business to take care of *themselves:* this is *my* hole: I dug it last night; and the cussed

Britishers can hit me if they kin — let 'em shute! Let the troops git under *their* sand-bank if they do n't want to git hit: *they* got one!' Was n't this an exhibition of the 'better part of valor' in a commanding officer?

Some months ago a person was committed to jail in Northampton, Massachusetts, and placed in a room with a maniac, who had been confined there temporially, previous to his being taken to the Insane Hospital at Brattleboro'. After the new-comer had 'turned in' for the night, his crazy chum ordered him up, and told him to dress himself, and then make a prayer, or he would choke him to death! There was no way but to obey, and after making what he supposed to be a sufficiently long prayer, he stopped. His inquisitor told him to keep on, and he actually kept him praying all night. The poor man was not relieved until the jailor carried in his breakfast. From the fact of his having been 'committed to jail,' probability favors the conclusion that he had not prayed for some time previously. Perhaps, however, he was a Massachusetts prisoner for debt. Be this as it may, it seems to us if he were not blessed with a great natural gift, being thus appealed to 'lead in prayer' must have 'come tough.' It would seem, at first sight, a dreadful situation to be kept praying all night, and *ex tempore*, too: but we well remember a good old wordy clergyman, of our 'boyhood's days,' who would have beaten the victim in an *involuntary* offering of the kind. His *hearers* were the victims, however, in *his* case: and when he came to pray for the bringing in of God's 'ancient covenant people, the Jews,' which was his last division, his audience always felt as rejoiced as did the aforesaid prisoner when the jailor came to deliver him from his unwilling service. 'Wo unto them that make long prayers!'—and, as a general thing, 'wo *is* unto them' who hear them!

NUMBER TEN.

FITFUL FOREBODINGS — OUR FIRST BABY: ROCHESTER JAIL — A 'VISIBLE SUPPORT': OUR 'QUARTER' TO A FOE: A YANKEE'S 'EYE TO TRADE': NEGRO ELOQUENCE: 'SWAYING' YOUNG TREES — HEARING 'SOMETHING DROP': 'JOHN SMITH' IN A QUANDARY: 'DOBB'S' IN SPRING-TIME: A 'FLAT-FOOTED' SIMILE: MURDER CONSIDERED AS 'MURDER': OF TURTLES AND THEIR 'ABUSES': A DYING WIFE TO HER HUSBAND: IRISH SHREWDNESS: AN IRISH BLUNDER: THE 'MORALITY' OF DECENT DRESS: ARTISTIC SMUGGLING,

DID you ever in your life see such a change in the feelings of any man, as is recorded below, in a couple of extracts from a letter of our correspondent 'JULIAN?' He is not well, is approaching 'New-Years,' and is altogether very sad indeed:

'It would be amusing, if one could laugh at any thing so sad, to observe the humors of the few who think upon the bearings of this solemn time. In the year to be, there are many to come, many to go, and but few to tarry; yet *all* have their ambitions of a life-time; those even, to whom the stars have grown dim, and life become almost a mockery under Heaven, dashing into the coming day with something of the old zest; while the many, the *oi polloi*, who have not yet made their grand move, are now ready, and think that therefore the earth is to take a new route in creation: forgetting that the old round must be the round for ever. Nights sleepless with joy, nights sleepless with pain, nights long with watching, feverish thought; crime that stings like an adder, and nights short with perfect rest; days long and weary, days bright and dashing, hot and cold, wet and dry, and days and nights with all of these — as hath been in the time that 's past, and will be in the time to come.

'There is something very pitiable in these humors; indeed very laughable, if your mouth is shaped to that effect; but as it happens with me to-night, my mouth refuses to twitch except in one direction. Its corners have the 'downward tendencies.' Perhaps it is because this is with me the anniversary of a day upon the events of which are hanging the movements of all after-life; it may be this, and there may be thereto added the coloring of a winter's day. The wind howls about the house-tops, and the air pierces like needles; even the stars, when they look down in thousands, as the rack goes by, seem to shiver in their high places; yet perhaps there is nothing so personal in all that, considering that just so the wind howled last night, and may for a month to come; but oh! as I am a nervous man, and look back upon the circling months, and feel the sting here and the stab there, in that galvanic battery; and as I look forward with eager eye, and ear open to the faintest whisper of the dim to-morrow, it is not as the stars shiver from excess of light, but with a shudder at the heart from the cooler blood of —— Good night, my kind EDITOR: that sentence is quite too long already, and there are some things too personal to tell.

. . . .

'P. S.—Whoop! hurrah! Light is upon the world again! Where are you, my dear friend? I say, Sir, I was an ass—do you hear?—an *ass*, premature, wise before my time, a brute, a blockhead! Did I talk of dust and ashes? Oh! Sir, I lied multitudinously. Every nerve, every muscle that did n't try to strangle me in that utterance, *lied*. No, Sir; let me tell you it 's a great world; glorious—magnificent; a world that can't be beat! Talk of the stars and a better world, but do n't invite me there yet. Make my regrets, my apology to DEATH, but say that I can't come; 'positive engagement; happy some other time, but not now.' Oh, no; this morning is quite too beautiful to leave; and beside, I would rather stay, if only to thank GOD a little longer for this glorious light, this pure air that can echo back my loudest hurrah. And then, my boy —— But have n't I told you? Why, Sir, I 've got a boy!—*a boy!*—ha, ha! I shout it out to you—A BOY; a ten-pounder, and the mother a great deal *better* than could be expected! And, I say, my old friend, it 's *mine!* Hurrah and hallelujah forever! Oh,

Sir! such legs, and such arms, and such a head!—and *he has his mother's lips!* I can kiss them forever! And then, Sir, look at his feet, his hands, his chin, his eyes, his every thing, in fact—so perfect! Give me joy, Sir: no you need n't either. I am full now; I run over; and they say that I ran over a number of old women, half killed the mother, pulled the doctor by the nose, and upset a 'pothecary shop in the corner; and then did n't I ring the tea-bell? Did n't I blow the horn? Did n't I dance, shout, laugh, and cry altogether? The women say they had to tie me up. I do n't believe *that;* but who is going to shut his mouth when he has a live baby? You should have heard his lungs, Sir, at the first mouthful of fresh air—such a burst! A little tone in his voice, but not pain; excess of joy, Sir, from too great sensation. The air-bath was so sudden, you know. Think of all his beautiful machinery starting off at once in full motion; all his thousand outside feelers answering to the touch of the cool air; the flutter and crash at the ear; and that curious contrivance the eye, looking out wonderingly and bewildered upon the great world, so glorious and dazzling to his unworn perceptions; his net-work of nerves, his wheels and pulleys, his air-pumps and valves, his engines and reservoirs; and within all, that beautiful fountain, with its jets and running streams dashing and coursing through the whole length and breadth, without either stint or pause — making altogether, Sir, exactly ten pounds avoirdupois!

'Did I ever talk brown to you, Sir, or blue, or any other of the devil's colors? You say I have. Beg your pardon, Sir, but you — are mistaken in the individual. I am this day, Sir, multiplied by two. I am duplicate. I am number one of an indefinite series, and there 's my continuation. And you observe, it is not a block, nor a block-head, nor a painting, nor a bust, nor a fragment of any thing, however beautiful; but a combination of *all* the arts and sciences in one; painting, sculpture, music, (hear him cry,) mineralogy, chemistry, mechanics, (see him kick,) geography, and the use of the globes, (see him nurse;) and withal, he is a perpetual motion — a time-piece that will never run down! And who wound it up? But words, Sir, are but a mouthing and a mockery.

'When a man is nearly crushed under obligations, it is presumed that he is unable to speak; but he may bend over very carefully, for fear of falling, nod in a small way, and say nothing; and then, if he have sufficient presence of mind to lay a hand upon his heart, and look down at an angle of forty-five degrees, with a motion of the lips — unuttered poetry — showing the wish and the inability, it will be (well done) very gracefully expressive. With my boy in his first integuments, I assume that position, make the small nod aforesaid, and leave you the poetry unuttered.'

It will take you but a minute to read this little sketch of what we heard and saw at the jail in Rochester, that wonderful new-old city, recently:

As we walked leisurely by a grated door, a flushed countenance and unquiet eye flashed suddenly upon us through the iron bars. It was a face to be remembered, for it had 'a smack of Tartarus and the souls in bale.' It was of a man in confinement for shooting his wife, in cold blood. She was still lingering upon the borders of the grave, and, woman-like, refused to criminate, by her testimony, her brutal husband. . . . As we were emerging from the prison, a representative from those conclaves of miscreancy in which crime is concocted, accumulations of humanity which ferment and reek like compost, in all large cities, was pointed out leisurely engaged in carrying out the plan of Mr. M'ADAM, with a long-handled hammer. He was a bit of a wag, we were informed, whose wit had often stood him in good stead. He had been repeatedly before the city authorities for divers misdemeanors, and each time promised well for the future; but although he always kept his countenance, he never kept his word. On one occasion, he was just about to be sentenced, with other sanculottists, as a common vagrant, when, with the most imperturbable *sang froid*, having suddenly harpooned a good idea, he pulled from a capacious pocket of his tattered coat a loaf of bread, and half of a dried codfish, and holding them up to the magistrate, with triumphant look and gesture, exclaimed: 'You do n't ketch me *that* way! I 'm no wagrant. An't *them* 'wisible means o' support,' I should like to know?' The argument was a *non sequitur*.

THE opinion has always extensively prevailed in the United States, and doubtless even now generally obtains, fostered as it is by many of our own writers, that the only feeling which an elderly Englishman, who happened to be 'out' in America, during our national contest, entertains toward this country and her people, is one of decided hatred and repugnance. We can call to mind, at this moment, some half dozen native fictions, and one or two indigenous works of a different character, in which this position is set forth as a prominent fact. Now, as a general truth, we believe the reverse to be the case; and we are sustained in this opinion by those who have had distinguished opportunities of judging of its correctness. An instance was recently related to us, by an illustrious American, known as well, and as highly honored, abroad as at home, which, without any infraction of social confidence, we shall here take the liberty to repeat, for the benefit of our readers.

'Old Admiral Sir —— HARVEY told me, at dinner, of

his serving on the American station, when he was a midshipman in 1776. He was cast away in the 'Liverpool,' in the month of February, on Rockaway beach. The boats were swamped in getting the crew to shore. The people of the neighborhood came down to the beach in wagons, took them up to their homes, changed and dried their clothes, and gave them supper. They remained quartered in this neighborhood for weeks, part of the time in tents, part of the time in the farm-houses. Nothing could exceed the kindness of the people, particularly of the Quaker family of the HICKS'S; and another family, who treated them always hospitably in their houses. They made great havoc among the bacon and beans, and passed their time pleasantly among the Quaker girls; who always, however, demeaned themselves with strict propriety; the old Quakers tolerating their youthful frolics. When they came to pay off scores, they expected to have 'a thundering bill.' The good people would take nothing but the king's allowance. 'You are people in distress,' said they; 'we will not take any thing out of your pockets.' The old Admiral declares he has never forgotten their kindness.

A GENIAL friend, in one of our south-county towns, which 'well we know,' as Mrs. GAMP says, tells the following: A map-pedler, in pursuance of his vocation, chanced to stop at the principal hotel in one of the pleasantest of our western state villages. A friend, whom he had known in former years in Yankee-land, seeing him at the hotel, invited him to a large party which he was to give the same evening. The old friend came; and when received by his host at the door, was found with three maps in his hand: 'How-de-du?' said he; 'got any nails? Thought as praps there was to be a good many fokes here to-night, I 'd hang up some o' my *maps* here, and let 'em look at 'em. Good chance — fust rate. May be some on 'em would like to buy 'em; and I could explain 'em as well as not; nothin' else to do, pooty much. Got a small hammer? Know where I 'd be liable to dispose of a few beans?' Sharp practice, that, eh?

THERE is a vast deal of a certain kind of originality about negro composition. Take this example of an illustration lately used by a colored exhorter at an evening conference-meeting in Montgomery, Alabama:

'MY bredren, GOD bless your souls, 'ligion is like de Alabama riber. In spring come de fresh, an' he bring in all de ole logs, slabs an' sticks, dat hab been lyin' on de bank, and carrying dem down in de current. Bimeby de water go down; den a log cotch here on dis island, den a slab get cotched on de shore, and de sticks on de bushes; and dare dey lie, wid'rin' and dryin' till comes 'nodder fresh. Jist so dere come 'vival of 'ligion; dis ole sinner bro't in, dat ole back-slider bro't back; an' all de folk seem comin'— an' mighty good times. But, bredren, GOD bless your souls! bimeby 'vival 's gone: den dis ole sinner is stuck on his ole sin; den dat ole back-slider is cotched where he was afore, on jus' such a rock; den one arter 'nodder, dat had got 'ligion, lies all 'long de shore, and dere dey lie till 'nodder 'vival. Beloved bredren, GOD bless your souls, get *deep* in de current!'

How many a white pulpit-bore has waded through the logical 'divisions' of a discourse, (a well-intended one, no doubt, but from its unconscionable length spoiling some hearer's Sunday turkey that was worth two of it,) which had not in its whole compass so forcible an illustration as this?

'*Remembrances of Boyhood*' shall appear: we *do* 'think the article worthy.' Speaking of boyhood, we may as well add, that we have recently had quite a practical illustration of the pleasure to be derived from certain of its reminiscences. During a recent visit to an esteemed friend in the country, whose hospitable mansion rises amidst its painted autumnal trees, within sound of the cataract of Cohoes, we joined a pleasant party to visit, over the Hudson, the lofty summit of '*Mount Rafinesque*,' (named after an old contributor to this Magazine,) from which a magnificent and most varied view may be commanded. As we alighted from our barouche, at the foot of the last great acclivity, and began to ascend through the forest that skirts its base, so it was that the fresh mountain air did greatly dilate the heart and expand the spirits of 'OLD KNICK.,' who left the 'honorable member,' his guests and the charming ladies of his household behind him, while ZACHEUS-like, he ran on in advance, and climbed some forty or fifty feet to the top of a small 'staddle,' having it in mind to perform a common feat of his boyhood; namely, to 'sway' the same by grasping its top and dropping slowly to the ground with the yielding trunk. Now look you what befel: 'Do me the favor to observe!' exclaimed 'OLD KNICK.,' as he threw himself free from the body of the sapling. Down he went, with a sensation as of sinking slowly in a balloon, when presently, while yet about fifteen feet from the ground, he suddenly '*heard something drop!*' The individual who emerged from under the bruised branches of that prostrate ash, (so unlike the lithe saplings familiar to his boyhood,) was rubbing several of his own limbs, for some cause or other; and we can answer for him, that when he saw the 'honorable member' smothering a titter, and his fair household suppressing a large amount of giggle; when he heard them say that they were '*sorry* that the tree had broken so soon; *very* sorry; did n't know the time, in fact, for several years, when they had been *quite* so sorry;' when 'OLD KNICK.' saw and heard this, he was discomforted within himself, and his countenance fell; for then he knew that they were laughing at him. There was a lame male 'human' about the house that night, doing something with laudanum and opodeldoc; yet he did not forget, amidst his thoughts of 'the toil to that mountain led,' the matchless view of city, village, mountain, 'field and flood,' which was commanded from its lofty summit, on that glorious October afternoon.

JOHN SMITH — we mention this gentleman's cognomen with some reluctance, for the reason that there are *two* persons of the same name in Gotham — JOHN SMITH was returning to town on one occasion about midnight, in a dark snow-storm. He was 'full of new wine,' and was quite unable, after riding for an hour, to find his own dwelling; but he drove up to a house which he thought must be at least in his neighborhood, and almost wrenched the bell-pull off with his hurried and repeated ringings. At length a neighbor's head peered from an upper window: 'What do you want, down there?' said not the best-natured voice in the world; 'what the d——l do you *want?* — ringing the bell as if the house was a-fire; *What do you want?*' 'Can you tell me where JOHN SMITH lives?' 'J-O-H-N S-M-I-T-H!?' answered the recognized neighbor, with a kind of exclamatory interrogation; 'why, *you* are JOHN SMITH, yourself!' 'I know *that*, as well *you* do,' hiccupped JOHN, 'but I do n't know where I live! — wan' to know *w-h-e-r-e I l-i-v-e!*' Somebody show'd him.

WE slipped up to 'DOBB his Ferry' the other day. It looked bleak there — all but the noble river and the grand old hills. There were no friends on the piazza fronting the sanctum, and no little people running down the hill to meet 'OLD KNICK.' half way, and pour into the porches of his ears much voluble discourse, on his farther way up. Down on the shore, however, was one of 'Young KNICK.'s' little shoes, and idly walking there, we picked up the tube of an old rocket. There was pleasure in thinking when that little old shoe was lost, and that signal-rocket fired. Winter has gone; the time of the singing of birds hath come; the trees are reddening with their newly-awakened life-blood; and soon 'DOBB'S' will put forth all its summer glories.

'I SHOULD like you to have seen,' said a friend to us the other day, 'a specimen of a green Yankee who came down the Sound in a Hartford steamer with me. He had never been 'to 'York' before, and he was asking questions of every body on board the boat. However, if he *was* 'green as grass' he was picking up a good deal of information, which will doubtless stand him in good stead hereafter. One of his comparisons struck me as decidedly original: 'Up to Northampton,' said he, 'I took breakfast, and they taxed me tew shillin's! 'Twas a pooty good price, but I 'gin it to 'em. 'Twas *enough*, any way. Well, when I come down to Har'ford, I took breakfast ag'in, next mornin', and when I asked 'em 'How much?' they looked at me and said, 'Half a dollar!!' I looked back at 'em pooty sharp — but I *paid* it; and *arter* I'd paid it, I sot down, and ciphered up inside how much it would cost a fellow to board long at that rate; and I tell you what, I pooty soon found eöut that 'fore the end of a month it would make a fellow's pocket-book *look as if an elephant had stomped onto it!*' 'SAM SLICK' himself never employed a more striking simile.

THE following specimen of judicial 'wisdom' was recently delivered to a 'Wolverine' jury: — 'Murder, gentlemen,' said our western SOLON, 'is where a man is murderously killed. The killer, in such a case, is a murderer. Now murder by poison is as much murder as murder with a gun. It is the *murdering* that constitutes murder, in the eye of the law. You will bear in mind that murder is one thing, and manslaughter another: therefore, if it is not manslaughter, it must be murder; and if it be not murder, it must be manslaughter. Self-murder has nothing to do in this case: one man cannot commit *felo de se* on another: that is clearly my view.

Gentlemen, I think you can have no difficulty. Murder, I say, is murder. The murder of a brother is called fratricide; but it is not fratricide if a man murders his mother. You will make up your minds. You know what murder is, and I need not tell you what it is not. I repeat, murder is murder. You can retire upon it, if you like!'

WE do not remember ever to have seen a more *appealing* look than one which was given us the other day by a Green Turtle at the door of a popular restaurant in Broadway. How he had effected so much, passes our comprehension; but he had actually backed up against the wall to an angle of about forty-five degrees; and his head was out, and bent round, apparently to see how the land lay. He regarded us with evident emotion; and the look of his eye, the gurgling in his throat, and a heavy sigh, which must have come from the very bottom of his shell, said as plainly as ever a Green Turtle spoke in the world: 'Friend, reverse me, for Pity's sake! Give me a chance for my life! I will do *you* as good *a turn*, if I ever find you on your back, with a label on your breast, setting forth that you are going to 'get into a stew' the next day!' For one moment we thought of 'liberty,' and heartily 'wished he might get it;' and he *would* have obtained it, too, if he had the same chance that a fellow-

Testudo had, with his English captors, as described by HOOK. It seems they were conveying a turtle in a boat on the river Tay, when somebody suggested the convenience of a sea-bath, and the refreshment the creature might derive from a taste of its native element. Accordingly Testudo was lifted over the side, and indulged with a dip and a wallop in the wave, which actually revived it so powerfully, that from a playful flapping with its fore-fins it soon began to struggle most vigorously, like a giant refreshed with brine. In fact, it paddled with a power which, added to its weight, left no alternative to its guardian but to go with it or without it. The event soon came off. The man tumbled backward into the boat, and the turtle plunged forward into the deep. There was a splash; a momentary glimpse of the broad back-shell; the waters closed, and all was over — or rather under.

'Is he *alive?*' inquired a little boy in our hearing the other day, as he gazed at a large turtle crawling in front of another restaurant, with a bill of his own fare on his back. 'Alive!' exclaimed a fat man who was also looking at the shell-monster with an expression of intense interest; 'sartingly, boy! He acts like a live turkle, do n't he?' 'Why yes, he *acts* like one,' answered the little querist; 'but I did n't know but he might be *makin' b'lieve!*' Is it possible that what a friend, just returned from New Zealand, tell us can be true? He says that he has many a time and oft seen a fat and tender white man lying before a cannibal eating-house, with '*Soup*' in large native characters, and the hour at which he was to be served up, inscribed on his breast. A man, says our friend, should see a sight like this, who would properly appreciate the frequent deep-drawn sigh which a poor turtle heaves while lying on his back, exposed to the rude gaze of hungry passers-by. Christian-men too, in good corporeal condition, has our traveller seen in Cannibal-land, driven around the lanes of the rude villages, their limbs decorated with parti-colored ribands, and the hour when they were to be killed marked on their backs! 'Mine GOTT! vat a peoples!'

THE following most touching fragment of a *Letter from a Dying Wife to her Husband* was found by him, some months after her death, between the leaves of a religious volume, which she was very fond of perusing. The letter, which was literally dim with tear-marks, was written long before the husband was aware that the grasp of a fatal disease had fastened upon the lovely form of his wife, who died at the early age of nineteen:

'WHEN this shall reach your eye, Dear G——, some day when you are turning over the relics of the past, I shall have passed away for ever, and the cold white stone will be keeping its lonely watch over the lips you have so often pressed, and the sod will be growing green that shall hide for ever from your sight the dust of one who has so often nestled close to your warm heart. For many long and sleepless nights, when all beside my thoughts was at rest, I have wrestled with the consciousness of approaching death, until at last it has forced itself upon my mind; and although to you and to others it might now seem but the nervous imaginings of a girl, yet, dear G——, *it is so!* Many weary hours have I passed in the endeavor to reconcile myself to leaving you, whom I love so well, and this bright world of sunshine and beauty; and hard indeed it is to struggle on silently and alone with the *sure conviction* that I am about to leave all for ever, and go down alone into the dark valley! 'But I know in whom I have believed,' and leaning upon HIS arm 'I fear no evil.' Do not blame me for keeping even all this from you. How could I subject *you*, of all others, to such sorrow as I feel at parting, when time will so soon make it apparent to you? I could have wished to live, if only to be at your side when *your* time shall come, and pillowing your head upon my breast, wipe the death-damps from your brow, and usher your departing spirit into its MAKER'S presence, embalmed in woman's holiest prayer. But it is not so to be — and I submit. Yours is the the privilege of watching, through long and dreary nights, for the spirit's final flight, and of transferring my sinking head from your breast to my SAVIOUR'S bosom! And you shall share my last thought; the last faint pressure of the hand, and the last feeble kiss shall be yours; and even when flesh and heart shall have failed me, my eye shall rest on yours until glazed by death; and our spirits shall hold one last fond communion, until gently fading from my view — the last of earth — you shall mingle with the first bright glimpses of the unfading glories of that better world, where partings are unknown. Well do I know the spot, dear G——, where you will lay me: often have we stood by the place, and as we watched the mellow sunset as it glanced in quivering flashes through the leaves, and burnished the grassy mounds around us with stripes of burnished gold, *each* perhaps has thought that some day one of us would come *alone*, and whichever it might be, *your* name would be on the stone. But we loved the spot; and I know you'll love it none the less when you see the same quiet sun-light linger and play among the grass that grows over your MARY'S grave. I know you'll go often alone there, when I am laid there, and my spirit will be with you then, and whisper among the waving branches, '*I am not lost, but gone before!*'

CURIOUS and odd things not unfrequently occur 'before the Mayor.' The other day, in attending to applications for situations in the police-force, the Mayor, it was supposed, was about to invest PATRICK MURPHY with a 'star,' when some of his Irish competitors outside the railing cried out: '*Are* ye goin' to 'pint PAT, yer Honor? He can't write his name, yer Honor.' 'I am only receiving applications to-day; in a fortnight we make appointments,' said the Mayor: and PAT was told to call on that day two weeks. The friend through whose influence PAT had been induced to apply for office said to him, as they came away from the Hall, 'Now, PAT, go home, and every night do you get a big piece of paper and a good stout pen, and keep writing your name. I 'll 'set the copy' for you.' PAT did as directed; and every night for a fortnight was seen running out his tongue and swaying his head over 'PATRICK MURPHY,' 'PATRICK MURPHY,' in the style of chirography generally known as 'coarse hand.' When the day for the appointment came, PAT found himself 'before the Mayor,' urging his claim. 'Can you write?' said that excellent functionary. 'Troth, an' it 's meself that jist *kin!*' answered PAT. 'Take that pen,' said the Mayor, 'and let us *see* you write. Write your name.'

He took the pen as directed, when a sort of exclamatory laugh burst from his surprised competitors who were in attendance: 'How-ly PAUL! — d' ye mind *that*, MIKE? PAT's a-writin'! — he 's got a quill in his fist!' 'So he has, be Jabers!' said MIKE; 'but small good 't will do him; he can't write wid it, man?' But PAT *did* write; he had recorded his name in a bold round hand. 'That 'll do,' said the Mayor. His foiled rivals looked in each other's faces with undisguised astonishment. A lucky thought struck them: 'Ask him to write *somebody else's name*, yer Honor,' said two of them, in a breath. 'That 's well thought of,' replied the Mayor: 'PAT, write *my* name!' Here was a dilemma; but PAT was equal to it. '*Me* write yer Honor's name!' exclaimed he, with a well-dissembled 'holy horror;' 'ME commit *a forgery*, and I a-goin' on the Pelisse! *I can't do it*, yer Honor!' And he could n't — but his wit saved him, and he is now 'a 'star' of the first magnitude.'

By-the-by, 'speaking of Irishmen,' CRANSTON, the popular host of the 'Rockaway Pavilion,' illustrates by a characteristic anecdote their inherent propensity to blunder. An Irish servant of his had been directed to awaken two gentlemen at six o'clock in the morning, who were to take the public conveyance to town. At *three* o'clock in the morning he awakened two *other* gentlemen from a sound sleep, who after anathematizing his stupidity, 'between sleep and awake,' for some hour and a half, at length fell into the refreshing slumber which had been so rudely dispelled; when there came another rap at their doors, which awoke them instanter. The blundering Irishman, having discovered his mistake, had 'come to *apologize* to the gintlemen for wakin' 'em up at the wrong hour!' 'Faix,' said he, in the most self-accusing spirit, 'it was n't yez that *was* to be waked, anny way!' With curses not loud, but of considerable depth, the restless guests resigned themselves to their fate—victims of an Irish servant.

AN eminent legal judge, and a preëminent judge of human nature, observes: 'It is an observation I have always made, that dress has a moral effect on mankind. Let any gentleman find himself with dirty boots, old surtout, soiled neck-cloth, and a general negligence of dress, he will in all probability find a corresponding disposition to negligence of *ad*-dress. He may, *en deshabille*, curse and swear, speak roughly and think coarsely; but put the same man into full dress, and he will feel himself quite another person. To use the language of the blackguard would then be out of character: he will talk smoothly, affect politeness, if he has it not; pique himself upon good manners, and respect the women: nor will the spell subside, until returning home, the old surtout, the heedless slippers, with other slovenly appendages, make him lose again his brief consciousness of being a gentleman.'

'*Running a Land Blockade*' reminds us of a trick played by a wag who, before the working of the saline springs of our own glorious State, made it a business to smuggle salt from Canada into 'the States.' One day, having got wind that he was suspected, he loaded his bags full of saw-dust, and drove past the tavern where the excisemen were waiting for him. He was ordered to stop, but he only increased his speed. At length he was overtaken, and his load inspected with many imprecations, after which he was permitted to pass on. A day or two after, he drove up again with a full load of salt, and asked banteringly, if they did n't want to search him again. 'Go on! go on!' said the excisemen; 'we 've had enough of you!'

NUMBER ELEVEN.

CLINGING TO LIFE: INSOLUBLE PROBLEMS: PREMONITIONS OF A CONSUMPTIVE: SUNSHINE OF THE GRAVE: DEATH OF HON. SILAS. HIGGINS: CALIFORNIA PILGRIMS: A 'LAID-UP' EAR: SUGGESTIVE EPITAPH: THE 'INNER LIFE' OF MAN: A ''NEW'-MILCH' COW: A VOICE FROM THE NURSERY: A CONDENSING CONVERSATIONIST: DOW AMONG THE TOMBS: A CITY SNOW-SCENE: LARGE 'UNDERSTANDING': WINTER IN THE COUNTRY: SOME THOUGHTS ON KITES.

MRS. NORTON, in '*The Child of Earth*,' has beautifully illustrated the tenacity with which poor Humanity clings to this shadowy existence:

FAINTER her slow step falls from day to day:
  Death's hand is heavy on her darkening brow!
Yet doth she fondly cling to earth, and say:
  'I am content to die — but oh, not now!
Not while the blossoms of the joyous Spring
  Make the warm air such luxury to breathe;
Not while the birds such lays of gladness sing,
  Not while bright flowers around my footsteps wreathe.
Spare me, great GOD! — lift up my drooping brow:
I am content to die — but oh, not now!'

The spring hath ripened into summer-time —
  The season's viewless boundary is past;
The glorious sun hath reached his burning prime:
  'Oh! must this glimpse of beauty be the last?

Let me not perish while o'er land and sea
  With silent steps the LORD of light moves on;
Not while the murmur of the mountain-bee
  Greets my dull ear, with music in its tone.
Pale Sickness dims my eye and clouds my brow —
I am content to die! — but oh! not now!'

Summer is gone; and Autumn's soberer hues
  Tint the ripe fruits and gild the waving corn;
The huntsman swift the flying game pursues,
  Shouts the halloo, and winds his eager horn.
'Spare me awhile, to wander forth and gaze
  On the broad meadows and the quiet stream;
To watch in silence while the evening rays
  Slant through the fading trees with ruddy gleam:
Cooler the breezes play around my brow —
I am content to die! but oh, not now!'

The bleak wind whistles: snow-showers far and near,
  Drift without echo to the whitening ground;
Autumn hath passed away, and cold and drear,
  Winter stalks on, with frozen mantle bound:
Yet still that prayer ascends: 'Oh! laughingly
My little brothers round the warm hearth crowd;
Our home-fire blazes broad, and bright, and high,
  And the roof rings with voices light and loud:
Spare me awhile — raise up my drooping brow!
I am content to die! but oh! — NOT NOW!'

PERHAPS two or three of the questions which ensue may be found difficult to answer. They are worse than HOOD'S '*Given C. A. B. to find Q.*;' for in that case the student had only to get a *cab*, and take a pleasant ride to *Kew*, near London, which was very easily accomplished, if we remember rightly:

'IF three men work ten days on a fertile farm, what is the logarithm?

'If three men, one of them a colored man, and the other a female, set out simultaneously, which 'll get there first?

Required also, from these premises, the time of starting, starting-point, destination, and the 'Natural Number' belonging to the other.

'*Explanatory Note:* X = O — B, the probable age of the parties multiplied into the distance travelled.

'Of what use is a compass without a needle, and which way does it point?

'*Note:* X = supposed use. S = South.

'What is the required length of a limited steel wire which runs the other way?

'*Note* — X + X + X = other way.'

In the solution of the problem, '*As a General Thing, which will do the most Good?*' an 'allegational formula' is given, which defies our types. The solution, however, it is but just to say, is as clear as the question itself. We annex two or three others:

'IN a large household neither father nor mother knew any thing. How was it with the family?

'Is a man ever justifiable in either case, and if so, *which?*

Note. — 2 C = Both.

'Two men, unable to travel, set out on a journey, at different times, in company with a third in the same condition. For three hours the first two kept ahead of each other, when, a violent snow-storm arising, all three lost their way. What 's required?

'If a hard knot be tied in a cat's tail, which way, how long, and with what success, will she run after it? Also, who *tied* the knot?'

The conditions of this last problem are extremely

vague: but we cannot help thinking that many minds have been 'disciplined' by mathematical problems which were of quite as much practical value as this, or any of the others which we have quoted. We beg leave to subjoin a few kindred questions, involving maritime law, the science of heat, scripture history, etc.:

1. SUPPOSE a canal-boat heads west-north-west for the horse's tail, and has the wind abeam, with a flaw coming up in the south: would the captain, according to maritime law, be justified in taking a reef in the stove-pipe without asking the cook?'

2. The chief property of heat is, that it expands bodies, while cold contracts them. Give a familiar example of this operation of a natural law. 'Yes, Sir: in summer, when it is hot, the day is long: in winter when it is cold, the day contracts, and becomes very short.'

3. How much did it cost per week to pasture NEBUCHADNEZZAR during the seven years that he was 'out on grass?'

4. Can there be a rule without an exception? 'Yes: the nasal organ is indispensable to a comely human countenance. 'How beautiful is the face of Nature!'—yet we look in vain for a nose!

Vive la Bagatelle!

THE water stood in our eyes, reader, (and it will stand in yours, if you have a heart to feel,) as we perused the subjoined eloquent passage of a letter from a friend to whom our readers have often been indebted for amusement, entertainment, and instruction. What a startling picture it presents of the first approaches of that 'hectic,' 'phthisic,' 'consumption,' or whatever be the favorite title of that most wily and fatal foe, who in one hand presents the insidious olive-branch, and in the other conceals his inevitable sword, cutting down Youth in its blossom and Manhood in its fruit! 'For very many years, from twelve to two have been my hours of retiring, and my exercise has been nothing, or nearly so, during the day. One result has been, that I have read one half of the Greek and Roman classics, and feasted largely in modern literature. A parallel result has been, that owing to corporeal sluggishness and nervousness, the curse of the sedentary, I have no doubt reaped less pleasure and profit than I might have done from half that assiduity coupled with a due regard to the wants of the body. The final result is, that an iron constitution is now largely disorganized: and from the constant presence of a dull, deep, stationary pain in my left side beneath the ribs, and fixed I fear upon the lungs, I begin to indulge in sad and deep forebodings. Often, when wakened by its painful urgency, I lie in the silence of the night, listening to my heart's deep beatings, and recall my early and yet unfilled dreams — dreams oh! how glorious! — and array before my unsated eyes this world, with all its lovely learning, and sweet poetry, and burning passion; and reflect how unfit I am to die, and try the conditions of a new existence, before I have fulfilled the duties and perused the mysteries of this, and then think of the wormy bed, and anticipate the hour when I shall lie there, closing my eyes to color and my ears to sound; the impatient longing I have sometimes felt for death is repaid by an indefinable horror: and between the tenderness of natural regret and the shudderings of unconquerable awe, passion masters pride, and both sink to meekness and humility in a flood of gushing tears!'

THE late Professor CALDWELL, of Dickinson College, a short time before his death, said to his wife: 'You will not, I am sure, lie down upon your bed and weep, when I am gone. You will not mourn for me, when GOD has been so good to me. And when you visit the spot where I lie, do not choose a sad and mournful time: do not go in the shades of evening, or in the dark night. These are no times to visit the grave of one who hopes and trusts in a risen REDEEMER! Come, dear wife! in the morning, in the bright sunshine, and when the birds are singing!'

NOTHING could more thoroughly impress us with the fact, that it is pretty impossible to communicate to others those ideas 'whereof we ourselves are not possess-ed of,' than the following funereal discourse, which was recently delivered in the Florida House of Representatives. The duty of making it was voluntarily assumed, and even insisted upon, by the speaker, to the no small wonder of the House, his utter incompetency being notorious:

'MR. SPEAKER: Sir! Our fellow citizen, Mr. SILAS HIGGINS, who was lately a member of this branch of the Legislature, is dead, and he died yesterday in the forenoon. He had the brown-creaters, (bronchitis was meant,) and was an uncommon individual. His character was good up to the time of his death, and he never lost his woice. He was fifty-six year old, and was taken sick before he died at his boarding-house, where board can be had at a dollar and seventy-five cents a week, washing and lights included. He was an ingenus *creetur*, and in the early part of his life had a father and mother. He was an officer in our state militia since the last war, and was brave and polite: and his uncle, TIMOTHY HIGGINS, belonged to the Revolutionary war, and was commissioned as lieutenant by General WASHINGTON, first President and commander-in-chief of the army and navy of the United States, who died at Mount Vernon, deeply lamented by a large circle of friends, on the 14th of December, 1799, or thereabout, and was buried soon after his death, with military honors, and several guns was bu'st in firing salutes.

'Sir! Mr. SPEAKER: General WASHINGTON presided over the great continental Sanhedrim and political meeting that formed our constitution: and he was indeed a first-rate good man. He was first in war, first in peace, and first in the hearts of his countrymen: and, though he was in favor of the United States' Bank, he was a friend of edication: and from what he said in his farewell address, I have no doubt he would have voted for the tariff of 1846, if he had been alive, and had n't ha' died sometime beforehand. His death was considered, at the time, as rather premature, on account of its being brought on by a very hard cold.

'Now, Mr. SPEAKER, such being the character of General WASHINGTON, I motion that we wear crape around the left arm of this Legislature, and adjourn until to-morrow morning, as an emblem of our respects for the memory of S. HIGGINS, who is dead, and died of the brown-creaters yesterday in the forenoon!'

WE wish to embalm this eulogy in these pages as a fine specimen of the '*Ironic Style*' of forensic eloquence.

'THE cry is still they' *go*—the crowded ships for California! Every steamer that arrives, bringing the 'precious metal,' returns with hundreds upon hundreds of eager adventurers after the 'dust,' beside inciting all sorts of water-craft and all sorts of people to follow in their wake: while innumerable land-companies and caravans are moving onward to the same land of promise. Ah! how few of these gold-seekers think of the discomforts, the privations, the perils, they may have to encounter!—or how many who have gone, with light and eager hearts, before them, worn down by disease and suffering, have 'laid them down in their last sleep!' And there, by the bleak sierra's side, or the rushing river's bank, they rest in their distant graves:

'No stone nor monumental cross
Tells where their mouldering ashes lie,
Who sought for gold and found it dross!'

THAT was an unfortunate member of the English Parliament whose seat, when Secretary, was the outside one, next to a passage-way. He said that so many members used to come perpetually to whisper to him, and the buzz of importunity was so heavy and continuous, that before one claimant's words had got out of his ear, the demand of another forced its way in, till the ear-drum, being overcharged, absolutely burst: which, he said, turned out conveniently enough, as he was then obliged to stuff the organ tight, and tell every gentleman that his physician had directed him not to use *that* ear at all, and the other as little as possible! Some of our office-givers had better adopt a similar ruse.

IN some grave-yards one shall scarcely see a stone that has not a pious verse, or a passage from Scripture, after the general inscription: and that these are not always appropriate, or in the best taste, we have sometimes shown in the KNICKERBOCKER. The following inscription may be seen on a grave-stone in the county of Greene, in this State: 'Here lies the body of JOHANNES SMITH, aged sixty-four years and two months. '*Go thou and do likewise!*'' Comprehensive, that!

'*The Inner Life of Man,*' delivered by Mr. CHARLES HOOVER, at Newark, New Jersey, is an admirable performance. From it we derive the following beautiful passage, which we commend to the heart of every lover of his kind: 'It is a maxim of patriotism never to despair of the republic. Let it be the motto of our philanthropy never to despair of our sinning, sorrowing brother, till his last lingering look upon life has been taken, and all avenues by which angels approach the stricken heart are closed and silent forever. And in such a crisis, let no counsel be taken of narrow, niggard sentiment. When in a sea-storm some human being is seen in the distant surf, clinging to a plank, that is sometimes driven nearer to the shore, and sometimes carried farther off; sometimes buried in the surge, and then rising again, as if itself struggling like the almost hopeless sufferer it supports, who looks sadly to the shore as he rises from every wave, and battling with the billow, mingles his cry for help with the wild, mournful scream of the sea-bird: Nature, in every bosom on the shore, is instinct with anxious pity for his fate, and darts her sympathies to him over the laboring waters. The child drops his play-things, and old age grasps its crutch and hurries to the spot; and the hand that cannot fling a rope is lifted to heaven for help. What though the sufferer be a stranger, a foreigner, an *enemy* even? Nature in trouble, in consternation, shrieks '*He is a man!*' and every heart and hand is prompt to the rescue!'

IT is amusing enough to remark the ignorance of town-bred children of the commonest matters of country life. A friend tells us that a little girl from the metropolis, who had visited a country town not a thousand miles from

New-York, was filled with surprise at the sight of a girl milking a cow. 'I did n't know that you did it *that* way!' she exclaimed, with 'round-eyed wonder:' 'I thought they took hold of the cow's tail and pumped the milk out of her! What's she got so long a tail for?' *There* was a wise child for this 'enlightened nineteenth century!'

Hearing faintly, just now, from the nursery overhead, the faithful nurse Mary-Ann rocking and plaintively singing to the little girl of two years in her arms, who is very fair and dear in the eyes and hearts of those who love her best, we opened the sanctum-door into the hall, and listened to hear the melody take shape in these words:

'Rock of Ages! cleft for me,
Let me hide myself in Thee!
Let the water and the blood
From Thy riven side which flowed
Be of Sin the double cure:
Cleanse me from its guilt and power!

'Not the labors of my hands
Can fulfil Thy law's commands:
Could my zeal no respite know,
Could my tears forever flow,
All for sin could not atone:
Thou must save, and Thou alone!

'Nothing in my hand I bring,
Simply to THY cross I cling:
Naked, come to THEE for dress,
Helpless, look to THEE for grace:
Foul, I to the Fountain fly,
Wash me, SAVIOUR! or I die!

'While I draw this fleeting breath,
When my eyes are closed in death,
When I soar to worlds unknown,
To meet THEE on THY judgment throne,
ROCK OF AGES! cleft for me,
Let me hide myself in THEE!'

Now as we closed the door, and resumed the pen, we were conscious of a glow of gratitude in our bosom, that GOD had made the heart of Woman tender and loving of infancy and childhood, and that the delegated guardian of our own little lambs reverently remembered the GOOD SHEPHERD, into whose fold we hope they shall one day be gathered.

DID you never meet with a condensing conversationist, like DICKENS's 'Mrs. GAMP?' We have heard many an old female gossip 'lump' the subjects of conversation in precisely the manner of that gentle and temperate nurse. Here is a fair specimen of her power of compression, and of her skill in hitting two or more birds with one stone:

'Now ain't we rich in beauty this here joyful afternoon, I'm sure! I knows a lady, which her name, I'll not deceive you, Mrs. CHUZZLEWIT, is

HARRIS; her husband's brother bein' six foot three, and marked with a mad bull in WELLINGTON boots upon his left arm, on account of his precious mother havin' been worrited by one into a shoemaker's shop, when in a sitiwation which blessed is the man as has his quiver full of sech, as many times I 've said to GAMP when words has roge betwixt us on account of the expense: and often have I said to Mrs. HARRIS, 'Oh, Mrs. HARRIS, Ma'am! your countenance is quite a angel's!'—which, but for pimples, it would be. 'No, SAIREY GAMP,' says she, 'you best of hard-workin' and industrious creeturs as ever was underpaid at any price, which underpaid you are—quite diff'rent. HARRIS had it done afore marriage at ten-and-six,' she says, 'and wore it faithful next his heart till the color run, when the money was declined to be give back, and no arrangement could be come to. But he never said it was a angel's, SAIREY, wotever he might have thought. If Mrs. HARRIS's husband was here now,' said Mrs. GAMP, looking round, and chuckling as she dropped a general courtesy, 'he'd speak out plain, he would, and his dear wife would be the last to blame him: for if ever a woman lived as know'd not wot it was to form a wish to pizon them as had good looks, and had no reagion give her by the best of husbands, Mrs. HARRIS is that 'ev'nly dispogician!'

A SHAKER friend at Hancock told us recently that he saw LORENZO DOW 'walking among the tombs,' alone, and muttering to himself, early one morning, in the principal grave-yard of a village in Connecticut. He soon collected a great number of lookers-on, when he mounted the stone-wall, and exclaimed in his peculiar voice: 'One year from this day I shall preach on this spot at six o'clock in the morning. And I want you to know that when I *say* six, I *mean* six: I do n't mean seven, nor eight.' Of course the news of this appointment soon spread 'through all the region of the country round about.' Just twelve months from that day, at precisely six in the morning, and in presence of more than twenty thousand people, LORENZO rose from the long rank grass of the grave-yard, where he had been sleeping, mounted the wall, and preached a fantastic, quaint, yet eloquent discourse, 'which will never be forgotten,' said our informant, 'by any who heard it.'

IT has been snowing since last night's gloaming: a soft, warm, driving, feathery snow: we felt a premonition of it 'in our bones' last evening, while we were scribbling: and this morning, lo! the bare trees in the street are all piled up with the 'gently-frozen rain:' so are the window-shutters and the lamp-posts; and there is a muffled sound of shovelling snow from the balconies, steps, and side-walks; and the ringing laughter of children, amid the faint banging of window-shutters in the gusty but attempered wind, is also heard: 'Young KNICK.' among them, too, with a pair of paternal boots, ('a world too wide' for his little 'supporters,') which he longs to be big enough to wear. Ah, well-a-day! 'When I am *a man?*' is the poetry of Childhood: 'When I was *a boy,*' is the poetry of Age!

A NORTHERN correspondent sends us the following, which was suggested by the 'Number twelve, pegged heel' anecdote in our last gossipry: 'An amazing pair of feet appeared in the bar-room of an ambitious village-inn, late one evening, the owner of which inquired anxiously for the boot-black. The bell rang nervously, and in a moment a keen Yankee illustrator of 'DAY AND MARTIN'S best' popped into the room. 'Bring me a jack!' exclaimed the man of great 'under-standing.' The waiter involuntarily started forward, but chancing to catch a glimpse of the boots, he stopped short, and after another and closer examination said, with equal twang and emphasis: 'I say yeöu, *you* aint a-goin' to leave this world in a hurry; you 've got too good a hold onto the ground. Want a boot-jack, eh? Why, bless your soul, there aint a boot-jack on airth big enuff for *them* boots! I do n't b'lieve that a jack-*ass* could get 'em off.' 'My stars! man!' cried our friend of the big feet, 'what 'll I do? I can't get my boots *off* without a jack?' 'I tell you what *I* should do,' replied 'BOOTS,' 'if they was *mine:* I should walk back to the *fork of the road*, and pull 'em off there! *That* would fetch 'em, I guess!' '

WE have had a taste of Winter: and we are ready to make affidavit, that sleighing is one of its greatest delights. There is scarcely any scene of *life*, that can surpass the bustle and excitement of a great city, in sleighing time.

Merry bells; gliding 'cutters,' sleighs, '*pungs*'—every thing that has runners, and can be drawn by cattle—bright faces, scores of parties, huddled in sweet hay, under warm buffalo-skins: mulled wine: what a delicious assemblage of pleasant matters! Reader, did you never engage in a sleigh-ride? Then is the elixir of life by you untasted. Go out on a *mild* morning in winter, ten miles from the city, over a well-trodden road, after a deep snow, which a slight north-east mist, dying away at last in a southern lull, makes damp and glib! Mark the brown woods: the blue hills, pale, clear, and stately in the distance: the imprisoned rivers, where the skater wheels on his shining heel; the whitened plains; the clouds, richly bedight with every hue! 'Tis a sight to remember:

——— 'Go when the rains
Have glazed the snow, and clothed the trees with ice;
While the slant sun of February pours
Into the bowers a flood of light. Approach!
The encrusted surface shall upbear thy steps,
And the broad arching portals of the grove
Welcome thy entering. Look! the mossy trunks
Are cased in the pure crystal: each light spray,
Nodding and tinkling in the breath of heaven,
Is studded with its trembling water drops,
That stream with rainbow radiance as they move:
But round the parent stem, the long low boughs
Bend in a glittering ring, and arbors hide
The grassy floor. Oh! you might deem the spot
The spacious cavern of the virgin mine,

Deep in the womb of earth — where the gems grow,
And diamonds put forth radiant rods, and bud
With amethyst and topaz — and the place
Lit up most royally, with the pure beam
That dwells within them. Or haply the vast hall
Of fairy palace, that outlasts the night,
And fades not in the glory of the sun:
Where crystal columns send forth slender shafts
And crossing arches: and fantastic aisles
Wind from the sight in brightness, and are lost
Among the crowded pillars. Raise thine eye:
Thou seest no cavern roof, no palace vault:
There the blue sky and the white drifting cloud
Look in. Again the wildered fancy dreams
Of spouting fountains, frozen as they rose,
And fixed, with all their branching jets, in air,
And all their sluices sealed. All, all is light —
Light without shade!

APRIL has come again: and the kite-season has opened with great activity. Did you ever remark, when Nature begins to waken from her winter-sleep; when the woods 'beyond the swelling floods' of the rivers begin to redden; when the snow has left us, and the city-trees are *about* leave-ing; when the first airs of spring assume their natural blandness; when ladies are out with their 'spring hats' and carmen with their spring-carts; how innumerous kites begin to thicken in the air? Yonder a big unwieldy fellow rises with calm dignity, trailing his long tail with great propriety behind him; here a little bustling creature ducks and dives, coquetting first on this side, then on that; until finally turning two or three somersets, it almost reaches the earth; but soon rises at a tangent, and sails far up into the bright blue firmament. Look! the air is full of them! It is a charming amusement, this kite-flying of the boys. We greatly affect it, even now, although we are 'out of our 'teens!' There is something ethereal in it; something that lifts up the young admiration.

> 'To that blue vault and sapphire wall
> That overhangs and circles all,'

and the mysterious realm that lies beyond its visible confines. Our metropolitan juveniles do n't know how to construct 'em. Thin, tissue-paper things, with no shape to them beyond that of a confused sexagon, no place for a head, and less for a tail, these are the machines you see fluttering and bobbing, ducking and sidling, in the sky of Gotham. How unlike the walnut-bow and cedar-shaft kite of the ked'ntry; with its red-worsted wings 'a flap-pink in the hair,' as YELLOWPLUSH says, its firmament of bright paper-stars gleaming in the sun; its long flaunting tail moving gracefully with the mass above it, its tasselled end waving like the tail-fin of a fish, that gracefullest of moving things. Ah! *those* were the kites; and it was from such specimens of 'high art' that we derived our love of them, which to this day has never left us; as many a lad can testify, who has been flying kites in our 'beat,' as we daily wend to and from the sanctum. We confidently ask our juvenile friends, did we ever see a kite, howsoever small or ignoble, lodged in a tree, or on a telegraph wire, or twisted round a telegraph-pole, or a chimney, without rendering immediate and 'valuable assistance?' Never!—and if the dyspeptic Wall-street broker, who called the attention of his sneering chum the other morning to 'Old KNICK.' descending a tree, a disabled kite in his hand, and a 'solution of continuity' in his trowserloons, will call up in our street, we will give him a little illustration of the 'luxury of doing good.' The bright, golden-haired boy who owned that kite, Mr. BROKER, knows how to be grateful; and if we should hereafter ever flourish in Wall-street, in your line, he would send us the best of shaving-'paper' to be had in 'the street;' and we can tell you too, Mr. POLITICIAN, that if in the progress of events, we should chance to be 'up' for some office in the gift of this our good old KNICKERBOCKER city, that lad would be 'good for' fifty votes. We can only say, that once *in* a municipal office, of the proper description, our best exertions shall not be wanting to 'put down' the telegraph-poles and wires. Electricity is a 'good institution,' no doubt, and enables us to 'enjoy our murders' in the morning papers to a greater extent than formerly; but telegraphs were never intended to interfere with the 'vested rights' of boys engaged in kite-flying: never! The destruction in this branch of business is greatly increasing. Look at the ragged skeletons, the almost fossil remains, that flap and writhe upon the wires and posts, where they have been gibbetted — 'lean, rent and beggared by the strumpet wind!' 'What 'underlies' all this evil? The telegraph system. Boys, 'To the poles! down with the poles!' should be the rallying cry. They are aristocratic: they are unconstitutional: they are worse than the 'WILMOT proviso!' Such and so many have been the wrecks of kites, 'sailing on the high seas of air,' that juvenile enterprise has been diverted to other channels; and a virulent eruption of whip-tops, 'groaning under the lash,' has broken out, and is spreading all over the metropolis; driving the aged from the walks, invading the delicate feet and ankles of our lovely female pedestrians, and playing the very deuce with the interior of their beautiful white under-dresses.

NUMBER TWELVE.

REFINEMENT OF IMPUDENCE: COMING-ON OF SPRING: WHAT IS GOING ON 'NOW': A 'DUMB ORATOR': THE ORNAMENTAL SEMPSTRESS: LIFE'S 'COMPENSATION': MONITORY 'MERACLES': LINES BY 'LORD NOZOO': THE MYSTERY OF SPRING: A LOCOMOTIVE ANTAGONIST: A 'MISTY' PUN: CRISPIN NONPLUSSED: A 'PATCHED-UP' SERMON: A PROTESTED REFERENCE: YANKEE 'CUTENESS IN WALL-STREET: A MODERN SACRED PORTRAIT: A DUBIOUS EULOGY: 'OLD KNICK'S.' PREDICTION: SWEARING 'IN NAME': FUNERAL-TREES OF THE INDIANS.

IN olden times there was a distinct class of itinerants in New-England, who were called 'cider-beggars.' One of them, on a Sunday morning, called at a farm-house, and finding only the 'woman of the house' at home, was quite importunate in his demands for 'Old-Orchard.' He was firmly and perseveringly denied. As a last resort, he reminded the pious lady that she should remember the Scriptural injunction to entertain strangers, 'for thereby many had entertained angels unawares.' 'I will risk that,' said she: 'for who ever heard of an angel going about Sunday morning begging for cider!'

'I advise you to go to work,' said an American in London to a beggar, who was pertinaciously beseeching him for a shilling: 'you are a hearty, hale fellow: I advise you to go to work.' 'I asked you for your *money:* I did n't ask you for your *advice!*' was the cool reply. Almost as impudent as the Spanish mounted beggar in Valparaiso, who replied to the remark of a pedestrian traveller, 'Why, Sir, you come to beg of me, who am compelled to go on foot, while you ride on horseback!' 'Very true, Sir; and I have the more *need* to beg, for I have to support my horse and myself too: so be so good as to hand over!' So *very* reasonable was this proposition, that it was at once complied with!

'COLD winter-ice is fled and gone,
And Summer brags on every tree:
The red-breast peeps among the throng
Of wood-brown birds that wanton be.'

Yes: and now how pleasant to the husbandman is 'all the land about, and all the flowers that blow:' the springing grass, the budding-trees, the smell of the fresh-ploughed earth, the transparent briskness of the spring-tide air! Season of hope and promise to the independent, happy cultivator of the soil! As a quaint old English poet says:

'THE earthe to entertaine him
Puts on his best arraye;
The loftie trees and lowly shrubbs
Likewise are fresh and gaye:

The birds to bid him welcome
  Doe warble pleasant notes:
The beaste, the fielde, the forest
  Cast off theire winter coates.'

DID you ever have the thought of WHAT IS NOW—at the moment while you happen to *think* that you are thinking—in Event and in Nature, in various and far-divided parts of the world? Say of scenery, for example: your imagination shall take you to the vast crackling ice-fields of Norway, or the rushing maëlstrom, circling and eddying day and night, as it 'sweeps its awful cycle:' or the vast Niagara cataract rolling its solemn roaring floods to Ontario and the Atlantic; or the sublime rocky heights that lie between us and the Pacific, and the boundless prairie-fields that stretch away from their 'giant feet:' or some transcendent villa in Italy, sleeping in the purple air under Alpine shadows, with groups of figures, such as are seen in antique marbles: or in some kindred scene in India, where the evening's breath is oppressive with perfume, and the rudest sound that breaks the stillness is the sweet coo of the wood-pigeon, or the sudden flight of a flock of gay parrots: or where the blessed Nile distributes along the vale of Egypt the gifts of the MOST HIGH, or the minarets rise from the midst of golden clusters of cassia-trees: or where the Arab gathers his harvest of yellow dates, or with the remote inhabitants of countries that the sun delays to look upon? Did you ever *think* of Nature in this way, at one and the same moment?—and in the like manner of Events? In one country, fierce battles raging; in another, the people just beginning to rejoice in the beams of peace; here national happiness and tranquillity; there discord and grief; a land 'rent with civil feuds, and drenched in fraternal blood?'

It is generally known, we believe, that a deaf person by watching the motions of a speaker's lips can understand what one is saying. We have heard of a Quaker woman, who was deaf, who used regularly to go to meeting, and without hearing a single word, could nevertheless report every thing that was said. One 'First-day' she came home without being able to give any account of the discourse. Her vision was impaired: and when asked in relation to the 'exercise,' she replied: 'I can't tell any thing about it: I went to meeting and forgot my spectacles!'

Read this, O daughter of Wealth! and ponder it well. Let it sink into your heart of hearts, and be the means of awakening there some sympathy for a toiling, suffering sister, who by no fault of hers is the serf she is:

'HARK, that rustle of a dress,
Stiff with lavish costliness;
Here comes one whose cheeks would flush
But to have her garments brush
'Gainst the girl whose fingers thin
Wove the weary broidery in:
And in midnight's chill and mirk
Stitched her life into the work:
Bending backward from her toil,
Lest her tears the silk might soil:
Shaping from her bitter thought
Heart's-ease and Forget me-not:
Satirizing her despair
With the emblems woven there!'

These lines, which would do honor to any poet in Christendom, are from the pen of JAMES RUSSELL LOWELL.

WE do not often envy any human being: but we confess to having entertained something of this feeling toward the possessor of a beautiful house and charming grounds, which we pass daily, in a fashionable quarter of the town, during the pleasant October days. But one morning we saw the owner among his grapes and flowers and fountains: a tall, care-worn, thin-visaged man, who stood tremblingly on 'his pins' and surveyed his beautiful possessions. Ah! thought we, there is a 'compensation' in every thing. 'What pleasure can it be to thee,' says an eloquent divine, 'to wrap the living skeleton in purple, and wither alive in cloth-of-gold, when the clothes serve only to upbraid the uselessness of thy limbs, and the rich fare only reproaches thee, and tantalizes the weakness of thy stomach! Sir 'let us to our mutton,' with that good digestion which waits on an appetite that is most like a hungry anaconda's.

A FRIEND of ours from the South, mentioned the other day a funeral sermon which he heard in North Carolina not long since, that set even our associate OWL a-winking. Parson S——, a rather eccentric character, was called upon to 'preach the funeral' of a hard case, named RANN, which he did in the following unique style: 'My beloved brethren and sistern: ef our dear departed brother RANN would a-wanted somebody to come here, and tell lies about him, and make him out a better man than he war, he would n t a-chose *me* to 'preach his funeral.' No, my brethren, he wanted to be held up as a burnin' and a shinin' light to warn you from the error of your ways. He kept horses, and he run'd 'em; he kept chickens, and he fou't 'em; he kept women, and there sits his widow who can prove it. (The widow sat directly in front of the pulpit, and here gave an affirmatory nod.) Our dear departed brother had many warnin's, brethren. The first warnin' was when he broke his leg, but he still went on in the error of his ways. The second warnin' was when his son PETE hung himself in jail; and the last and greatest warnin' of all was when he died himself!' The preacher enlarged on these topics until he had sunk RANN so low that his hearers began to doubt whether he would ever succeed in getting him up again, and, as is usual in 'funerals,' landing him safely in ABRAHAM's bosom. This was the object of the second part of the sermon, which started off thus: 'My brethren, there 'll be great meracles, *great* meracles in HEAVEN. And the first meracle will be, that many you expect to find there you won't *see* there. The people that go round with long faces, makin' long prayers, won't be there; and the second meracle will be, that many you do n't expect to find there, as perhaps some won't expect to find our dear departed brother RANN, you 'll see there: and the last and greatest meracle will be, to find *yourselves* there!' 'There is not one single word of exaggeration,' said the narrator, 'in this. It is a literal transcript.'

THE following lines were penned by Lord Nozoo, in 167–. They first appeared in the ———, about the time of the reign of the first ———, in England:

'FOR years, upon a mountain's brow,
A hermit lived — the LORD knows how.

'Plain was his dress, and coarse his fare;
He got his food — the LORD knows where.

'His prayers were short, his wants were few;
He had a friend — the LORD knows who.

'No care nor trouble vexed his lot;
He had a wish — the LORD knows what.

'At length this holy man did die;
He left the world — the LORD knows why.

'He 's buried in a gloomy den,
And he shall rise — the LORD knows when!'

HAVE you never felt, just at the season of mid-March, the force and truth of the ensuing observations? Our only wonder is, that another should have expressed so perfectly our own thoughts and emotions, a hundred times awakened and experienced, in the early 'spring-time of the year:' 'There is a certain melancholy in the evenings of early spring, which is among those influences of nature the most universally recognized, the most difficult to explain. The silent stir of reviving life, which does not yet betray signs in the bud and blossom; only in a softer clearness in the air, a more lingering pause in the slowly lengthening day; a more delicate freshness and balm in the twilight atmosphere; a more lovely yet still unquiet note from the birds, settling down into their coverts; the vague sense under all that hush, which still outwardly wears the bleak sterility of winter — of the busy change hourly, momently at work — renewing the youth of the world, re-clothing with vigorous bloom the skeletons of things; all these messages from the heart of Nature to the heart of Man may well affect and move us. But why with melancholy? No thought on our part connects and construes the low, gentle voices. It is not *Thought* that replies and reasons: it is *Feeling* that hears and dreams. Examine not, O child of man! — examine not that mysterious melancholy with the hard eyes of thy reason: thou canst not impale it on the spikes of thy thorny logic, nor describe its enchanted circle by problems conned from thy schools. Borderer thyself of two worlds — the Dead and the Living — give thine ear to the tones, bow thy soul to the shadows, that steal, in the season of change, from the dim Border Land!'

'Not long since,' writes an old friend and correspondent, 'as I was returning from Buffalo, I was amused, while the cars made a momentary stop, at a demonstration made by a crazy man, on his way to the State Lunatic Asylum, at Utica. He was standing on the track, in front of the 'iron-horse:' 'You think you are something!' he said, looking wildly at the locomotive, and assuming a boxing attitude; 'but look o' here: I can whip you! I 've flogged the fiery bulls of Bashan, and broken their horns off! Say! — do n't you stand there, whistling and smoking, like a blackguard in a bar-room: jest jump to *me*, and *I'll* take the conceit out of you, you d——d old *cooking-stove on wheels!*'

ELLIOTT, the eminent portrait-painter, 'laid himself out' on a pun the other morning, as he was walking down town with a friend, in a faintly-drizzling mist, so fine as scarcely to be perceptible to the naked eye: 'If it should stop altogether,' said 'CHARLIE,' 'it would n't be *missed!*' This has been carefully kept from the daily journals, and 'now first appears in print.' P. S. Mr. ELLIOTT has recovered, and may still be found at his rooms, 'first floor from the roof' of the Art-Union Building, where may also be seen numerous new pictures from his industrious and facile pencil; each one informed with that perfectly life-like individuality of expression, whether in color, lineament, position, or drapery, which will render his portraits as lasting as the canvas upon which they are painted.

WE heard to-day a laughable '*Anecdote of a Man with a big Foot.*' He was a Buffalonian, who must be living now, for a man with so good a hold upon the ground is not likely to 'drop off' in a hurry. He stepped one day into the small shop of a boot-maker's in the flourishing capital of old Erie, and asked CRISPIN if he could make him a pair of boots. Looking at his long splay pedal extremities, and then glancing at a huge uncut cow-hide that hung upon the wall, he said, 'Well, yes, I guess so.' 'What time will you have them done? To-day is Monday.' 'Well, it 'll depend on circumstances; I guess I can have 'em done for you by Saturday.' On Saturday, therefore, the man called for his boots: 'Have you got 'em done?' said he, as he entered the little shop. 'No, I have n't — I could n't; it has rained every day since I took your measure.' 'Rained!' exclaimed the astonished patron; 'well, what of that? What had *that* to do with it?' 'What had THAT to do with it?' echoed CRISPIN; 'it had a *good deal* to do with it. When I make your boots *I 've got to do it out doors*, for I have n't room in my shop, and I can't work out doors in rainy weather!' It was the same man of 'large understanding' whom the porters used to bother so, when he landed from a steamer. They would rush up to him, seize hold of his feet, saying, 'Where shall I take your *baggage*, Sir? Where 's this *trunk* to go, Sir?'

WE shall not be so indiscreet as to name the popular clergyman against whom a correspondent inveighs bitterly, in that, 'having heard great things of him, he went to hear him, and came away disappointed.' The subjoined lines are quoted at the conclusion of our correspondent's commentary, as 'expressing exactly what the writer desired to describe.' If the limning be faithful, the divine must have won the suffrages of those who affect 'interesting preachers:'

'O YE ruling Powers
Of Poesy sublime, give me to sing
The splendors of that sermon! The bold a-hem,
The look sublime, that beamed with confidence,
The three wipes with the cambric handkerchief;
The strut — the bob — and the impressive thump
Upon the HOLY BOOK!
'No notes were there:
No, not a scrap. All was intuitive,
Pouring like water from a flashing fountain,
With current unexhausted. Now the lips
Protruded, and the eye-brows lowered amain,
Like KEAN'S in dark OTHELLO.
'But let us hear
Somewhat of this same grand and flowery sermon.
Aha! there comes the rub! 'T was made of *scraps!*
Sketches from Nature; from old JOHNSON some,
And some from JOSEPH ADDISON and GOLDSMITH;
BLAIR, WILLIAM SHAKSPERE, YOUNG'S Night Thoughts, The Grave;
GILLESPIE on the Seasons; even the plain
Bold energy of ANDREW THOMPSON here
Was pressed into the jumble. Plan or system
Had it none: no gleam of mind or aim;
'A thing of shreds and patches!' Yet the blare
Went on for twenty minutes, haply more.'

THE subjoined anecdote of a demagogue-candidate for the Legislature of a western State, a man of low moral stature, has been sent us by a new correspondent: 'There was a 'stump-speaking,' and ABNER G. D—— had the platform, enlightening 'the unterrified' long and loudly. 'Fellow-citizens,' said he, 'I now come to a slanderous rumor which has been most dastardly circulated against me from one end of the county to the other. My enemies, not content with endeavoring to ruin my political prospects, have assassin-like attempted to blast my good name by their insidious reports.' 'ABNER' then stated what the rumor was, and continued: 'I rejoice, fellow-citizens, to have it in my power instantly to fasten the lie upon this malicious and atrocious slander. I see among you one of the most estimable citizens of this county, whose character for truth and integrity is above all question. Squire SCHOOLER, to whom I allude, is acquainted with all the facts, and I call on him here to state whether this rumor is true or false. I pause for a reply.' Whereupon Squire SCHOOLER slowly arose, and in his strong, slow, and sonorous voice said: 'I rather think you *did* it, ABNER!' You old scoundrel!' exclaimed ABNER, 'why do you interrupt me, while I am discussing great constitutional questions, with your low personalities?' And he accompanied this objurgatory exclamation with such a 'surge' of gesticulation, that he stepped back beyond the platform, fell backward on a big dog, amid the howls of which, and the deafening roars of the 'sovereigns,' the meeting was effectually broken up.

'If you wish to hear a little specimen of Yankee 'cuteness, just listen to this colloquy, which we heard the other day in the counting-house of a mercantile friend: 'A man kind o' picks up a good many idees abeöut. I larnt a few in Wall-street.' 'In Wall-street?' 'Yes; 'see, I studied it eöut while I was stage-drivin'. I got a little change together; did n't know where to place it; could n't hire it eöut hum, 'cause I was pleadin' poverty all the time; that, 'see, would n't deu: so I goes deöwn and claps it in the Dry Dock Bank; got five per cent., tew. Had a brother thair who was teller. One day I 'gin a check for fifty dollars: all right. At last the bank got in trouble: I had some four or five thousand dollars: I goes to my brother and draws eöut my money: he pays me in Bank of ——— notes. Well, I took 'em hum, but they forgot to take eöut my check of fifty dollars. So I goes, and sez I, 'I owe you fifty that you haint charged me; will you take your own notes?' 'Sartin,' sez they; so I pays 'em in notes that I bought at twenty-five off. 'That 's a good spec,' sez I; so I goes areönd and buys up abeöut tew hundred Dry Dock notes. When I got to the city I could n't pass 'em off. I tried a good many banks — no go. At last they creöwded me off the pavement in Wall-street, the creöwd was so big, and I stood in the middle of the street, and *cal'lated.* I've got the idea,' sez I; 'I 'll come country over 'em.' So I walked into the Bank of ———, took off my hat, and looked areöund as if did n't know what I was abeöut. I knowd the cashier; so he comes up: 'SAM!' sez he, 'what neöw? — how 's the family?' 'All well,' sez I; 'but what 's the matter with your banks? I do n't know who to depend on. Here 's your neighbor, the Dry Dock 's gone, and may-be *you 'll* go next; and I've got abeöut five thousand dollars of your money; and I guess I 'll come deöwn and draw the specie.' I expect I must a-looked as if I was frightened to death; for he said to-once, 'Deönt do that, SAM!' sez he; 'you 'll frighten the hull country, and they 'll come and run us.' 'Can't help it,' sez I: 'Here 's abeöut tew hundred dollars of the Dry Dock, and if I do n't get the money *somewhere* before I go hum, I 'll draw on you sëoon.' 'Heöw much?' sez he. 'Abeöut tew hundred.' 'We 'll take it, SAM,' sez he, 'and you keep our paper.' 'Well,' sez I, 'on that condition I 'll keep still.' I guess I made my twenty-five per cent. eöut of Wall-street *that* time, 'if I *am* Dutch,' as the sayin' is!' There is not a great deal of *honest* financiering done in Wall-street that is more shrewdly performed than was this 'fair business transaction.'

'I WAS walking through Trafalgar-Square in London, one morning,' said a travelled friend to us the other day, 'when I was accosted by a man who was selling an engraved picture of *Christ Examining the Tribute-Money*. He urged me so piteously to purchase one, that I was tempted to do so. I wish I had it now to show you. Our SAVIOUR was dressed in as natty a swallow-tailed coat as you ever saw in a tailor's report of the fashions; his pantaloons were strapped down over a pair of exquisite little boots, and he wore on his head a small low bell-crowned hat, much in fashion about that time. His apostles were dressed in the same fashion; only that it was evidently intended that the principal figure should in this respect quite exceed them. I thought of the value of 'keeping' in art, as I looked at that scriptural picture, and the text which it was supposed to illustrate; and, sacred as was the subject, I could not help guffawing obstreperously in the crowded square.'

WE have not encountered any thing better than the following vindication of a friend by a western editor, since the eulogy pronounced upon Mr. THOMAS HIGGINS and

General Washington by a member of the legislature of Florida. The friend in question had been arrested for stealing sheep: 'We have known Mr. Thomas for twelve years. Our acquaintance commenced with the great storm which blew down our grandfather's barn. At that time he was a young man in the prime of life, and we think raised the best marrow-fat peas we ever eat. He was a good mathematician, kind to the poor, and troubled with fits. In all the relations of a husband, father, uncle, and trustee of common lands, he has followed the direct standard of duty. Mr. Thomas is at this time forty-three years of age, slightly marked with the small-pox, an estimable citizen, a church-member, and a man of known integrity, for ten years. As to sheep-stealing, that he would have done it if he could get an opportunity, is without foundation in point of fact. Mr. Thomas could have stolen our lead-pencil several times, but he did n't do it.'

Fifteen years ago we placed upon record the following vaticination, in a review of Parker's Travels to the Rocky Mountains:

'No insurmountable barriers exist to the construction of a rail-road from the Atlantic to the Pacific. No greater elevations would need to be overcome than have been surmounted on the Portage and Ohio rail-road. *And the work will be accomplished.* Let this prediction be marked. This great chain of communication will be made with links of iron. The treasures of the earth, in that wide region, are not destined to be lost. The mountains of coal, the vast meadow-seas, the fields of salt, the mighty forests, with their trees two hundred and fifty feet in height, the stores of magnesia, the crystallized lakes of valuable salts, these were not formed to be unemployed and wasted. The reader is now living, who will make a rail-road trip across this vast continent. The granite mountain will melt before the hand of enterprise; valleys will be raised, and the unwearying fire-steed will spout his hot white breath, where silence has reigned since the morning hymn of young creation was pealed over mountain flood and field. The mammoth's bone, and the bison's horn, buried for centuries, and long since turned to stone, will be bared to the day by the laborers of the Atlantic and Pacific Rail-road Company: rocks which stand now as on the night when Noah's deluge first dried, will heave beneath the action of 'villanous saltpetre;' and where the prairie stretches away, 'like the round ocean, girdled with the sky,' with its wood-fringed streams, its flower-enamelled turf, and its herds of startled buffaloes, shall sweep the long hissing train of cars, crowded with passengers for the Pacific sea-board. The very realms of chaos and old night will be invaded; while in place of the swarm of wild beasts, or howl of wilder Indians, will be heard the lowing of herds, the bleating of flocks; the plough will cleave the sods of many a rich valley and fruitful hill, while 'from many a dark bosom shall go up the pure prayer to the GREAT SPIRIT.'

SOMEBODY (Captain DONOWHO, if we *must* give names) mentions an old saw-miller in Maine, whose profane ob-structure of the stream which 'carried' his mill was itself carried away by a sudden freshet. The mill was old; the machinery in its decadence; the whole establishment 'tottering to its fall.' The owner was regarding the 'flood-wood' of his fortunes with a sad and wistful eye, when a friendly by-stander consolingly said to him: 'Build *another:* 't wont take you three weeks to do it.' 'Ah,' said the *ci-devant* miller, looking at the old naked edifice, which had no more 'back-water' for a background, '*it aint worth a dam!*' Mentioning this the other evening to a friend, he said it reminded him of a d — m which stopped the waters of a river between the mountains in one of our northern States, and which, by a sudden 'fresh,' was swept away during the night. The owner of the works thereon was a well-known gentleman of honor and intellect, but irritable, notwithstanding, and apt at times to give vent to his aroused emotions. The neighbors, as usual, gathered around, awaiting the arrival of the owner, and speculating as to the manner and language he would adopt, under the strong provocation to his 'pheelinks.' He soon after arrived, and probably suspecting, from movements and signs about him, that the assembly was waiting for an out-break, very coolly surveyed the rushing river, and the sluice-way it had opened, and turning to the people with a bland smile, he said: 'I think, neighbors, you will all agree with me that this river ought to be dam—d!'

THE voyager up the Saint MARY'S river, after reaching a distance of some thirty miles from the Huron, will begin to observe, crowning the green ridges that rise amphitheatrically from the stream, and at intervals of five or seven miles, single trees of great height, standing like verdant cones above the general level of the unbroken forest around them. The aboriginal tradition is, that these are the funeral-trees of Indian chiefs who have been buried beneath them. When a great 'brave' died it was the custom of the survivors to bend or 'sway' to the ground a tall young tree, and in the cavity occupied by the displaced roots and earth, to lay the body of the dead warrior, and then release the tree, to spring back to its former position. WHITTIER, in a poem several years since in the

KNICKERBOCKER, described a similar observance in the instance of a Sokokis chief, on the banks of the Sebago lake, in the State of Maine:

'WITH grave, cold looks, all sternly mute,
They break the damp turf at its foot,
And bare its coiled and twisted root.

'They heave the stubborn trunk aside,
The firm roots from the earth divide —
The rent beneath yawns dark and wide.

'And there the fallen chief is laid,
In tasselled garb of skins arrayed,
And girdled with his wampum-braid.

'The silver cross he loved is pressed
Beneath the heavy arms, which rest
Upon his scarred and naked breast.

''Tis done: the roots are backward sent,
The beechen tree stands up unbent —
The Indian's fitting monument!

'When of that sleeper's broken race
Their green and pleasant dwelling-place
Which knew them once, retains no trace:

'Oh! long may sunset's light be shed
As now upon that beech's head —
A green memorial of the dead!

'There shall his fitting requiem be,
In northern winds, that cold and free
Howl nightly in that funeral tree.

'To their wild wail the waves which break
Forever round that lonely lake
A solemn under-tone shall make!

'And who shall deem the spot unblessed
Where Nature's younger children rest.
Lulled on their sorrowing mother's breast?'

The western tradition, when related to us on board the little 'St. Clair' steamer, while she was struggling up the rapid rushing current of the St. MARY'S, brought instantly to mind the foregoing beautiful lines; and a single pencil-word, just seen on our little memoranda of some of the incidents of our last summer's memorable trip, has again brought the subject out from a back-shelf of Memory's 'catch-all.'

NUMBER THIRTEEN.

THE INEBRIATE — A WARNING: AN ORNAMENT TO SOCIETY: ANECDOTE OF HON. THOMAS CORWIN: A CHILD'S LAST 'GOOD-NIGHT': A RICH RESTAURANT 'CARTE': FLUCTUATIONS IN NATURE: FORE-RUNNERS AND GHOSTS: A 'DREADFUL SCED'NE' IN VERSE: THE 'POOR RICH MAN': BURCHARD ON TOBACCO: THE INFIDEL'S 'WORLD TO COME': 'FOUR TO THE POUND' — STRICT CONSTRUCTION: NEW BOTANICAL PLANTS: A RETORT COURTEOUS: A POETICAL QUANDARY: AN IMPROMPTU 'CROW-BAR'.

WALKING along the Battery, on our return this evening from a delightful trip down the Lower Bay, in the '*Orus*' steamer, we beheld a young man whom we had known many years since, but whom we had not seen for many months, zig-zag-ing along the middle walk, with a friendly supporter hold of each arm. He was 'boozy,' he was 'swipsed,' he was 'cut,' he was 'tight,' he was 'cizzled,' he was 'building,' he had 'a stone in his hat,' he was 'intoxicated' — *he was drunk!* He glanced at us with an unrecognizing, lack-lustre eye, and shambled on — his two friends seemingly ashamed of their burthen; an object of compassion to friends, of derision to foes; scrutinized by strangers, and stared at by fools. O! that the weak, the nervous, who 'feel a daily longing for some artificial aid to raise their spirits in society to the ordinary pitch of all around them without it,' could have seen that spectacle; could have seen that young man 'struggling with the billows that had gone over him!' Where were his pride, his self-respect, his love of the world's esteem? It has always seemed inexplicable to us, that a man with the garb and feelings of a gentleman, conscious of what belonged to the character, should go on from day to day rivetting the chains of habit, until at length he finds himself going down a precipice with open eyes and a passive will; seeing his destruction, without the power to stop it, yet feeling it all the way emanating from himself; bearing about the piteous spectacle of his own self-ruin, the 'body of death, out of which he cries with feebler and feebler outcry to be delivered;' until at last, forgetful of *all* self-respect, he falls into that taste for low society which is 'worse than pressing to death, whipping, or hanging,' and finally falls to rise no more. Wine, properly and moderately used, is 'a good familiar creature,' but 'every *inordinate* cup is unblessed, and the ingredient is a devil;' and he who cannot avoid, or finds himself in any degree approaching, the 'inordinate cup,' should eschew it utterly: for at the last it 'will bite like a serpent and sting like an adder!'

A FRIEND of ours, not long since in England, relates a characteristic anecdote of CHARLES LAMB, which he heard there, and which we think worth repeating here. At a dinner-table one evening, a sea-faring guest was describing a terrific naval engagement, of which he was a spectator, on board a British man-of-war. 'While I was watching the effects of the galling fire upon the masts and rigging,' said he, 'there came a cannon-ball, which took off both legs from a poor sailor who was in the shrouds. He fell toward the deck, but at that moment another cannon-ball whizzed over us, which, strange to say, took off both his arms, which fell upon deck, while the poor fellow's limbless trunk was carried overboard.' 'Heavens!' exclaimed LAMB; 'did n't you *save* him!' 'No,' replied the naval MUNCHAUSEN; 'he could n't swim, of course, and he sank before assistance could be rendered him.' 'It was a sad, sad loss!' said LAMB, musingly; 'if he *could* have been picked up, what *an ornament* to society he might have become!'

WE record here an anecdote of Hon. Secretary CORWIN, because it admirably illustrates the potency of forms' in political meetings, and the absence of '*entoosy-mussy*,' as BYRON would term it, in some partizan auditories. Mr. CORWIN, in the early part of his political career, had been addressing some ten or twelve thousand of his matter-of-fact fellow citizens, at a place called 'New-England Settlement,' in the Western Reserve. He never made a better speech, nor uttered one more impressively, in his life; but it was not interrupted during its delivery by a single encouraging word or gesture: and when it was finished, an awful pause ensued; until a tall thin Yankee, on the outskirts of the crowd, rose and said, in a thin drawling voice: 'Mr. Chairman, I move that, in consideration of the spirited and patriotic speech of Mr. COR-WINE, this meeting give him three cheers!' Another awful pause followed; when a little man jumped up on the other side of the crowd, and jerked out: 'I second that motion!' The chairman rose with great deliberation and dignity: 'Gentlemen,' said he, 'you have heard the resolution: it is moved and seconded, that in consideration of the spirited and patriotic speech which we have heard from Mr. COR-WINE, this meeting proceed to give him three cheers!' An irregular '*Hoorah!*' was returned, and then all was silence. The chairman rose again: 'The resolution, it should not be forgotten,' said he, 'contemplated *three* cheers; you will therefore now proceed to give a *second* cheer;' and a second 'cheer,' such as it was, was given; and a third followed, with the same forms; and the 'large and *enthusiastic* meeting' dispersed.

IF you are a mother or a father, reader, and hear nightly from rosy, innocent lips the prayer of childhood mentioned in the following account of the death of a missionary's little girl, you will feel in your 'heart of hearts' the touching pathos which it embodies. It is an extract from a letter of Rev. Mr. LAWRENCE, at Dindigul, in India, announcing the death of a lovely child, between three and four years of age: 'Dear LOUISA went as calmly to her last repose as the shutting up of a flower at twilight. As her sight began to fail, though about four o'clock in the afternoon, she said to me, '*Good night, father*,' her usual words on going to sleep, and then went on to repeat:

'Now I lay me down to sleep,
I pray the LORD my soul to kee — eo — p;
A — a — men!'

'And so she left us to weep and rejoice, and now to long almost for a reünion: not here; oh, no, not here! Sweet, blessed child! a more fitting prayer thou couldst not have offered, had thy lips been then, as now, the lips of an angel! Thou wert indeed lying down to sleep, and sweet shall be thy rest, for the LORD will keep thee: thou shalt sleep on HIS breast and wake in HIS arms. She did not live to say,

'IF I should die before I wake,
I pray the LORD my soul to take!'

but the LORD took her in the midst of her evening prayer,

when she mistook the darkness of death gathering over her for the shades of evening, and bidding her friends 'Good night,' calmly committed her sweet spirit to her heavenly FATHER's care.'

WE were not a little amused the other day, on sitting down with a friend at a 'foreign-kept' café, not a thousand miles from Broadway, at finding on our plate the annexed bill of fare. Some wag had obtained possession of one of its blank bill-heads, and by way of a parody upon the frequent errors committed at that restaurant in transferring French edibles to English, as well as by way of satire upon the 'entertainment' sometimes to be met with there, had substituted the following for the regular 'carte' of the day:

LIST OF VICTUALS

AND THINGS LYING UNCOOKED AND COOKED AT THIS CAFE-HOUSE.

	s.	*d.*
SOUP-Maigre, (four pails water to turnip and ingen,)	2	6
Soups from different theatres, ...	3	
Fishes (assorted sizes) biled, ...	2	6
Fishes' Balls, ...	2	
Exposed Frogs — naked, ...	3	
" " dressed, ...	4	
Fillet de Bœuf, Campanalogian sauce, ...	1	6
Line of an Old Bull, ...	2	
Round of Beef, ...	1	

Flat of Beef,	1	
Calvé's Head,	2	6
Rost Mutting, Pico sauce,	2	6
Spring Chickin,	6	6
Summer do.,	5	
Autumn do.,	10	
Winter do., (hard to keep,)	12	
Hay and Straw Berries,	1	
Extra Bread,		3
Extra Herald,		2
Root-beer, on draft, p'ts.,		6
Pot o' Stout, (Pôt de Robuste,)		8
Lobsters in the chell,	2	6
Oystees, ror or scalded,	1	
" without opening,	2	6
Bifstek de Mutting,	2	
Mutting Chaps,	1	6
Stewed Heels,	2	6
Swashingers,	1	
Cabidg, (ad lib.,)	7	
Indian Pudding, (made by OSCEOLA, rare,)	5	

Considering the juxtaposition of some of the above articles, and the syle of spelling, we have come to the conclusion that Mr. YELLOWPLUSH must be travelling *in cog.* in this 'wooden country.'

WE took a short 'sally-out' this morning ''cross lots toward the Hudson, from the Bloomingdale Road, with a protecting umbrella against the burning rays of the sun.

How hot and still it was! No sound came from the landscape, save where myriads of

> 'PITTERING grasshoppers, confus'dly shrill,
> Piped giddily along the glowing hill.'

Since we have come back, a cloud which was no bigger than a man's hand when we reached home, has proved to be pregnant with wind and rain, of which there has been a very 'general delivery:' and now, how different is the air! We have been thinking of what CARLYLE says somewhere: 'The expression of the fluctuations and modifications of feeling in the heart of the heavens is made audible and visible and tangible on their face and bosom. O Heavens! what have I not felt in a summer shower! The dry world all at once made dewy!'

'Do you believe in fore-runners?' asked a nervous lady of old Deacon J——. 'Yes Ma'am,' replied the Deacon; 'I 've *seen* them!' 'Bless me!' exclaimed the lady; 'do tell!' 'Yes,' continued the Deacon, fixing his eyes with a solemn stare on a dark corner of the room: '*I see one now!*' 'Mercy! mercy on me!' shrieked the lady; 'where!' 'There! there!' said the Deacon, pointing to where his eyes were directed. 'That cat, Ma'am, may be called a fore-runner, for she runs on all-fours!' Speaking of apparitions: that is rather a forcible argument urged against the theory of their existence by one of the characters in 'The Grimsby Ghost:' 'Ghosts be hanged! It 's too late in the day for 'em, by a whole century: they 're quite exploded; went out with the old witches: No, Sir; workmen may rise for higher wages; the sun may rise, and bread may rise, and the sea may rise, and the rising generation may rise, and all to some good or bad purpose; but that the dead and buried should rise, only to make one's hair rise, is more than I can credit. What should they rise for? Some say they come with messages or errands to the living; but they can't deliver 'em for want of breath, and can't execute 'em for the want of physical force. If you come up out of your grave to serve a friend, how are you to help him? And if it 's an enemy, what 's the use of appearing to him if you can't pitch into him?' To which an interlocutor replies, 'To show your *spirit*, of course;' and he goes on to declare *his* belief in ghosts; for he was 'knowing to' a case of the kind, where a figure-head of a vessel called the Brittania had appeared to a retired sea-captain in London, on the very night that she found a watery grave off Cape Horn!'

'COB'ME all my nab'rin peepil waäte
Whid'le I a d'n-dreadful sced'ne relate,
Of wod'n bright youth as e'er you see,
Was kid'l'd id'n Hartford by a tree,
Id'n Hartford by a tree!'

Now when we heard this affecting stanza suddenly sung, during a slight pause in the conversation, etc., of a pleasant evening party at B——, we pricked up our ears for the 'full and particular account' of the 'dreadful sced'ne,' so pathetically alluded to. S——, with befitting nasal twang, and 'linked sweetness long drawn out,' went on:

'Od'ne ISAAC ABBOTT was his nab'me,
Who late-ly id'nto Hartford came;
Residin' with his brother JAB'MES,
Od'ne day at nood'n went, as it seems,
At nood'n went, as it seems.

'To cut sob'me timber for a sled;
The snow bein' deep, he had to wade
Near forty rods to ad'n ash-tree;
The top was dry, as you shall see —
Was dry, as you shall see.

'He cut it off all frob'm the stub'mp,
The top bein' dry, threw back a chunk,
Which flew ad'nd hit-tim on his head,
Ad'nd crush'd hib'm, yet he was not dead —
Hib'm, yet he was not dead.

'There the poor suff'rer sed'nseless lay
Ad'l the remaid'nder of that day,
'Till Deacon JAB'MES ad'nd his sod'n,
Alarb'm'd, set out upon a rud'n,
Set out upon a rud'n.

'They sood'n behed'ld him with surprise,
Ad'nd gaz'd od'n hib'm with steadfast eyes;

They took hib'm up ad'nd bore hib'm hob'me,
Put hib'm to bed id'n a warb'm roob'm,
To bed id'n a warb'm roob'm.

'His fried'nds ad'nd na'bers gather'd round,
The sermon preached by Ed'lder BROWD'N:
His corpse with care were bord'ne away,
To biggle with its dative clay,
'Gle with its dative clay!'

'THERE are some people,' says a modern author who has a keen eye for the weaknesses and absurdities of 'the world,' 'there are some people, who have no reverence except for prosperity, and no eye for any thing beyond success.' These are the men who fasten on to rich folks so naturally, and whom the richer folks than themselves, for that very reason, always despise. These are the men who, when told that the young man next them at dinner, or whom they encounter at their club, has recently become the heir of half a million, regard him with an 'interest' that *he* sees through with half an eye, and speaks of elsewhere with an appropriate sneer. These men, who know their own fortuitous gains to be vastly overrated; whose affections rush out to meet and welcome money; whose sentiments awaken spontaneously toward the interesting possessors of it; these men do n't consider themselves at liberty to indulge in friendship for any individual who is not richer than themselves; in consequence of which, it is difficult to say whether they are most despised by those who are above or those who are below them in a pecuniary point of view; while the irrepressible self-consciousness that they are mere DOMBEYS makes them even more distasteful to themselves than to others. These are the '*poor rich men*' whom Miss SEDGWICK has so well described.

A CASUAL correspondent in Watertown, (N. Y.,) senas us the following extract from a temperance-lecture by BURCHARD, the eccentric 'revivalist,' lately delivered in that village. We mentioned in a recent anecdote the manner in which the speaker once obtained a quid of tobacco in church; and it seems but fair that we should set forth his subsequent trials in es-chewing the weed: 'I was once,' said he, 'an inveterate lover of tobacco, and I know how difficult it is to break off the habit of using it; still it *can be done.* I indulged in the use of the weed to a great excess; I *loved* it; but knowing that its effects were bad, and especially ill-becoming a minister of the gospel, I made one almighty resolve to quit it. With that resolution I took a tremendous 'cud,' which was to be my final wind-off. I chewed it and chewed it, and 'rolled it as a sweet morsel under my tongue,' and from one cheek to the other, for three weeks. 'Pears to me tobacco never tasted so good before; and I almost shed tears when I recollected that it was to be my last indulgence. When its strength was all gone, I threw it away: 'There, BURCHARD,' said I, 'there goes your last—your omega of quids!' Well, for a while it was very hard doing without it, and I was often sorely tempted to try it again. Old tobacco-chewers would pull out their rusty steel-boxes, give them a scientific snap, and say, 'BURCHARD, have a chew?'—and for a long time, whenever I heard the click of a tobacco-box, I involuntarily put my hand in my trowse's to get hold of my pig-tail. In fact I am afraid I sometimes blundered dreadfully in my sermons, my thoughts being more perhaps upon tobacco than upon the LORD. But I stuck to my resolution; and neither 'cavendish' nor 'pig-tail' has ever been between my teeth from that day to this!'

THE article entitled '*Infidelity in New-York*' magnifies, we must hope and believe, what would otherwise indeed be a 'dangerous moral enemy.' Infidelity, such as our correspondent describes, can gain few adherents. What is *substituted* for what is disbelieved, must prevent any great extension of such vague and wicked assumptions. 'Let any of those who renounce Christianity write fairly down in a book all the absurdities which they believe *instead* of it, and they will find that it requires more faith to reject Christianity than to embrace it:

'If all our hopes and all our fears
Were prisoned in life's narrow bound;
If, travellers in this vale of tears,
We saw no better world beyond;
Oh what could check the rising sigh,
What earthly thing could pleasure give?
Oh who would venture then to die —
Oh who would venture then to live?'

If men, says LACON, have been termed pilgrims, and life a journey, then we may add, that the Christian pilgrimage far surpasses all others in the following important particulars; in the goodness of the road, in the beauty of the prospects, in the excellence of the company, and in the vast superiority of the accommodation provided for the Christian traveller who has finished his course.

TALK about the 'progress of the age,' the 'barbarism of the past,' and the like! Where, in any country, save such as makes its own laws directly through the people, could an occurrence like the following take place? A legal friend of ours, passing recently through the charming village of Canandaigua, was struck with the appearance of an oblong frame building by the road-side, a little way out of the town, open by gratings on all sides, and presenting the appearance of an ornamental corn-house. He was attracted toward the spot by repeated calls from the interior; and on reaching it, what was his surprise to find the place occupied by four respectable citizens of the village! They were confined in the town-pound, hitherto a sort of 'sponging-house' for animals having no visible means of support, and indebted for past 'keep' to the corporation grounds. They were sadly in want of food, and their beards had assumed an appearance not unlike that of the gentleman's who staid so long at Jericho, beyond the termination of the 'long stage' from Dan to Beersheba. On inquiring the cause of their incarceration, our friend was informed that they were the Trustees of the village; that they had been confined there for more than a week, under a section of the 'Laws of New-York,' of 1820; and that at the end of four days they were to be sold into bondage! One of the unhappy wretches here thrust through the grating a dirty, crumpled piece of paper, on which was written with a blunt pencil the 'section' by virtue of which they were held in duress. It ran as follows, and may be found at page two hundred and forty-four of the 'State Laws:'

'WHEREAS it is suggested by petitions from the inhabitants of the village of Canandaigua, that doubts exist upon the true construction of the third section of the act hereby amended, and the said petitions pray for a declaratory law, and for certain amendments in the said act, *Therefore*,

'BE IT ENACTED, That the said Trustees, or the major part of them, as often as they shall make, ordain and publish any by-laws for restraining animals, *may be seized and impounded, and after reasonable delay may be sold at public vendue*, to pay the penalties imposed for the violation of any such ordinance, together with cost and charges.'

Some private citizens, aware of this section of the act, as it stands even now on the statute-book, and actuated by private pique against the trustees, had taken the law into their own hands, and put it in force against them. Its 'plain meaning and intent' were not matters to be considered. There stood the statute; they followed it 'to the etter;' and —here stood its victims! It was a hard case, to be sure; but then, on the other hand, such mistakes sometimes result in *favor* of the accused; as in an instance reported in 3 HARR. Delaware Reports; where a man was indicted for stealing 'one pair of boots.' The theft was proved: but the thief was acquitted, the evidence showing that the boots were not a pair. They were the 'better-halves' of two pairs of 'rights-and-lefts;' and being both 'rights,' the Judge decided that it was '*all* right,' and the prisoner left. What will the 'monarchical press' say to these legal abuses of the model republic?

MR. C——, the distinguished agriculturist of Patterson, New-Jersey, was remarking recently to a lady-friend of his, that he could wish, for one, that the Latin terms used in agricultural chemistry and botany could be reduced to English, so that their meaning might be more generally understood by the great mass of farmers, and persons fond of botany. 'Well,' observed the spinster, 'I *have* changed all the Latin names in *my* herbarium to English; all except two, and I could n't *find* names for them.' 'What were they, Madam?' 'They was the '*Ory-Bory Allis*' and the '*Delirian Trimins!*'

'Do I understand the counsel for defendant,' asked a *very* far-western judge, 'to say, that he is about to read his authorities, as *against* the decision just pronounced from the bench?' 'By no *means!*' responded the counsel 'aforesaid.' 'I was merely going to show to your honor, by a brief passage which I was about to read from the book which I hold in my hand, what an old fool Blackstone must have been!' 'Oh, ay!' said the judge, not a little elated: 'and there the matter ended.'

Let us try to give you very briefly, reader, a little story that was told us the other night in the sanctum. We will endeavor to present it as nearly as possible in the words of the narrator: 'Did I ever tell you,' said he, 'about my first and last poetical effort? Reckon not. Well, thus it was: A considerable long time ago, when I was pursuing the law, (*haud passibus æquis,*) and which I never overtook, I was sitting with my feet on a line with my nose, 'my custom always in the afternoon,' when at the opened door a veritable client appeared. His inimitable hitch at the waist-band spoke at once his occupation on the briny deep. 'Do you ever write letters here?' was his first question. 'Sometimes,' said I, 'although I am not exactly a man of letters.' 'Well, then,' said he, looking round carefully to see that his communication was confidential, 'I want a first-rate one.' 'To whom, and on what subject?' I asked. 'To a gal in Kittery,' said he. 'She aint acting right, and I want to tell her so. She 's been and gone to a singing-school with another chap sence I left. Now take a sheet of paper and give her my mind strong!' I did my best, and put down in our good vernacular some emphatic expressions of indignation, and some hard knocks against the interloper of the singing-school. 'Hold there!' says he, 'that is rather too much sail on that tack! Now put her off a few p'ints on another tack, and give her some soft biscuit, for I do n't want to break off entirely; only to *score* her, so that she will mind her helm and steer straight.' So I eased off, and put in some 'soft sawder' and love-sick nonsense. I read it to him. '*That* will do,' said he; 'but tell her, after all, it will be as she behaves!' So I qualified the honey with a little vinegar. 'That 's all right,' said he; 'but I want you to put in some verses, to wind up the yarn.' 'Such as what?' said I. 'This:

'MY pen is poor, my ink is pale,
My love for you shall never fail.'

'I wrote at his dictation until I came to the word 'pale.' 'That will never do,' said I, 'for this ink is most particularly black'— and it *was* 'black as Erebus,' or 'the ace of spades.' This was a poser. He scratched his head in most amusing perplexity. 'I must have the poetry,' said he, 'at any rate; and what if it aint exactly true? Will that hurt it?' 'Not as *poetry*,' said I, refining, 'but as *fact*. It will be a false statement of a matter of fact, and the falsehood will be apparent on the face of the record, and *falsus in uno, falsus in omnibus*, you know JACK! How can BETSEY believe a word you say, with such a black falsehood staring her in the face?' (I was young, and fresh from BLACKSTONE, and talked learnedly.) 'What shall we do?' cried JACK; 'you must fix it somehow.' 'How will this answer, JACK?' I asked:

'MY pen is poor, my ink is black,
My love for you shall never slack!'

'First-rate!' exclaimed JACK; and so it went, and so ended my first and last attempt at poetry. I wish I had kept a copy of that letter!'

THE 'BACHELOR' was in a 'reverie:' 'RALPH SEA-WULF' was silent: 'RICHARD HAYWARDE' was musing, and 'Old KNICK.' was drinking in the exhilarating air of the sweet Spring morning—('we four, and no more,' were being wheeled to Huntington, Long Island, over a beautiful road, through pleasant villages, in a fine vehicle, drawn by a pair of 'fast bays')—when HAYWARDE, noting a long neck of land pushing out into the Sound, bare at low tide, and thickly besprinkled with crows, inquired, 'What is that?—'Long-Neck,' 'Horse-neck,' 'Cow-Neck,' 'Little-Neck,' 'Rye-Neck,' or *which* of the Long-Island 'Necks' is it?' 'Neither, I fancy,' answered 'one of us;' 'it is only a nameless bar putting out into the Sound: but I should think '*Crow-bar*' would be a good designation for it.'

NUMBER FOURTEEN.

A REVERSED WASH-TUB: A RAIL-ROAD LYRIC: A PERSONAL FUNERAL: THE TOPER'S SPECTACLES: REV. JOHN MASON — QUAINT TABLE 'GRACES': A MILITARY DILEMMA: MATRIMONIAL INDIFFERENCE: STANZAS — 'SNOW': 'FUNNY MEN': A HOPEFUL SON: ANECDOTE OF WHITFIELD: THE — GALLOWS: THE VORK-'OUSE BOY — A PARODY: OLLAPOD'S EPISTOLARY POETRY: ANECDOTE OF ALVAN STEWART: A 'BORE' IN THE PILLORY.

THE horrors of '*Washing Day*' have composed a time-hallowed theme for grumblers, and have elicited the soft numbers of the poets. But according to an amusing traveller, whose 'Letters' we have recently read, they remove far off the annoyance in some parts of the old world. At Ouchy, near Lausanne, he writes: 'I saw to-day for the first time in my life a converse of the washing-tub theorem. In the common case, the washing-tub contains water and the linen, but not the washer-woman, who is at some point without the tub: in this case the tub contained the washer-woman, but neither water nor linen. The women were standing in tubs in the lake, and were washing clothes which were on the outside of the tub in the water. The mode they have of subsequently smacking the linen on the stones is a most uncharitable and un-christian proceeding. Far from hiding the defects of an old shirt, it puts them immediately in a very striking light, and makes the most of all its little weaknesses.'

THE ensuing lines are quite in the style of THACKERAY'S 'PEG of Limavady;' yet they are perfectly original, and do not even verge upon parody. The reader will observe how completely the measure chimes with rail-road motion:

SINGING through the forests,
  Rattling over ridges,
Shooting under arches,
  Rumbling over bridges:
Whizzing through the mountains,
  Buzzing o'er the vale —
Bless me! — this is pleasant,
  Riding on a rail!

Men of different 'stations'
  In the eye of Fame,
Here are very quickly
  Coming to *the same!*
High and lowly people,
  Birds of every feather,
On a common level
  Travelling together.

Gentlemen in shorts
  Looming very tall;
Gentleman at large
  Talking very small;
Gentlemen in tights
  With a loose-ish mien;
Gentlemen in gray
  Looking rather green:

Gentlemen quite old
  Asking for the news;
Gentlemen in black
  In a fit of 'blues;'
Gentleman in claret
  Sober as a vicar:
Gentleman in snuff
  Dreadfully in liquor:

Stranger on the right
  Looking very sunny,
Obviously reading
  Something rather funny;
Now the smiles are thicker:
  Wonder what they mean?
Faith! he 's got the KNICKERBOCKER Magazine!

Stranger on the left
  Closing up his peepers;
Now he snores amain,
  Like the Seven Sleepers!
At his feet a volume
  Gives the explanation,
How the man grew stupid
  From 'Association!'

Market-woman careful
  Of the precious casket,
Knowing 'eggs are eggs,'
  Tightly holds her basket:
Feeling that 'a smash,'
  If it came, would surely
Send her eggs to pot
  Rather prematurely!

Ancient maiden lady
  Anxiously remarks,
That there must be peril
  'Mong so many sparks:
Roguish-looking fellow,
  Turning to the stranger,
Says it 's his opinion
  She is out of danger.

Woman with her baby
  Sitting vis-à-vis;
Baby keeps a-squalling,
  Woman looks at me:
Asks about the distance,
  Says it 's tiresome talking,
Noises of the cars
  Are so very shocking!

Singing through the forests,
  Rattling over ridges,
Shooting under arches,
  Rumbling over bridges:
Whizzing through the mountains,
  Buzzing o'er the vale—
Bless me!—this is pleasant,
  Riding on a rail!

THE well-known anecdote of 'JARVIS and the melancholy Frenchman' with the segar-box had its parallel here a short time since. A gentleman of bituminous complexion, dressed all in sables, with black coat, black vest, black gloves, black pantaloons, and black hat, with a very long black streamer depending therefrom, was walking alone through Broadway 'with solemn step and slow,' bearing a very small baby's coffin under his right arm. A brother 'darky' coming from the opposite direction, with a recognitive grin, èxposing a row of teeth like the keys of a piano, hailed him: 'Well, JOE! where is you bound dis mornin' wid yu box?' 'SAAM!' said the mourner, with a look of offended dignity, and a 'stand-aside' wave of the arm, 'Go 'way!—do n't you see dat I is *a funeral?*'

'WHO hath redness of eyes!' This interrogative 'portion of divine scripture' is forcibly illustrated by an anecdote, related with most effective dryness by a friend of ours. An elderly gentleman, accustomed to 'indulge,' entered the bar-room of an inn in the pleasant city of H——, on the Hudson, where set a grave Friend toasting his toes by the fire. Lifting a pair of green spectacles upon his forehead, rubbing his inflamed eyes, and calling for a hot brandy-toddy, he seated himself by the grate; and as he did so, he remarked to Uncle BROADBRIM that 'his eyes were getting weaker and weaker, and that even spectacles did n't seem to do 'em any good.' 'I 'll tell thee, friend,' rejoined the Quaker, 'what I think. I think if thee was to *wear thy spectacles over thy mouth* for a few months, thy eyes would get sound again!' The 'complainant' did not even return thanks for this medical counsel, but sipped his toddy in silence, and soon after left the room, 'uttering never a word.'

IT is related of the celebrated clergyman, JOHN MASON, that sitting at a steam-boat table on one occasion, just as the passengers were 'falling to' in the customary manner, he suddenly rapped vehemently upon the board with the end of his knife, and exclaimed: 'Captain! is this boat out of the jurisdiction of GOD ALMIGHTY? If not, let us at least thank HIM for his continued goodness;' and he proceeded to pronounce 'grace' amidst the most reverent stillness. It is to be hoped, however, that his 'grace' was not like the few set words handed down from father to son, mumbled without emotion, and despatched with indecent haste, which one sometimes hears repeated over country repasts. 'Bless this portion of food now in readiness for us; give it to us in thy love; let us eat and drink in thy fear — for CHRIST'S sake —— LORENZO, *take your fingers out of that plate!*' was a grace once said in *our* hearing, but evidently not in that of the spoilt boy, 'growing and always hungry,' who could not wait to be served. We should prefer to such insensible flippancy the practice of an old divine in New-England, who in asking a blessing upon his meals, was wont to name each separate dish. Sitting down one day to a dinner, which consisted partly of clams, bear-steak, etc., he was forced in a measure to forego his usual custom of furnishing a 'bill of particulars.' 'Bless to our use,' said he, 'these treasures hid in the sand; bless this ——' But the bear's-meat puzzled him, and he concluded with: 'Oh! LORD, *thou only knowest what it is!*'

OUR readers will remember the order given by the Chinese Emperor to a corps of Mandarins, who were to exterminate the 'barbarian Englishers' in the harbor of Canton, by going down to the bank of the river in the night, and then and there 'dive straight on board those foreign ships, and put every soul of them to death!' Subsequently, however, the red-bristling foreigners managed to land, when, as it since turns out, it became necessary to adopt more sanguinary measures. The Emperor called up one of his 'great generals,' and gave him his orders: 'You must dress your soldiers,' said he, 'in a very frightful manner, painting their faces with the most horrid figures, and depicting dragons and monsters on your banners: you must then rush upon the barbarians with fearful outcries, and terrify them so that they will fall down flat on their faces; and when they are once down,' said the Imperial potentate, '*their breeches are so tight that they can never get up again!*'

'DRESS always and *act* to please your partner for life, as you were fain to do before the nuptial-knot was tied.' This is an old maxim, and here is 'a commentator upon it.' A newly-married lady is suddenly surprised by a visit from a newly-married man, when she straightway begins to apologize: 'She is horribly chagrined, and out of countenance, to be caught in such a dishabille; she did not mind how her clothes were huddled on, not expecting any company, there being nobody at home but her husband!' The husband meanwhile shakes the visitor's hand, and says: 'I am heartily glad to see you, JACK: I do n't know how it was, I was almost asleep: for as there was nobody at home but my wife, I did not know what to do with myself!'

THE lines entitled '*Snow*' are imbued with true feeling. It is easy to see that they came from the writer's *heart*. 'I looked out of the window,' said our correspondent, in the note which encloses the lines to us, 'through a thick, sluggish snow, the *first* of the season, that was falling softly across the river; and there I saw a house, and over the door was one of those rose-trees that grow so large and luxuriantly in this meridian. The snow was falling upon it; and certain memories came into my heart of a hand that plucked roses, flushed with beauty and damp with dew, in 'the days that are no more!' The buds and the leaves of the bush had vanished; the air of those evenings had floated away; and *she* fled!'

FALL thickly on the rose-bush,
Oh! faintly-falling snow!

For she is gone who trained its branch
And wooed its bud to blow.

Cover the well-known pathway,
Oh, damp, December snow!
Her step no longer lingers there,
When stars begin to glow.

Melt in the rapid river,
Oh, cold and cheerless snow!
She sees no more its sudden wave,
Nor hears its foaming flow.

Chill every song-bird's music,
Oh, silent, sullen snow!
I cannot hear her loving voice,
That lulled me long ago.

Sleep on the Earth's broad bosom,
Oh, weary, winter snow!
Its fragrant flowers, and blithesome birds
Should with its loved one go!

IT is our private opinion that a *merely* 'funny man' is one of the biggest bores in all the land of Boredom. Wit and humor, united to general discernment, plain common sense, a love of the beautiful, and warm sensibility, these constitute the true 'man of wit.' Of such was SYDNEY SMITH and HOOD, and of such, preëminently, in these 'latter days,' is DICKENS.

'MILK FOR BABES,' an elaborately-concocted satire upon a certain class of 'learned and pious hand-books for urchins of both sexes,' is not without humor, and ridicules what indeed in some respects deserves animadversion. We affect as little as our correspondent what has been rightly termed 'a clumsy fumbling for the half-formed intellect, a merciless hunting down of the tender and unfledged thought,' through the means of 'instructive' little books, wherein an insipid tale goes feebly wriggling through an unmerciful load of moral, religious, and scientific preaching; or an apparently simple dialogue involves subjects of the highest difficulty, which are chattered over between two juvenile prodigies, or delivered to them in mouthfuls, curiously adapted to their powers of swallowing. 'The minor manners and duties,' says our correspondent, 'are quite overlooked by misguided parents now-a-days;' and this he illustrates by an anecdote: 'THOMAS, my son,' said a father to a lad in my hearing, the other day, 'won't you show the gentleman your last composition?' 'I do n't want to,' said he. 'I *wish* you would,' responded the father. 'I wont!' was the reply; 'I'll be goy-blamed if I do!' A sickly, half-approving smile passed over the face of the father, as he said, in extenuation of his son's *brusquerie:* 'TOM do n't lack manners generally; but the fact is, *he's got such a cold, he is almost a fool!*' Kind parent! happy boy!

THERE is in these humane and benevolent days an increasing sympathy in the public mind for a man condemned to 'march sorrowfully up to the gallows, there to be noosed up, vibrate his hour, and await the dissecting-knife of the surgeon,' who fits his bones into a skeleton for medical purposes. 'There never was a public hanging,' says a late advocate of the abolition of capital punishment, 'that was productive of any thing but evil.' There is an anecdote recorded of WHITFIELD, however, which seems to refute this position, in at least one instance. This eloquent divine, while at Edinburgh, attended a public execution. His appearance upon the ground drew the eyes of all around him, and raised a variety of opinions as to the motives which led him to join in the crowd. The next day, being Sunday, he preached to a large body of men, women and children, in a field near the city. In the course of his sermon, he adverted to the execution which had taken place the preceding day. 'I know,' said he, 'that many of you will find it difficult to reconcile my appearance yesterday with my character. Many of you will say, that my moments would have been better employed in praying with the unhappy man, than in attending him to the fatal tree, and that perhaps curiosity was the only cause that converted me into a spectator on that occasion: but those who ascribe that uncharitable motive to me are under a mistake. I witnessed the conduct of almost every one present on that occasion, and I was highly pleased with it. It has given me a very favorable impression of the Scottish nation. Your sympathy was visible on your countenances, and reflected the greatest honor on your hearts: particularly when the moment arrived in which your unhappy fellow-creature was to close his eyes on this world for ever, you all, as if moved by one impulse, turned your heads aside and wept. Those tears were precious, and will be held in remembrance. How different was it when the SAVIOUR of mankind was extended on the cross! The Jews, instead of sympathizing in his sorrows, triumphed in them. They reviled him with bitter expressions, with words even more bitter than the gall and vinegar which they gave him to drink. Not one of them all that witnessed his pains, turned the head aside even in the last pang. Yes, there was one; that glorious luminary, (pointing to the sun,) veiled his bright face and sailed on in tenfold night!' *This* is eloquence! Would that we could have seen the beaming features, the 'melting eye, turned toward heaven,' which indelibly impressed these words upon the heart of every hearer!

EVERY body has heard or seen '*The Mistletoe-Bough*,' that Radcliffian story in song, of a bride who had hid herself in an old oak chest (which 'closed with a spring') on the night of her marriage, and who was seen no more, until years had rolled by, when her skeleton, in its bridal gear, was accidentally discovered in the living tomb which she had sought in merriment. There is a capital parody on this very Germanic tale, entitled '*The Vork-'Ouse Boy*,' which is set to the same music, and sung with a particularly lugubrious and 'dying fall' in the chorus. It would 'create a soul under the ribs of Death' to hear it 'executed' in the voice and with the instrumentation of a certain friend of 'Old KNICK.'s,' who in rendering it preserves the original pathos and irresistible cockneyism, to a charm. The last verse brought tears to our eyes:

THE VORK-'OUSE BOY.

THE great-coats hung in the vork-'ouse hall,
The vite-'ats shone on the vite-vashed wall;
And the paupers all were blithe and gay,
A-keepin' their Christmas 'oliday:
Ven the Master he cried, with a savage leer,
'You 'll all get soup for your Christmas cheer!'
Oh! the vork-'ouse boy!
Oh! the vork-'ouse boy!

At length all ov us to bed vas sent;
But a boy vas missing — in search ve vent!
Ve sought him above and ve sought him below,
And ve sought him vith faces of grief and vo!
Ve sought in each corner, each kettle, each pot —
In the vater-butt looked — but found him not!

And veeks rolled on, and ve all vore told
That the vork-'ouse boy had been Burked and sold!
Oh! the vork-'ouse boy!
Oh! the vork-'ouse boy!

But ven the soup-coppers repair did need,
The copper-smith come, and there he seed
A dollop of bones lie grizzling there,
In a leg of the trowse's the boy did vear!
To gain his fill the lad did stoop,
And dreadful to tell, he vas b'iled into soup!
And ve all ov us said, and ve said it vith sneers,
That he was pushed in by the overseers!
Oh! the vork-'ouse boy!
Oh! the vork-'ouse boy!

THE death of the late SAMUEL WOODWORTH should not pass unnoted. He has written many beautiful poems, which will live as long as the language; witness his 'Old Oaken Bucket,' that will be sung by millions yet unborn. Mr. WOODWORTH was a warm-hearted man, a good husband and father, and blameless in all the relations of life. One characteristic of his style was a sort of treble-rhyming, which we at one time fancied to be a very difficult species of composition; but 'OLLAPOD' (may he rest in peace!) undeceived us, by throwing off almost impromptu stanzas in this kind. Resisting all entreaties, on one occasion, to prolong a winter-visit in New-York, on the plea that the Delaware would be frozen, and his return to Philadelphia rendered difficult, he thus referred to the truth of his prophecy, in the opening of a poetical epistle by the next mail after his arrival at home:

'I AM glad, as it is, that so soon I departed
  To this goodly city at once to return;
For immediately after, old BOREAS had started
  To scatter the snows from his locks and his urn:
If I'd staid till Monday, or come home on Sunday,
  I should have had one day of pleasure, 't is true;
But the steam-boat ceased running, and therefore 'cunning'
  I think 't was, my shunning to tarry with you.'

This measure, poor 'OLLAPOD' was wont to say, could be 'run off the reel' faster than any other with which he was acquainted.

THERE is a pleasant anecdote related of Mr. ALVAN STEWART, of Central New-York, which strikes us as worthy of preservation. He was dining one day at one of our fashionable hotels; and after selecting from a bill-of-fare in French a piece of roast-beef, he despatched one of the sparse corps of servants to procure it. He waited for some time, but the servant 'came not back.' At length, observing him assisting at an opposite table, he beckoned to him, and having caught his eye, exclaimed, in a sonorous voice, '*Young man, I am hungry!*' 'Ay, ay, Sir,' replied the waiter, and departed a second time for the plate of beef. After some time had elapsed, the beef was placed before the hungry gentleman, who turned a solemn face to the servant, and asked, 'Are you the boy who took my plate for this beef!' 'Yes, Sir, I be,' said the waiter. 'No!' exclaimed Mr. STEWART: 'why, *how you have grown!*'

WHO can withhold his assent to the justice of this estimate of the deserts of that class of persons (happily small) who, having acquired some notoriety as 'conversationists,' are continually striving to be striking or profound; who say things in ten words which require only two; and who fancy all the while that they are making a great impression? 'It is easy to talk of carniverous animals and beasts of prey; but does such a man, who lays waste a whole party of civilized beings by prosing, reflect upon the joy he spoils and the misery he creates, in the course of his life?—and that any one who listens to him through politeness, would prefer ear-ache or tooth-ache to his conversation? Does he consider the extreme uneasiness which ensues, when the company have discovered that he is a *bore*, at the same time that it is impossible to convey, by words or manner, the most distant suspicion of the discovery? And then who punishes this bore? What sessions and what assizes for him? What bill is found against him? Who indicts him? When the judges have gone their vernal and autumnal rounds, the sheep-stealer disappears; the swindler gets ready for the Bay; the solid parts of the murderer are preserved in anatomical collections. But after twenty years of crime, the bore is perhaps discovered in the same house; eating the same soup; unpunished, untried, undissected.' Have you not encountered, reader, in the course of what Mrs. GAMP would term your 'pilgian's progess through this mortial wale,' an occasional bore of this stamp; a man whose disquisitions (touching mainly perhaps his own literary opinions and writings, published or unpublished,) beat lettuces, poppy-syrup, mandragora, hop-pillows, and the whole tribe of narcotics, all to nothing? If you have not, you are lucky. We know who has.

NUMBER FIFTEEN.

OPENING OF AN ANCIENT VAULT — REFLECTIONS: AN EGG-PERSUADER: AN ACTOR 'CORNERED': INQUISITIVE PEOPLE: A VERITABLE YANKEE STORY: VICISSITUDES IN 'GETTING TO YORK': 'IN THE NAME OF THE' OCEAN — 'FIGS!': A SELF-DEPENDENT PHILOSOPHER: A 'STRAWBERRY DITTO': SITTING AND LYING FOR A BUST: THE METROPOLITAN STONE-GAME: THE CHRISTIAN WAY-FARER.

JUST after you pass from Broadway into Wall-street, citizen reader, you will perceive on your left a wide open space, covered with rubbish and dotted with laborers. Turn aside for a moment and survey the scene. It is a space of ground occupied by two sacred edifices, in succession, the latest of which has just been taken down. The numerous arches which you see around, some almost demolished, and others slowly yielding to the crow-bar and pick-axe, were the vaults of the dead. Advance a few yards and examine them more attentively. The workmen are removing all that remains of the forms that once tenanted them; sometimes so little as scarcely to be perceptible; a spade-full or so of dust, a shapeless lump of porous bone, and perhaps a dank piece of worm-eaten mahogany, being all that is left. In the two or three small pine boxes which you see in the centre of the square are deposited, in a promiscuous heap, the few bones, large and small, which were found commingled together in the vaults; and where the lines of graves ran on each side of the church, are also now and then found similar 'trophies of the dead and gone.' Pause at this spot, reader—as by an eddy that slowly revolves in the curve of some rushing stream—pause for a moment, and ere you hasten on to mingle with 'multitudes commercing' in the crowded mart of traffic, solemnly meditate, and commune with yourself: What am I? and whither am I tending? Men with spirits as buoyant and hopes as bright as my own; who once met daily in the busy thoroughfares of the metropolis; who mingled with each other in fraternal intercourse; who sat side by side in the same house of prayer; where are they now? 'Shrunk to this little measure!' their very remains commingled together in the dust, and dwindled into indistinctness and inextricable confusion:

'AND is it thus!—*is* human love
So very light and frail a thing!
And must life's brightest visions move
For ever on Time's restless wing?

'Must all the eyes that still are bright,
And all the lips that talk of bliss,
And all the forms so fair to sight,
Hereafter only come to this?'

Even so! When the rattling earth is cast upon our

coffin, it sends up a hollow sound, which after a few faint echoes, dies and is buried in oblivious silence. That fleeting noise is our posthumous renown. 'The earth itself,' says the great MILTON, 'is a point, not only in respect of the heavens above us, but of that heavenly and celestial part within us. The mass of flesh that circumscribes me, limits not my mind. That surface that tells the heavens they have an end, cannot persuade me *I* have any. There is a divinity within us: something that was before the elements, and owes no homage unto the sun.' Bear this well in mind, therefore, that 'affections well-placed and dutifully cherished; friendships happily formed and faithfully maintained; knowledge acquired with worthy intent, and intellectual powers that have been diligently improved as the talents which the great Author of Mind has committed to our keeping; will accompany us into another state of existence, as surely as the soul in that state retains its identity and its consciousness.' No one, says SOLON, can truly be called happy, until his life has terminated in a happy death; and surely his death will be the happiest, who in his day and generation has done the most good to his fellow-men. Seek out, then, those unhappy wretches who are shunned because penniless and forlorn; oppressed and wronged, because weak and powerless; who endure poverty without pity, age without reverence, want without succor, and pain without sympathy; seek them out, and relieve them. Then will the 'blessing of him that was ready to perish' cheer your last hour. Then there will be joy in the thought that

> ——'our living bodies (though they seem
> To others more, or more in our esteem)
> Are but the shadow of that real Being,
> Which doth extend beyond the fleshly seeing,
> And cannot be discerned until we rise
> Immortal objects for immortal eyes.'

IF any man among us lacks pride in his country, or in the ingenious handicraft of his fellow-citizens, we counsel him to step into the *Fair of the American Institute*, at NIBLO's Garden. *Is* there any nation under heaven, with the experience that our's has had, that can excel us in the useful arts? How vain-glorious soever the assumption may seem, we think not. There are *some* inventions on exhibition at the Fair which will provoke a smile from the observant visitor; but we shall not name them, lest our motives should be misinterpreted. The truth is, *we* have had an invention 'thrown out' by the managers; and any adverse remarks of ours upon the 'improvements' of other exhibitors, would be placed to the account of private pique. Our appeal lies to the public. The '*Ekkalaeobion*,' or Chicken-Hatching Machine, suggested to us an improved plan for supplying the increased demand for eggs, created by that unique steam-hen. It was called '*The Self-acting Back-Action Egg-Persuader*,' and was upon the following principle: A nest, in the usual form, was made of bent pieces of whale-bone, supported at their upper ends by a circular hoop, and terminating in very thin points at the bottom of the nest. Below the nest was suspended a circular thread-netting. The *modus operandi* of the invention was as follows: The veritable nest being concealed by the usual matériel, the hen mounts in good faith, settles down, and deposits her egg, 'in the full glow of conscious security.' The pliant centre of the nest feels the weight of the new burthen, yields gently to the pressure, and the egg is safely deposited in the netting below. The hen finding after all her labor 'a product of *nil*' in the nest, renews her maternal endeavors; nor does she cease, until the lower basket of net-work is filled with eggs, and there remains *one* in the veritable nest. Such, fellow-citizens, is the useful invention which was 'thrown out' by the Accepting Committee of the American Institute!

DID you never meet, reader, on board a steam-boat, in a rail-road car, or in society, with one of those perking, nquisitive persons, who try to pick the brains of every man who will submit to the process? When *next* you encounter such an one, adopt the 'interrupting game,' as played by a traveller upon an inquisitive inn-keeper: 'Good morning, Sir; how do you do? I suppose you are going to ——' Here BONIFACE paused, expecting the name of the place to be supplied; but the traveller answered: 'You are quite right, Sir; I generally go there at this season.' 'Ah! ahem! do you? And no doubt you are now come from ——' 'Right again, Sir; I live there.' 'Oh! ah! do you? Well, your face is familiar to me; I have met you somewhere, I am quite ——' 'Very likely, Sir; I 've been there often. Good morning, Sir.' 'Good morning.' 'Not much information elicited from *that* witness!' as MEDDLE says in the play. WALCOTT, that very clever and most versatile of actors, tells us that he was once shut up in an apartment of a New-England country inn, with a 'ginoowine' female inquisitor, who had just alighted from a stage-coach. While her male attendant had gone to get her 'some *'fresh'ents*,' he was left in the room with her. Being engaged with a book he did not notice her particularly. Presently she observed, looking at a daub of portrait hanging against the wall, 'Do yoëu kneöw whuse picter that is? It looks like a fine moral creetur.' 'I am afraid you mistake the character of the original,' replied Mr. WALCOTT; 'I am informed that he was a lodger, who was leaving clandestinely, without paying his board, and that his portrait was detained as security in part for his dues.' 'Yoëu do n't say so!'—and the lady passed on to another rude painting, and the only other one in the apartment. Surveying it a moment, she again inquired: 'Whuse is *that* paintin'? It's a pleasin' picter, but he wears his hair cur'us.' 'That,' said the player, 'is a copy of our SAVIOUR.' 'Now du tell—I want to know! Well,' she continued, 'it *does look sun'thin' like him, do n't it?*' Reflection as to the implied familiarity with the original face, which enabled the 'inquisitor' to detect at a glance a *general* resemblance, was interrupted by the appearance of the ''fresh'ents,' in shape of 'nut-cakes and cider;' and presently, says our informant, 'the pair went on their way, and I saw them no more.'

'A FEW days since a raw-looking genius, carrying a cheap hair-trunk, made his appearance on board a sloop which plies between New-York and a small port on the Connecticut coast, and inquired for the captain. He hailed from Coos county, New-Hampshire, and presented in his appearance a perfect specimen of a fresh-caught Yankee. He wore a mixed coat of home-made fabric, with short square skirts, such as are usually called 'bob-tail,' lead-buttons, and sleeves about six inches too short at the wrists. His pantaloons were striped, and his legs were thrust a long way through them, leaving the interval between the legs of the trowsers and his heavy laced boots arrayed in a substantial pair of pepper-and-salt yarn stockings. On a head, adorned with a luxuriant growth of coarse sandy hair, tallowed to a nicety, was perched a hat much worn but in an excellent state of preservation, with a narrow brim and huge bell-crown, serving the purpose of a travelling valise in addition to the other uses of that article of wearing apparel. An immense collar, rigid with starch and erect to the ears, supported by a cotton cravat of variegated yellow and black, completed the adornment of his outer man. He seemed about twenty-five years of age; was a lean, cadaverous-looking individual, standing some six feet when erect, but having a stoop of the shoulders which reduced him to about five-feet-nine. A small pinched-up mouth, peaked nose, high cheek-bones, sunken cheeks, prominent chin, and a pair of bright twinkling eyes, of an indescribable color, gave an air of extreme 'cuteness' to his physiognomy.

This was obviously his first visit to the salt water; but as he stood upon the sloop's deck whistling Yankee-doodle, his arms thrust into his pockets up to the elbows, one leg thrown forward, his eyes cast upward scanning the rigging with the air of a connoisseur, he seemed as much at home as though he was a veritable 'ocean-child.' In reply to a question as to his business, he drawled out:

'Capting, what 'll yeöu charge to take a feller tu York city?'

He was informed that the fare was one dollar and fifty cents.

'I s'spect yeöu mean yeöu charge a feller that when yeöu *find* him; what 'll yeöu take a feller for, when he finds *himself?*'

The price of passage without board, he was informed, was seventy-five cents.

'Then I shall have to foot it tu York; you see, I 'm scant on 't for funds, and I *must* have a leetle somethin' left to feed me a'ter I get there; can 't get along without victuals.'

'Can 't help it,' replied the captain; 'that 's our lowest; we ha' n't but one price.'

'Neöw just take a feller for half-a-dollar, capting; come, neöw; if yeöu will, I 'll help du up the chores while I 'm aboard.'

'No, Sir, I can 't take you for *that* price.'

The green-horn squirted a long stream of tobacco-juice upon the deck, resumed his tune of Yankee-doodle, shouldered his hair-trunk, and walked off. In about an hour he returned, and with a grin addressed the captain:

'Neöw, look o' here, capting, I 'm in distress; I positively haint got but tew dollars in the world; I must get tu York, or I shall starve; I can 't get nothin' to du here.

Neöw, du, capting; I 've always hear'n tell that you sailors was generous chaps.'

This appeal to the captain's professional pride had its effect; and he agreed to take the persevering mendicant for fifty cents, provided he would supply himself with provisions, and render such assistance as he could in managing the vessel.

The passage was unusually long, being delayed by contrary winds nearly a week beyond the ordinary time of starting. On the second day the Yankee ran out of provisions; and the captain, as an act of charity, furnished him from the vessel's stores. About thirty-six hours before their arrival, in the exuberance of his exultation at having outwitted the captain, he disclosed to a fellow-passenger that he had 'lots o' cash,' and he made quite a display of loose change. This soon came to the ears of the captain, who was so indignant at the imposition which had been practised upon him, that he was about setting the tricky customer ashore, to 'foot it to York' the best way he could; but on reflection, he concluded that it would be a worse punishment to keep him on board, stop his rations, and put him to hard work. From this time until their arrival, the Yankee's situation was no sinecure. Furnished with a cloth, and a bucket of sand, he was set to *scouring the anchor!* Being inured to labor, that did not trouble him much; but to work on an empty stomach for thirty-six hours, and endure the curses of the enraged captain, and the taunts and jeers of the passengers and crew, and all for the small matter of twenty-five cents, he thought was 'paying rather dear for the whistle!' Great was his joy, therefore, when they hauled into the slip at New-York; and before the sloop's side had touched the dock, he jumped ashore. Leaving the little hair-trunk to be removed after he had satisfied his hunger, he hastened to the nearest place where food could be procured. This happened to be a huckster's stand at the head of the slip; where, among other eatables, were displayed some fine-looking boiled lobsters. Our verdant genius had often heard lobsters spoken of as excellent food, although he had never tasted any; this seemed a good opportunity to satisfy his hunger, and at the same time to enjoy a rare luxury; so after bargaining awhile, and beating the old woman down in her price some three or four cents, he bought three lobsters and as many Boston 'crackers,' with which he returned to the sloop.

Meanwhile one of the passengers, a wag of the first order, having been up into the city, returned on board and noticed the Yankee, at the heel of the bowsprit, seated on his hair-trunk, and 'goin' into' his bargain tooth and nail. It was a greedy spectacle! He wrenched the jaws and claws of the lobsters apart with unnecessary strength, drawing out with voracity sharp splinters of the meat, and biting them off close down to the sockets which held them. Such a smacking and cracking was never heard before. Carelessly sauntering within hearing, the waggish passenger gave the captain a wink, and remarked:

'This is a horrible business, captain!'

'*What* is a horrible business?' asked the skipper.

'Hain't you heard the news? All the papers are full of it. Some Jersey fishing-smacks have been taking lobsters on the copperas-banks off Barnegat, and have sold them all over the city. Every person who has eaten any of them is p'isoned. Fifty-three have died since morning; there is a tremendous excitement about it. As I came down, I saw an officer arrest the old woman who keeps a stand at the head of the slip, for selling some of the same lobsters.'

The Yankee, who had already devoured one and part of another, paused at the narration, as if suddenly paralyzed; then dropping the fragment which he held, with the untouched prize, into the water, his mouth filled with cracker-and-lobster, his enormous palms extended over his abdomen, his face pallid with terror, he exclaimed:

'Oh golly! what shall I du! What shall I du! I'm sartingly a dead man! Darn York! Cuss the lobsters! I wish I 'd staid tu hum! Oh, my beöwels! my beöwels!'

'If that d—d green-horn has n't been eating some of 'em! — run for a doctor!' exclaimed the captain. Some one started ashore for a physician. In the mean time the Yankee continued to groan and lament, attracting a large crowd of spectators by his cries: 'Oh, SUKE! if I had only taken your advice, and kept clear of this tarnal York city! I 'm dying — I know I am! My mouth tastes jest like a rusty cent! The doctor 'll charge an all-fired price to cure me, I s'spect. There, I 'm spitting green! — that 's the copperas! I shall die before the doctor gets here! Murder! murder! murder!'

Some one personating a physician now made his appearance, felt of the patient's pulse, examined his tongue, and pronounced it a clear case of poisoning from eating copperas lobsters. He prescribed a powerful emetic, which was immediately administered in the form of a quart of luke-warm salt water. The effect was powerful beyond explanation. It produced a prodigious paroxysm, and kept him in a continual shudder for more than an hour, during which his case seemed to be very doubtful. He kept girding his stomach with his two hands, squeezing his viscera, and bowing down as the contending forces racked his whole inner man. In the pauses of his pangs he uttered sundry exclamations, such as, 'Oh, SUKE! damn lobsters! cuss York city! Oh, my beöwels! If I ever get hum again you 'll never catch —— There it is again! I *shall* die! Parson DULITTLE! Parson DULITTLE! if I had n't neglected your preachin'!' etc., to the great edification and amusement of the by-standers. At length the doctor pronounced him free from danger and convalescent. The next thing was the payment of the fee, which he was informed was five dollars. He groaned in spirit, and his 'beöwels' yearned worse than ever at the thought of parting with such a sum of money. There was no help for it, however; so he 'forked over' the V, and shouldering his hair-trunk, went growling on his way.

WE have often heard of persons talking with angry vehemence to inanimate objects which displeased them; and we have even heard of these same objects being 'put upon their good behavior,' as in the case of the sailor who reminded his staunch craft, when she was sailing beautifully before the wind, that if she would behave equally well during the voyage, she should have a handsome coat of paint the very day after she arrived at her destined port. One of the best things in this kind, however, which we remember to have heard, was told us the other day by a friend, whom no 'good thing' ever escapes. A vessel in the Mediterranean, loaded to the gunwale with a rich cargo of figs, was wrecked in a tremendous storm; the captain and mate being saved by a miracle. The next day, by one of its sudden changes, the blue ocean was as smooth as glass: scarcely a cat's-paw of wind could be traced, as far as the eye could reach. The captain of the wrecked vessel, however, walking along the coast near Lisbon, surveyed the scene with a jaundiced eye. 'Oh! yes!' said he, 'mighty still *now;* smooth enough *to-day;* but I see through you; *I* know what you want — *you want more figs!* You do n't catch me *ag'in*, though, mind I tell you!'

'*The Changeless Philosopher*' is not bad; nay, it is very good — but not *quite* original. GOLDSMITH has a character so much like the 'philosopher,' that we hardly think *both* can be original creations. Part of our 'peripatetic' hero's reasoning seems also to have been borrowed from the bankrupt 'WYLDE OATES' argument in extenuation of stealing a conveyance in town, and making an inroad upon the larders and bars of sundry suburban houses of entertainment, 'without regard to expense:' 'I do n't know whether things are not funnier when you 've got no money at all, than when your pockets are brimful. Take all you can, and no responsibility; no forking down or settling up; a free blow, every-which-way. Get kicked a little sometimes; but that mends itself cheap; and when you 've had a ride and trimmings, whisky-punch and fried oysters, a dance, an upset, and a fight with chairs and decanters, why what can they do with you then, if you are independent in your circumstances, and have n't got a red cent? They can 't unride a fellow; no, nor undance him neither. When you 've had something to drink, you 're a fixed fact, and can 't be unpunched!'

WE were not a little amused the other evening at NIBLO'S, by a dialogue which we overheard between a verdant-looking biped and a colored 'gemman' officiating as waiter. Taking up a little bill from one of the small tables, the white youth ran over the items, as 'Vanilla cream,' 'Strawberry, do.,' 'Raspberry, do.,' etc. At length, 'Bring me,' said he to the waiter, 'some o' your '*Strawberry Do!*'' The 'colored person' looked at the dish indicated by the finger of his interlocutor: 'Oh!' he explained, 'that means *ditto;* it means that it 's the same thing, you see.' 'Very well, then, bring me a Strawberry *Ditto;* you 've *got* it, ha'nt ye? There 's a man there 's jest sent and had one fetch'd. Jest bring *me* one on 'em!' At that moment we heard the tones of Mrs. MOWATT'S most musical voice; the curtain was up; and we left the intelligent inquisitor thrusting into his very throat large heaps of 'Strawberry Ditto.'

MR. FOWLER, 'practical phrenologist,' has issued an elaborate work on his 'science.' It contains the engraved busts of a good many men remarkable for their bumps. *We* once 'lay' for our plaster-portrait to Mr. FOWLER, and kept a very sober face in our coffin-like box until he had piled the liquid matériel around our smoothly-greased head and face, to within a half an inch of the mouth; but when he began to feed the adjacent features with a spoon, and we saw only a nose sticking out of the warm white hasty-pudding, 'human-natur'' could n't stand it; and just as far as those features *could* laugh they *did*; the muscles below however were 'stuck;' and the result in the cast was a face solemn as an owl's up to the outer line of a small circle embracing the mouth and muscles immediately adjacent, which were themselves 'full of mirth.' 'Picture it, think of it,' reader! And yet Mr. FOWLER had the audacity to exhibit that bust in his window (PETER ROBINSON the murderer on one side and our friend Colonel WEBB on the other!) until we extracted a promise from him to remove it and break the mould which had been worse than an 'iron mask' to us.

OUR Tinnecum friend and correspondent saw an adroit trick 'done and performed' the other day in the vicinity of Washington-market. A fellow loaned a countryish-looking man a gold watch for ten dollars, with the privilege of redeeming it in two days, for a dollar premium. 'It was worth sixty;' 'belonged to his father,' etc.; but then he *must* have the ten dollars. He took it from his pocket, wrapped a paper round it, gave it to the countryman, and got his ten dollars. 'Halloo! stranger!' said an accomplice over the way, after the fellow had gone off with the money, 'what 'll you bet that ain't a stone you have just bought?' 'I 'll bet you tew dollars 't ain't. Did n't I see him wrap it up?' 'I 'll stand you!' said the accomplice; 'money down.' The money was deposited in the hands of a by-stander, the package was unrolled, and a flat rounded stone was all its contents! The countryman staid about the market for several days — but he has gone home now!

THAT was an affecting conclusion of a speech by a venerable Methodist clergyman at one of our late religious anniversaries. He had been depicting the sufferings of his youth and manhood in proclaiming the 'glad tidings' of CHRIST in the western wilds; often riding in storm and tempest through the forest, when it was so dark that he could not see the beast on which he rode, and frequently sleeping in the dense woods; his own hands mean time ministering unto his necessities. He was a poor wayfaring man, he said, with no cottage in the wilderness, but wandering like the Israelite, and lodging awhile in tents, till he should reach the heavenly Canaan. The fervor with which the following lines were given from the lips of the speaker brought tears to many an eye:

'NOTHING on earth I call my own:
A stranger to the world unknown,
I all their goods despise;
I trample on their whole delight,
I seek a city out of sight,
A city in the skies.

'There is my home and portion fair,
My treasure and my heart is there,
And my abiding home;
For me my elder brethren stay,
And angels beckon me away,
And JESUS bids me come.'

A Word at Parting.

We must now 'speed the parting Guest.' He has sat at our 'Table,' and partaken of the numerous dishes which we had prepared, as well as of several which had been sent in by friendly neighbors, that it might be decided whether or no they would please the palate of that many-neaded monster, 'The Public.' If our guests should not deem the present fare too simple and homely, it may be that we shall again invite them to sit at our board, and partake of a repast, in which by-gone errors in choice of dishes, or modes of cookery, may be avoided.

Good-bye, Friends!—and may peace and happiness be with you!

AMERICAN AND ORIGINAL.

THE

Knickerbocker Magazine:

EDITED BY

LOUIS GAYLORD CLARK.

THE FORTY-FIRST VOLUME of this oldest Magazine in America commences on the *First of January*, 1853. The work has been so long before the public, that it is not deemed necessary to enlarge upon its widely-acknowledged claims to general favor. The annexed list of contributors to the Magazine, and a few notices of the press, (out of many thousands,) will sufficiently attest its character and its popularity:

WASHINGTON IRVING,
WILLIAM C. BRYANT,
FITZ GREENE HALLECK,
PROF. H. W. LONGFELLOW,
J. K. PAULDING,
MISS C. M. SEDGWICK,
HON. LEWIS CASS,
CAPT. F. MARRYAT,
SIR E. L. BULWER,
REV. ORVILLE DEWEY,
R. H. STODDARD,
J. H. PRESCOTT, ESQ.,
HON. R. M. CHARLTON,
JAMES G. PERCIVAL,
HON. W. H. SEWARD,
JARED SPARKS,
'HARRY FRANCO,'
NATH. HAWTHORNE,
MRS. L. H. SIGOURNEY,
REV. DR. BETHUNE,
MRS. C. M. KIRKLAND,
FREDERICK S. COZZENS,
MISS LESLIE,
W. D. GALLAGHER,
HON. JUDGE CONRAD,
DR. O. W. HOLMES,
THOMAS W. PARSONS,
PROF. HITCHCOCK,
MRS. E. C. EMBURY,
WILLIAM B. GLAZIER,
HON. D. D. BARNARD,
J. P. BROWN, (Constantinople.)
F. W. EDMONDS, ESQ.,
REV. MR. GANNETT, (Mass.)
MRS. GILMAN, (S. C.)
E. T. T. MARTIN,
H. W. ELLSWORTH,
H. J. RAYMOND, ESQ.,
H. R. SCHOOLCRAFT,
CHARLES G. LELAND, ESQ.,
REV. J. PIERPONT,
HON. G. C. VERPLANCK,
ALBERT MATHEWS, ESQ.,
COL. T. S. M'KENNY,
JOHN T. IRVING,
ALBERT PIKE, ESQ.,
'IK MARVEL,'
CHARLES SPRAGUE,
RICHARD B. KIMBALL, ESQ.,
PARK BENJAMIN,
THEODORE S. FAY,
MRS. FANNY K. BUTLER,
DONALD MACLEOD,
MISS CHARLOTTE CUSHMAN,
HON. JAMES KENT,
PRESIDENT DUER,
JOSEPH BARBER,
MISS H. F. GOULD,
E. W. B. CANNING,
PROF. CHARLES ANTHON,
ALFRED B. STREET,
JOHN WATERS,
CONSUL G. W. GREENE,
JAMES BROOKS,
REV. DR. SPRING,
J. N. BELLOWS,
PROFESSOR FELTON,
STACY G. POTTS,
MR. F. PARKMAN, (Boston.)
J. G. WHITTIER,
JAMES RUSSELL LOWELL, ESQ.,
H. W. ROCKWELL,
WILLIAM PITT PALMER,
CHARLES M. LEUPP, ESQ.,
PROFESSOR BECK,
HON. CHARLES MINER,
REV. FREDERICK W. SHELTON,
EDWARD S. GOULD,
JOSEPH G. CANNING,
CHARLES GOULD,
MRS. E. F. ELLET,
J. H. GOURLIE, ESQ.,
HORACE GREELEY,
REV. DR. PISE,
ALBERT MATTHEWS, ESQ.,
MR. THOMAS W. STORROW,
GEORGE LUNT,
REV. J. GILBORNE LYONS,
H. T. TUCKERMAN,
MRS. M. E. HEWITT,
PROF. JAMES J. MAPES,
JAMES LINEN,
REV. R. H. BACON,
J. H. SHELDON, JR.,
J. G. SAXE, ESQ.,
JOHN HENRY HOPKINS, (Vt.)

THE foregoing list included also ROBERT SOUTHEY, Rev. TIMOTHY FLINT, Miss LANDON, JUSTICE MELLEN, TYRONE POWER, ROBERT C. SANDS, WILLIS GAYLORD CLARK, JOHN SANDERSON, the 'American in Paris,' NICHOLAS BIDDLE, Miss MARY ANNE BROWNE, (Mrs. GRAY,) England, Rev. Dr. BRANTLEY, South-Carolina, WILLIAM L. STONE, J. H. HILLHOUSE, J. FENIMORE COOPER, Rev. WM. WARE, J. H. STEPHENS, Hon. R. H. WILDE, JOSEPH C. NEAL, PHILIP HONE, ESQ., Rev. HENRY BASCOM, Rev. WALTER COLTON, HENRY BREVOORT, ESQ., WILLIAM WORDSWORTH, A. BRIGHAM, Dr. JOHN NEILSON, JR., J. K. KENNARD, JR., Mass., Hon. JUDGE HALL, (Illinois,) Rev. W. B. O. PEABODY, with other distinguished writers who have 'paid the debt of nature.' The following notices of the KNICKERBOCKER are from the American and English press, and from American and British writers of distinction:

'THE KNICKERBOCKER holds its own remarkably well. Nobody can complain that he does not have his money's worth in so great a variety of pleasant reading at three dollars a year.'—BOSTON DAILY ADVERTISER.

'WE never read the KNICKERBOCKER but we feel as if we were reading a letter from a cherished friend. Here's a health to thee 'Old KNICK.!' If the fates should ever send thee to 'Old Virginia,' there is one hand that will give thee a cordial grasp, and one heart a friendly greeting.'—PETERSBURGH (Va.) DAILY EXPRESS.

'THE KNICKERBOCKER is quite the ablest

repertory of original American literature of all periodicals of its class. Among its contributors, from the commencement of its career, have been the ablest and most popular authors that the country has produced. But that feature which has always most attracted us, in this entertaining Magazine, is the *Editor's Table.* Though occupying the last pages of the work, we always open to it first; and wherever in its genial, cheerful, single-minded 'Gossip,' the eye falls, thence it is led forward by irresistible attraction from topic to topic, till the end.'—N. Y. JOURNAL OF COMMERCE.

'No periodical published in America will compare, for unflagging, sustained interest and variety, high literary character and general popularity, with this universal favorite. It is at once the ablest and best magazine of its class this side of the Atlantic; and on some accounts we know of none across the 'big pond' that we prefer before it.' . . . 'There is not, on either side of the Atlantic, so elegantly, so delicately printed a periodical as is our 'Old KNICK.' It is refreshing to wander over its faultless pages.'—ALBANY DAILY REGISTER.

'THIS glorious argosy from prose and verse-land, full freighted, luscious and spicy, is just anchored at our desk. Amid the stubble of politics and dry-as-dust news, it comes like clover-scented zephyrs, fragrant, balmy, but not, like most delicious things, surfeiting. The KNICKERBOCKER is *the* American Magazine: 'Long may it wave!''—EVENING MIRROR.

'No number of the KNICKERBOCKER has ever been issued under CLARK'S supervision that did not bear indubitable evidence of editorial care, and anxious thought and well-directed labor enstamped upon its pages. We have known no monthly, of this country or Europe, so thoroughly *edited*, in the strictest sense of the term. In variety, in richness, in mingled gayeties and gravities, it has never been surpassed.'—N. Y. DAILY TRIBUNE.

'The KNICKERBOCKER comes to us in advance, with its budget of good things and things of beauty. Surely, the EDITOR is inexhaustible. His 'Table' is supplied from the Cornucopia itself.'—N. Y. DAILY TIMES.

'NOTHING is more remarkable than the unfailing promptitude of this old Monthly, except perhaps its constant and constantly increasing excellence.'—N. Y. DAILY COURIER AND ENQUIRER.

'I PERUSE the numbers of the KNICKERBOCKER with high gratification. They seem to me of an order of merit quite above the average of the periodicals of its class, English or American.'—HON. EDWARD EVERETT.

'I HAVE always felt a deep interest in the KNICKERBOCKER, and taken pleasure in bringing it to the notice of my friends. The manner in which it is conducted, and the great merit of many of its contributors, place it in the highest rank of periodicals.'—HON. J. K. PAULDING.

'THE KNICKERBOCKER stands high in this quarter. It is infinitely superior to most of the English magazines, and well deserves its large list of subscribers.'—PROFESSOR LONGFELLOW.

'THE KNICKERBOCKER is the best American periodical I have yet seen.' . . . 'I take pleasure in enclosing you some lines, which were penned expressly for your work.'—SIR EDWARD BULWER LYTTON.

'THE KNICKERBOCKER is an honor, and a high one, to the literature of our country. I always feel that I am conferring a favor on the persons to whom I recommend it, rather than upon the proprietors.'—HON. R. M. CHARLTON, Georgia.

'I HAVE read a good many of the articles in the KNICKERBOCKER, and find them to possess great merit. Some of its papers, it is true, were too light for my serious turn of mind; yet the whole appears well calculated to gratify the tastes of the general mass of readers.'—REV. DR. DICK, Scotland.

'THIS very clever Magazine is the pleasantest periodical in the United States. Its articles are numerous and short, various and interesting, and well worthy of imitation by our Magazines on this side of the Atlantic.'—LONDON EXAMINER.

'THE KNICKERBOCKER is one of the most valuable Magazines of the day, and out-strips all competition in the higher walks of literature. It is rich, racy, and varied; exhibiting industry, taste, and talent at the helm, equal to all it undertakes.'—ALBANY ARGUS.

'JUDGING from the numbers before us, we are inclined to consider this the best of all American literary periodicals. Its contents are highly interesting, instructive, and amusing.'—LONDON MORNING CHRONICLE.

'THE taste and talent which the KNICKERBOCKER displays are highly creditable to American writers, and very agreeable for English readers.'—LONDON LITERARY GAZETTE.

TERMS.

THREE dollars a year, INVARIABLY in advance. Two copies for Five Dollars: Five copies, and upward, Two Dollars each. Postmasters will act as Agents. Specimen numbers sent gratis, on application, post-paid. To CLUBS, the KNICKERBOCKER, HARPER'S, GRAHAM'S, or GODEY'S Magazines will be sent one year for FIVE DOLLARS. The KNICKERBOCKER and 'HOME JOURNAL,' or any other New-York, Philadelphia, or Boston two-dollars'-weekly, for FOUR DOLLARS a year. POSTAGE on the KNICKERBOCKER is two cents per number: paid, optionally, by the subscriber or the publisher. All *Literary Communications*, or inquiries in regard to them, to be addressed to the EDITOR: all *Business Communications* to the PUBLISHER,

SAMUEL HUESTON,

139 NASSAU STREET, NEW-YORK.

www.ingramcontent.com/pod-product-compliance
Lightning Source LLC
LaVergne TN
LVHW010202110826
845151LV00002B/585

* 9 7 8 1 4 2 5 5 3 5 5 6 8 *